Psychological Interventions in Medical Practice

Contributors

Gladys Witt Strain, Ph.D., R.D.

Research Nutritionist
Montefiore Hospital and Medical Center
Bronx, New York

Nutrition Consultant
Obesity Research Center
Department of Medicine
St. Luke's Hospital Center
New York, New York

David Hamerman, M.D., F.A.C.P.

Professor of Medicine
Albert Einstein College of Medicine

Chairman, Department of Medicine
Montefiore Hospital and Medical Center
Bronx, New York

Psychological Interventions in Medical Practice

James J. Strain, M.D.

Director of Liaison Service
Montefiore Hospital and Medical Center

Associate Clinical Professor of Psychiatry
Albert Einstein College of Medicine
Bronx, New York

ACC Appleton-Century-Crofts/New York

For Jay, Jeffrey, and Jamie

---

78 79 80 81 82 / 10 9 8 7 6 5 4 3 2

Prentice-Hall International, Inc., London
Prentice-Hall of Australia, Pty. Ltd., Sydney
Prentice-Hall of India Private Limited, New Delhi
Prentice-Hall of Japan, Inc., Tokyo
Prentice-Hall of Southeast Asia (Pte.) Ltd., Singapore
Whitehall Books Ltd., Wellington, New Zealand

Library of Congress Catalogue Card No: 78–4850

Cover art: *Hands,* a scultpure by Henry Moore.
From the Collection of Mr. and Mrs. Allan D. Emil.

PRINTED IN THE UNITED STATES OF AMERICA

ISBN 0-8385-8014-9

Contents

Foreword

Why have the psychological aspects of medical practice lagged behind the biological and technical aspects in this century? There is little doubt that such is the case. What new understandings of human psychology can compare with the irradication of diphtheria and polio, the discovery of penicillin, or the development of organ transplantation? As a matter of fact, one can argue that the mental health of our citizenry has become worse instead of better in the past 75 years. To support such an argument, one would only have to adduce the national data on crime, violence, alcoholism, suicide, delinquency, and child abuse.

What is surprising and contradictory about all this is that it has occurred in spite of enormous public interest in psychology. From the earlier eager acceptance of the teachings of Freud to the latest preoccupations with eastern mysticism, the people of the United States appear to be psychologically sophisticated—except when it applies to their own health. Newspapers and magazines abound with columns of psychological counsel, but the individual reader finds it difficult to change his own life.

The medical profession has not been immune to this paradox. On one hand, doctors have shown intense interest in the biology and technology of mental illness while, at the same time, there has been steady attrition of the quality of our interpersonal relationships with patients. Impersonality is one of the chief epithets against modern physicians and their medicine.

Lately, however, there has been a renascence of interest in the psychological dimensions of medical practice. Part of the interest can be attributed to the recovery of a generalist vocation in medicine, or as it is frequently referred to, primary medical care. The generalist has always had to deal with the immediacy of human suffering, mental as well as physical, and to recognize the absurdities and irrationalities of human behavior. The generalist is also confronted with a host of problems that, strictly speaking, are not diseases, problems that can be evaded or ignored by those physicians who deal only in diseases. Moreover, the generalist also inherits patients with multiple diseases who have been "processed" technologically without cure or relief. These come back for whatever help is left in the desperate hope that in the end they will not be abandoned.

This book is for the physician who functions near the "front entrance" to medical care, where the patients' problems are not neatly sorted into diseases, where the complaints are often vague and undifferentiated, or the language is mistakenly physical when the suffering is mental. The authors understand this setting and its unique demands on the physician. They know that it is not easy to be a "front-door physician," and they do not demean the role by offering a bag of magic psychological tricks.

What they offer is an approach to understanding psychological problems in ambulatory patients as a basis for rational action by the physician—even when the problems themselves are not rational. Fundamental to this understanding is a dynamic psychology that respects the biography of each person and values the relationship between patient and physician. They do not ignore the contributions to patient care that derive from the academic social sciences, but they clearly avoid identification with one or another of the popular psychologies. Their experience is medical, and they write for physicians; however, their approach is valuable for any health professional whose work is mainly clinical.

I have had the privilege of reading this book in its manuscript stage and offering my comments to Dr. Strain. It is particularly appropriate for the family physician whose commitment is uniquely to primary medical care. I recommend this book not only to those who teach family medicine, but equally to those who practice it.

G. Gayle Stephens, M.D.
Professor and Chairman
Department of Family Practice
School of Medicine
University of Alabama in Birmingham

Prologue

On the Aims of This Book. The psychiatrist who works closely with his medical colleagues, and is aware of the difficulties they typically encounter in the management of their patients' psychological needs, is confronted with two major issues.* First, the question arises as to the precise nature and extent of his responsibility to the medical community regarding this critical aspect of patient care. Second, the psychiatrist's desire to disseminate psychological concepts is often undermined by his awareness of the demands that are currently made on the physician. Spokesmen for every specialty clamor for the physician's attention to one or another sector of the patient's body, and his problems are compounded by the amount of "new" medical information he is expected to assimilate. Consequently, the psychiatrist is understandably reluctant to urge the physician to assimilate still another body of knowledge and techniques which, all too frequently, are thought to lie outside the primary province of medicine. This book has emerged from my own efforts to grapple with these issues, and hopefully to propose some viable solutions to the dilemmas they present.

The psychiatrist can take some comfort from the fact that, regardless of the extent and nature of their preoccupation with physiological issues, most physicians concede the importance of psychological issues in the onset, course, and outcome of physical disease. Unfortunately, even when he is strongly committed to this stance, the physician is often unable to provide routine psychological care for his patients. The most glaring impediment to the incorporation of psychological concepts and interventions in medical practice lies, I think, in the fact that, by and large, the physician does not know enough about psychological care—what it can consist of and how it should be administered. It is precisely because of this lack of psychological knowl-

* It occurs to me that some readers may be offended by my use of third person pronouns in the masculine gender to refer to physicians, patients, etc., throughout this book. No alternative occurs to me that would not create confusion, be unnecessarily clumsy, or seem artificial.

edge and skills that his efforts in the psychological sector so often take the form of "humanism"—demonstrations of caring about the patient —rather than offering him "real" psychological help. This is the problem to which the psychiatrist must address himself.

It is a problem that might best be alleviated, in my opinion, through the dissemination of a clinically useful model of psychological medicine. Such a model, if it is to be effective, might be based on three premises:

First, the physician's overriding psychological goal in the medical setting is to foster the patient's adaptation to a life style compatible with his illness; and his assessment of the behavior of the individual patient and interventions on his behalf are geared toward the achievement of this goal.

Second, the patient's behavior cannot always be fully understood if it is evaluated solely in terms of its superficial manifestations. In any event, the meaning of behavior takes on greater clarity when the patient's latent (unconscious) responses—the instinctual reactions that medical illness typically evokes, i.e., rage, aggression, hostility, self-destructiveness—are taken into account as well.

Third, a critical prerequisite for the effective psychological management of the medically ill patient is the physician's ability to acknowledge the possibility that his own conscious and unconscious response to that patient may have contributed to the patient's psychological dysfunction.

My aim in this book is to delineate such a model of psychological medicine and demonstrate its applicability to a particular segment of the patient population, namely, the chronically ill who are treated in an ambulatory setting. Chronic illness demands certain changes in the patient's life style, his perception of self and others, etc.; psychological interventions on behalf of such patients may demand changes in the physician's customary mode of relating, in his perception of self, etc.

Orientation. An author has license in the prologue of his book to go beyond the specific content of his text, where he has sought to be objective, to expand on issues and concepts so that they reflect his own judgment and biases. A discussion of the orientation on which this book is based might well begin with a more precise definition of the terms of reference that are used throughout. I am concerned here soley with those medical patients who do not present gross psychiatric pathology, in addition to their physical disease, and the means by which these "normal" patients can be helped to adapt to their illness. Adaptation to chronic illness places great demands on the patient as well as the physician. The capacity for work and sex, which are not only criteria of, but enable adaptation to life in the healthy, are frequently unavailable to the chronically ill. Other measures need to be employed to evaluate the chronically ill patient's capacity to adapt—to life in general, but to his illness in particular.

I believe that adaptation, at least as it applies to chronic illness, can best be defined as the ability of the patient to function within his physical limitations with minimal conflict. Ideally, in time, the patient's enforced dependency will not cause him undue mental anguish, to the degree that he ignores his physical constraints or excessively mourns the loss of his physical capacities. If, in short, he finds a dependent posture tolerable, then he has achieved an important measure of adaptation to his illness. The physician may thwart the patient's efforts to achieve even such minimum adaptation if he places a high premium on independence and self-sufficiency, if he cannot, for a variety of reasons, accept the specter of a full-grown adult who relies on others for his most basic needs. And, in that event, the physician must examine these attitudes. Only after he has resolved his own conflicts, has come to terms with his own unconscious fantasies, and is able to adapt to his patient, will the physician be able to foster adaptation in the patient by helping him accept his limitations, alter his ego ideal, be proud of himself for his ability to accept his disease—the blow that fate has dealt him.

This concept of adaptation, and references to unconscious fantasies and attitudes will, of course, immediately bring to mind the psychoanalytic model of behavior. I hasten to reassure the physician that this volume is not intended to serve as a textbook of psychoanalysis. Rather, I have attempted to extract from the body of psychoanalytic theory those concepts that have specific relevance for the physician's understanding of his patient and himself, and, on the basis of these concepts, to develop an approach that might most accurately be described as psychodynamic in orientation. I would also hasten to reassure the physician that he is not expected to function in the capacity of psychoanalyst or psychotherapist. However, he does have to be well-versed in the psychodynamics of the doctor–patient relationship and all that this implies. For this model proceeds on the premise that, if properly managed, the doctor–patient relationship is the most effective psychological tool available to the physician.

If the physician is to establish a therapeutic relationship with the patient, he needs to have contact with him at regular intervals over a period of time; he needs to have some familiarity not only with the patient's intrapsychic environment, but with his external environment as well. Such knowledge is essential if he is to understand and help the patient modify his maladaptive behavior. Because the primary care physician provides comprehensive are over the long term, he is in a unique position to foster adaptation to chronic illness. However, these characteristics apply to physicians engaged in other forms of practice as well: such as the internist, the family physician, and the pediatrician. In fact, although the primary care physician is the protagonist of this book, any physician, regardless of his specialty, might be so designated. If he recognizes the need for psychological medicine in medical practice, sees his goal as helping the patient adapt to illness, while promoting his own adaptation to the patient, he is, in a sense, practicing primary care medicine.

The crucial question now arises as to the psychiatrist's role in facilitating the psychological care of the medically ill in general, and encouraging adoption of the model of psychological medicine described above in particular. The psychiatrist can fulfill one of many roles vis-à-vis his medical colleagues. At times, he may be expected to serve as a consultant, to collaborate with the physician in the treatment of a medically ill, emotionally troubled patient. Or he may function primarily in an educational capacity. In this book, my role is that of an educator. Specifically, I have attempted to fill some of the major gaps in the physician's knowledge of psychological medicine, gaps that arise primarily from deficiencies in his medical education and training. Thus, I have sought to illuminate the matrix of the doctor–patient relationship—its components, assessment, evaluation, and its appropriate utilization. I have attempted to outline the means by which the physician can deepen his understanding of what the patient is saying, and assess his psychological status within the realistic constraints imposed by a busy medical practice. And I have tried to clarify certain misconceptions that have long impeded the effective psychological care of patients with chronic medical illness.

Scope and Format. The volume is divided into three sections. Part I, the Conceptual Framework, is intended to provide certain background data which are more or less essential to the reader's understanding of the propositions advanced here. Thus, Chapter 1 sets the stage by describing the current status of psychological medicine. Chapter 2 consists of a summary of developmental theories that are critical to the comprehension of psychological reactions to disease in general, and have particular relevance for the elucidation of psychological responses to chronic illness. My efforts in Chapter 3 are directed toward the provision of a schema for the detection of psychological dysfunction in the medically ill, and general guidelines for the treatment of such dysfunction.

Part II consists of discussions of problematic clinical issues that are commonly encountered among the chronically ill patient population seen in the ambulatory medical setting.

Finally, in Part III, mechanisms for the implementation of psychological medicine are proposed for other settings as well, namely, the inpatient hospital ward and the institution-based tertiary medical care unit. Because the success of such attempts hinges, in large measure, on the organization and structure of these settings, these variables require some discussion. If only by implication I am saying that the adoption of a psychological approach to medical care in these environments depends not only on the predilection of the individual physician, but also, to a large extent, on the philosophy and organization of every sector of the teaching hospital, for that is where the future of psychological medicine will ultimately rest.

An author also has license in the prologue of his book to reply to anticipated criticisms of his effort. For one, the many modes of psychological intervention that have proven effective with the medically ill are not discussed at length; nor does the book include a detailed discussion of interview techniques. With regard to the first criticism, I feel that psychological intervention based on psychodynamic principles currently constitutes the most comprehensive approach to the management of the normal medically ill. Second, although I concede that a detailed discussion of interview techniques might be helpful, I also have the impression that when the physician uses the structured interview, he becomes so preoccupied with asking the "right" questions and getting the "right" answers that he frequently loses touch with the patient—and with himself.

I am also well aware of the criticisms that may accrue from other limitations I have imposed in regard to both the scope and format of this book. For example, in Part II, I have omitted discussion of such core issues as sexual dysfunction in the chronically ill; substance abuse, including alcoholism; psychopharmacology; and so forth. This volume was not intended to serve as an encyclopedic presentation of the multiple issues that are subsumed under the psychosocial problems encountered in the chronically ill. In any event, these specific issues have been discussed by experts at great length in the literature. This is not to say I have selected only "virgin" topics for consideration, or provided comprehensive discussions of these topics. The aged patient, noncompliance, obesity have all been dealt with in much greater detail elsewhere in the literature. In each instance, however, I have tried to add a new dimension to current thinking on these topics, and in these and every other issue discussed in this book, that new dimension is the extent to which the physician may unconsciously contribute to the maintenance of the patient's aberrant psychological and sometimes physical behavior.

Obviously, this orientation makes a certain amount of repetition inevitable. This is by intent; I believe the psychological approach I advocate graphically illustrates the universality of certain reactions in patient and doctor alike. Hopefully, the repetition of these reactions, however monotonous, will foster the physician's inclination toward self-observation. This is not to say that I regard the approach proposed here as definitive. No entirely satisfactory curriculum or model for the psychological care of the medically ill has yet been developed; this goal has only been approximated, and the model outlined herein is no exception.

I hope that this book will prove useful to physicians at every phase of their professional development. A new practitioner will learn quickly that 50 to 70 percent of all the patients who visit his office will present with a primary psychological problem or manifest psychological dysfunction secondary to the physical illness. An established practitioner, who has had ample exposure to the psychological reactions to chronic illness, should benefit from the systematic overview I have attempted to provide.

Psychiatrists, who as a group are more and more involved with teaching medical psychology to their nonpsychiatric colleagues, may find that *Psychological Interventions in Medical Practice* will assist them in their pedagogic pursuits.

I believe that knowledge of the psychological responses which are universally evoked by chronic illness, and the means by which these responses can be managed effectively, will make the physician's professional life more rewarding and enhance its quality by reducing the psychological pressures to which he is exposed daily.

James J. Strain

Acknowledgments

This book is the result of my collaboration with Elaine Cohen. In the cross-fertilization, the feedback, the ultimate unfolding of ideas, her involvement has been invaluable. Elaine Cohen's insight and understanding of psychoanalytic theory enabled the translation of complex ideas into cogent statements; her unique editorial skills allowed her to assume a major responsibility for the organization and format of the book. But her distinctive talent consisted in her capacity to move beyond manifest clinical data, to add a creative dimension to my theses. Last, but not least, her dedication to and interest in my work enabled this book to reach the light of day.

In a sense, this book is also a result of the special relationship I have enjoyed with the Chief of a department of internal medicine at a prestigious teaching hospital: Dr. David Hamerman has made me aware of the medical problems he and his staff encounter every day on the wards and in the clinics at Montefiore Hospital and Medical Center. He has allowed me to make him aware of the psychological components of these problems. Moreover, he has encouraged me to disseminate the principles of psychological medicine at several levels within his department of medicine. Through the years we have discussed countless medical patients, their psychological reactions to their illness, and the psychological reactions they engender, not only in the "students," i.e., house staff, but in the "teaching" attending as well. From this vantage point over the last decade, I was able to observe the patient, the doctor-in-training, and the doctor's teacher, and the nature of and sequelae of their interactions; this volume is an account of these observations.

I am also indebted to Dr. David Duffy, Director of the General Medical Clinic (Primary Care Clinic) at Montefiore, for giving me an opportunity to observe psychosocial teaching rounds and preceptor teaching sessions geared to train the new physician to detect and manage the adverse psychological reactions of his medically ill patient. And I would express my appreciation to Dr. Mary Ann

Cohen, liaison psychiatrist assigned to that Clinic, for helping to create a setting conducive to medical psychological teaching. The choice of clinical issues described in Part II of this book was prompted by consideration of the kind of problems these patients bring to their doctors.

Specific clinical issues discussed in this book have been influenced by my professional contact with other colleagues at Montefiore as well. Lenore Zohman, Head of the Work Physiology Unit, enhanced my understanding of the physiological as well as the psychological problems that confront the coronary patient throughout his illness. Kurt Elias, Attending Physician on the Oncology Service, conducted psychosocial teaching rounds prior to their formal institutionalization within our medical division. And Robert Soberman, Director of the Renal Dialysis Satellite Unit, invited us to experiment with new patient care and teaching models, and made it possible thereby to establish a medical–psychological program in that setting that could serve as a paradigm not only for the nephrologist and his staff, but also for the psychiatrist.

However essential medical programs may appear to their progenitors, the implementation of such programs requires support and money. The administration of Montefiore Hospital and Medical Center, and Dr. Martin Cherkasky in particular, have developed a policy that advocates and actively promotes a bio-psycho-social approach toward the understanding and treatment of medical illness. In addition to the monetary support from the hospital budget per se the Psychiatric Manpower Branch of the National Institute of Mental Health, under the direction of Dr. James S. Eaton, Jr., has since 1972 generously supported our experiments in training for primary care physicians, nonpsychiatric health care professionals, and psychiatrists, in psychological medicine.*

I would be remiss if I neglected to express my gratitude to the liaison fellows I have been fortunate enough to teach who have helped me hone and expand my thinking about medical psychology. My thinking has also been shaped in no small measure by my staff: Frank Baudry, Leslie Gise, Jimmie Holland, Richard Marks, Alfred Wiener, and Zebulon Taintor. My prior work with Stanley Grossman and James Spikes, Associate Director of the Division of Liaison Psychiatry at Montefiore, gave rise to many of the thoughts and ideas that have been developed further in this book. The Division of Liaison Psychiatry is committed to the promulgation of a new approach to

* Psychiatry–Liaison Training 2 TO–1 MH 13041–05 and Training in Psychosocial Aspects of Primary Care 1 TO–1 MH 14368–01.

medical care in which at times must inevitably be a hostile environment. The strength of our joint commitment and our shared triumphs and disappointments in the pursuit of that commitment have transformed my relationship with my staff and colleagues; I count them as my friends.

Several of my colleagues from both medicine and psychiatry have read this book in manuscript. Drs. Frank Baudry, David Duffy, Leslie Gise, Lewis Goldfrank, Kathy Degen, George Avery Ellsworth, Ira Lazar, Harry Mendelsohn, Philip Rogal, James Spikes, Zebulon Taintor, and Alfred Wiener all made comments and suggestions that have undoubtedly made the book more readable—and relevant. But my thanks go, in particular, to Drs. Arnold Drapkin and G. Gayle Stephens who gave countless hours of their valuable time to the analysis of this manuscript, and who helped me to see how this book could best serve the interests of physicians engaged in the general practice of medicine.

I also want to express my appreciation for help I received from Danny McKinney whose assistance over the years has freed me from innumerable chores so that I could write; Maureen Pons, who faithfully typed and retyped the manuscript through many long nights; to my secretaries, Ms. Denise Churba, Phyllis DeNome, and Irene Freemerman, for their untiring support of my efforts; to Kathy Gallo, who searched through the references; and to Richard Lampert and Sophia Prybylski, at Appleton-Century-Crofts, who tolerated my idiosyncracies with good humor during the processing of the manuscript; and Rodelinde Albrecht for her creative forbearance in designing the cover.

Finally, I would like to express my gratitude to Mrs. Allan D. Emil for giving me permission to use her sculpture for the cover of this book and for her continuing interest in my work.

Part I

The Conceptual Framework

Chapter 1

The Uses of Psychology in the Medical Setting

The battle for improved health care is currently being fought on many fronts—political, economic, and social. And there is no doubt that reforms in each of these sectors are sorely needed. Within the past decade, however, it has become increasingly evident that even if such reforms were implemented, patient care would still fall far short of the ideal. Unless medical practice is restructured to accommodate psychological as well as physiological medicine, it will remain unresponsive to the needs of the patient.*

Recent research findings attest to the validity of this contention. It has been established beyond doubt that a relationship exists between soma and psyche—and, to varying degrees, between psyche and soma—and that these relationships are operative in every disease. It follows, then, that psychological care is coordinate with medical care.

It is our impression that the great majority of clinicians subscribe to this hypothesis in principle; yet, for a variety of reasons, the mandate it carries to adopt a psychophysiological approach to medical care has not always been followed. Some physicians believe that the nature and organization of their medical practice precludes detailed consideration of the psychological components of disease. Others, who are strong proponents of the view that disease cannot be treated effectively unless the patient's psychological status is taken into account, may nonetheless

* The terms, *psychological medicine, psychological care,* etc., as they are used in this book, should be understood to connote the identification and management of social and cultural, as well as psychological issues in physical disease.

lack sufficient psychological knowledge and skills to provide effective psychological care for their patients. Physicians in both "categories" reflect the deficits that currently exist in medical training. The failure of medical educators to disseminate core psychological concepts, to provide training in the application of these concepts, and to emphasize their relevance at every level of medical practice has undermined efforts to provide psychological care, and resulted in a widespread tendency to view "humanism" as a viable substitute for psychological medicine. This tendency must, inevitably, detract from the quality of medical care, for humanism, in itself, is grossly inadequate to the task of fulfilling the psychological needs of the medical patient.

In medical parlance, "humanism" seems to mean little more than interest, kindness, and sympathy. It is an approach that is reminiscent of the medieval effort, which, instead of seeking a solution to the suffering of the individual, advocated charity (i.e., caring) as a proper response to all human misery. Human misery was regarded as a given; the emphasis was on its palliation rather than its alleviation. Similarly, the current "humane" approach to the medically ill accepts the psychological response of the patient who must cope with illness and pain as a given, and deals with this response on a superficial level.

Thus one can speculate that the physician who considers his humanism a potent psychological tool would limit his interventions on behalf of his patients to the reduction of manifest psychological symptoms via expressions of reassurance, support, and sympathy—and routine psychopharmacological intervention where indicated. But such efforts cannot, in themselves, foster adaptation to illness, which is the major goal of psychological care in the medical setting. The achievement of this goal requires a model of psychological medicine that moves well beyond a shallow, parochial humanism. It requires a model that addresses itself to the sources of the patient's maladaptive behaviors, to the stresses, conflicts, and regression that he inevitably experiences as a consequence of his illness, rather than the overt symptomatic expression of these phenomena; that rejects the concept that psychological symptoms (or their sources) can be treated in isolation. It is the combination of the physician's knowledge of his patient's physical status on the one hand, and his understanding of the dynamics of his patient's psychological responses on the other, that form the cornerstone of psychological care. Finally, a model of psychological medicine that promotes optimal care of the medically ill seeks to foster adaptation on the part of the physician, as well as the patient. It incorporates the proposition that once disease develops, certain personality changes inevitably occur in the patient which can be managed most effectively within the context of the doctor-patient relationship, provided the doctor is able to adapt to the patient and his illness.

The components of a model of psychological medicine gain clarity when they are viewed within a specific frame of reference. Our discussion has relevance, in particular, for the chronically ill ambulatory patient for whom comprehensive care must be provided over an extended period of time. Our protagonist is the primary care physician whose practice is structured to facilitate the implementation of a "bio-psycho-social" approach to medical care. Consequently, he is in an ideal position, given the knowledge and skills essential to this task, to attend to the psychological needs of the chronically ill patient, and thereby demonstrate the efficacy of such an approach.

Within this frame of reference, the model of psychological medicine will be discussed from three vantage points: (1) The rationale for its construction; (2) its underlying precepts; and (3) the factors that may impede its implementation.

RATIONALE FOR THE CONSTRUCTION OF A MODEL FOR PSYCHOLOGICAL CARE IN THE MEDICAL SETTING

The Bio-Psycho-Social Theory of Disease

Recent research has provided compelling evidence that psychological, social, and cultural—as well as biological—factors are involved, to varying degrees, in the initiation, course, and outcome of pathophysiological processes.* For example, such life stresses as bereavement, crowding, etc., are now considered to play a critical role in the onset and exacerbation of certain forms of physiological dysfunction. This thesis acquires clinical currency when it is considered in specific relation to one of the most commonly encountered diseases in medical practice, namely, coronary heart disease.

For schematic purposes, coronary heart disease can be divided

* Lipowski,[1] for example, has proposed an ecological viewpoint which states that ". . . the study of every disease must include the person, his body, and his human and non-human environments as essential components of the total system. . . ." Reiser's [2] bio-psycho-social field theory of disease emphasizes the interaction and interrelationship of all systems—physical, mental, psychological, environmental, etc. Finally, Engel [3] has vigorously urged the adoption of a bio-medico-psycho-social model of disease that would be applicable to psychological as well as physiological dysfunction, and would recognize that complex interactions between the individual and his total environment are major determinants of health and disease states.

into six distinct phases: (1) pre-illness, (2) acute illness (prior to establishing medical contact), (3) acute illness (initial medical contact), (4) acute illness—coronary care unit, (5) acute illness—inhospital convalescence, and (6) posthospital convalescence. It is commonly acknowledged that psychosocial issues play a role at every phase (Fig. 1). It is less commonly recognized, however, that the meaning and nature of these psychological issues change at various phases of the illness, that they assume different degrees of importance, and require different modes of psychological intervention. Most important, it is not sufficiently recognized that the effectiveness of psychological intervention at particular phases of this illness may well determine its course and outcome.

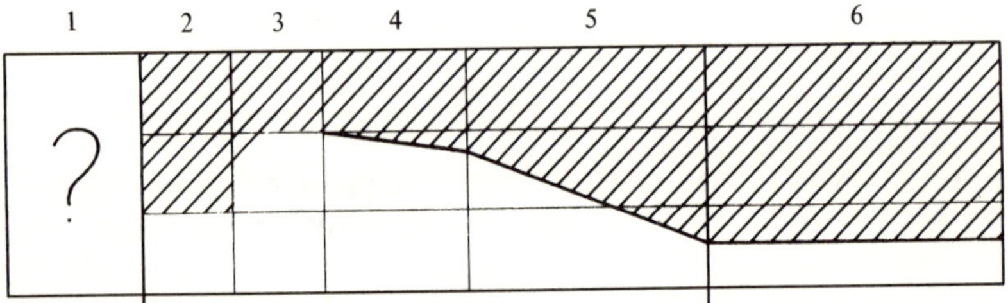

Pre-Illness	Acute illness	Convalescence
Primary prevention	Secondary prevention	Tertiary prevention
Predisposing factors a) psychological stress b) smoking c) diet d) blood pressure	Initiating factors a) affects b) exaggerated character traits	Psychological sequelae a) inhibitions b) phobias c) disturbance of affect e.g., anxiety, depression

Psychological.
Physiological.

FIGURE 1

Phases of coronary heart disease: psychological and physiological components. 1, pre-illness; 2, acute illness—prior to establishing medical contact; 3, acute illness—initial medical contact; 4, acute illness—coronary care unit; 5, acute illness, inhospital convalescence; 6, posthospital covalescence.

The pre-illness phase. The physiological factors that are thought to predispose to coronary heart disease, e.g., smoking, high serum lipids, diet, excessive body weight, the presence of other illnesses (diabetes, hypertension), inadequate regular exercise, and genetic endowment, have been discussed at length in the literature. Certain predisposing psychological factors, e.g., psychological stress; a particular personality type (Type "A"), described by Friedman and Rosenman [4] as driving, competitive, time conscious, and the like; and socioeconomic phenomena, have been implicated as well. Admittedly, the precise nature of the interrelationship between these psychological variables and the physiological risk factors mentioned above is not yet fully understood. Nor has it been determined which combination of these variables is most pernicious in terms of the predisposition to this illness. Nevertheless, to the degree that these risk factors are known to exist, the physician is in an ideal position to counsel the vulnerable patient, and thereby reduce their potential impact.

Acute illness (prior to establishing medical contact). It has also been established that a variety of psychosocial factors can cause a delay in the patient's prompt response to the signs and symptoms of coronary heart disease. Obviously, the psychological mechanism of denial is involved, but various fantasies and unconscious wishes may also contribute to the patient's aberrant and self-destructive behavior: Among these we would include the patient's need to defend himself against fears of helplessness and passivity, of being damaged; his wish to suffer because of unconscious feelings of guilt; and/or his belief that he is invincible. Or the patient may believe, on a conscious level, that he is making too much of his symptoms, that these, like others he has had in the past, e.g., cough, fever, etc., will pass in time. (And, in that event, his behavior may be a product of family attitudes toward illness—or of his relationship with his doctor.)

In the meantime, the patient's fears and anxiety continue to mount as his chest pains persist—with dire physiological consequences. There is irrefutable evidence that volatile emotions, and anxiety in particular, result in the production of excess amounts of catecholamines (epinephrine and norepinephrine), which, in turn, increases the oxygen requirements of the heart, causes tachycardia and perhaps arrythmias, and can result in an increase in the size of the myocardial infarction, in hypotension or shock, peripheral vasoconstriction, etc., all of which will have a deleterious effect on an already compromised cardiovascular system.

It follows, then, that if patients were encouraged to respond promptly to their symptoms, control of affects, e.g., anxiety, would reduce cardiac stress, and thereby reduce morbidity and mortality in this phase.

Acute illness (initial medical contact). Since heightened anxiety contributes to autonomic arousal and concomitant cardiovascular effects, efforts to diminish the patient's anxiety by any means—pharmacological or psychological intervention, or environmental manipulation—are mandatory. It has been demonstrated that such efforts should be instituted immediately in the acute care triage setting after the physician arrives at a diagnosis of myocardial infarction.

Acute illness (coronary care unit). Although, as pointed out, denial may militate against seeking medical care promptly, this mechanism often fosters adaptation in the coronary care unit: Patients who can deny an excessively pessimistic outcome (but do not deny the existence of their illness) have diminished affective arousal and decreased morbidity. This thesis is supported by several studies. Stein [5] has shown that "gloomy" patients in a coronary care unit have increased morbidity. And Cassem and Hackett [6] found that the mortality rate from coronary heart disease was significantly diminished in patients referred for psychiatric consultation.

The patient's psychological reactions to his coronary heart disease are shaped by his pre-illness emotional conflicts, earlier hospital experiences, the meaning the illness holds for him, and the nature and quality of his relationships with his earliest caretakers, e.g., parents, pediatrician, etc. Thus, during this phase, aberrant or bizarre behavior may arise from fears of excessive dependency, morbid fears of bodily damage, concerns about the loss of sexual identity (i.e., the patient's fear that he will emerge from his illness "half a man"—a shadow of his former self). On the other hand, because coronary heart disease often has a sudden onset, it may overwhelm the patient, leaving him confused, panic-stricken, and numb. Or the patient may manifest a variety of aberrant behaviors—anxiety reactions, depressive reactions, exaggerated character traits (e.g., hyperactivity)—that ultimately put more stress on his heart. Whatever their source and nature, if the patient's maladaptive psychological responses to coronary heart disease are not dealt with in the acute phase of this illness, they can result in a deteriorating cardiac status or plant the seeds for a cardiac neurosis.

Acute illness (inhospital convalescence). At this stage of the illness, psychological intervention focuses on the patient's concerns about leaving the protective hospital environment and returning home, and specifically on his concerns about re-entry into his family and the resumption of work and sex. The patient's anticipatory anxiety in this regard needs to be alleviated via reality-testing, reduction of misconceptions, education with regard to commonly experienced apprehensions, and so forth.

Posthospital convalescence. During this phase, the possible psychological sequelae of coronary heart disease—work and/or sex inhibitions or phobias, and disturbances of affect, i.e., anxiety and/or depression—must be dealt with in order to reduce these sources of psychological stress—and secondary physiological stress. Psychological intervention at this phase will help the patient to adapt to his physiological limitations, thereby reducing the possibility of a recurrent myocardial infarction, angina, congestive heart failure, and arrhythmias. Furthermore the physician can help to reduce the impact of those factors that are thought to predispose to, initiate, and sustain coronary heart disease.

The data presented above attest to the validity of the bio-psycho-social theory of disease, and to the need for a model of psychological medicine that will make that theory operational, that will enable the physician to deal effectively with the psychological issues that arise and may complicate the patient's physiological status, not only in coronary heart disease but in every disease. The rationale for the construction of such a model has been underscored by other events in medicine as well.

The Technological Revolution

Technological advances in medicine have given rise to new human problems and highlighted existing ones. For example, almost invariably, the intensive care unit evokes psychological stress and taxes the coping capacities of the acutely ill patient. Being on renal dialysis presents major psychological, as well as physiological hazards. These problems defy resolution by means of the traditional humane approach to patient care. They require the physician's understanding of the psychodynamics of the patient's response to his illness—and his treatment—and the formulation of a management plan that incorporates psychological concepts.

The technological revolution has also resulted in a marked increase in the number of chronically ill and/or aged, who currently constitute the bulk of the patient population seen in medical practice. Although funding has been made available for the medical care of these populations, it is generally conceded that existing systems do not fulfill the criteria of adequate physiological care; nor do they make provision for routine evaluation and management of the psychological problems these patients typically present.

THE PRECEPTS OF PSYCHOLOGICAL CARE OF THE CHRONICALLY ILL

Delineation of the precepts that underlie the model of psychological medicine presented here follows naturally from the content of the preceding subsections of this chapter.

1. The physician sees as a major goal of his efforts on behalf of the chronically ill facilitation of the patient's adaptation to his illness, which is contingent, in turn, on his own capacity to adapt to the patient.
2. In general, his efforts to foster such adaptation proceed within the broad framework of the bio-psycho-social theory of disease.
3. Specifically, his interventions to this end are based on his knowledge of core psychological concepts.
4. Finally, he recognizes as essential the creation of an ecology that will facilitate the incorporation of psychological concepts into medical practice.

Facilitation of the Patient's Adaptation to Chronic Illness

The importance of the patient's ability to adapt to his illness is not a new concept, of course. But the ways in which the physician can foster such adaptation, and the ways in which he may, albeit unwittingly, impede the adaptive process, have not been sufficiently explored in the literature to date. Since, as noted above, the most sophisticated therapeutic instrument at the physician's disposal is the physician himself, it is his task to use a concordant doctor–patient relationship to full therapeutic advantage; to modify a fluctuating or discordant relationship, when feasible; and, when the differences between patient and doctor have become irreconcilable, when the physician's negative feelings toward the patient are protracted, cannot be altered, and diminish the quality of treatment, to dissolve the doctor–patient relationship.

Ideally, in the course of their long-term relationship, the primary care physician will have an opportunity to correct the misconceptions and misperceptions of reality that prevent the patient from developing a disease-compatible life style. What needs to be emphasized is that if he is to help the patient learn to live with his illness, the doctor may have to "correct" his own misconceptions and misperceptions of reality. Thus, an essential prerequisite for the effective management of the chronically ill is the formulation of realistic treatment goals. However determined his therapeutic efforts, the physician will not be able to help some diabetic patients to reduce; he cannot hope to restore optimal cardiac function in some coronary patients; he cannot expect to mobilize arthritic joints in some aged patients. And regardless of these patients' attempts to adapt to their altered physiological, psychological, and social status, inevitably, the quality of their lives will be altered by their disability. The physician must be prepared to adapt to their situation. He needs to accept the fact that a relationship, based on sound psychological principles, is often the prescribed treatment for the aged, the dying, and some chronically ill patients. And he can take comfort from the fact that a concordant doctor–patient relationship remains a powerful therapeutic tool even under the most unpropitious conditions.

The Bio-Psycho-Social Theory of Disease

The concept of the interdependence of physiological variables, on the one hand, and psychological, social, and cultural variables on the other, stands at the center of our model of psychological medicine. Thus the physician proceeds on the premise that effective management begins with his understanding of the psychobiology of physiological states. Hopefully such understanding will dispel the myths and misconceptions that frequently surround them. His efforts are based on the precept, demonstrated in our discussion earlier of coronary heart disease, that his physiological interventions should be guided, at times, by his awareness of the patient's unique psychological needs at a given phase of his illness, and vice versa.

The Incorporation of Core Psychological Concepts into Medical Practice

Obviously, the primary care physician is not expected to function as a traditional psychotherapist (or family therapist). But this does not gainsay the fact that the therapeutic effectiveness of his relationship with his patient ultimately depends upon his possession of certain basic psychological knowledge. This knowledge, which has heretofore been identified with psychiatrists, psychologists, sociologists and social workers, can be readily incorporated into primary care practice.

The physician who is conversant with the psychodynamics of medical illness will not equate expressions of kindness, caring, and sympathy with psychological care. He perceives the psychological manifestations of the patient's physical illness, and his psychological behavior secondary to that illness, as the product of his past and current psychological, social, and cultural experiences. And, given this orientation, the physician recognizes that blanket reassurance will not allay the coronary patient's anxiety about returning to work and/or sex; that telling a patient to "tough it out" will not relieve his depression, that telling him that nothing is wrong with him will not automatically put an end to his complaints. By the same token, the physician who equates psychological care with permissiveness, or believes that the chronically ill patient is "entitled" to engage in behavior that would ordinarily be regarded as socially unacceptable, is not acting in the patient's best interests.

This permissive approach is reminiscent of the tendency of some physicians to view the doctor–patient relationship as essentially a parent–child relationship, with the patient assuming minimal responsibility for the course and outcome of his illness. In contrast, in the context of the model of psychological medicine presented here, the patient is perceived as the doctor's partner in the pursuit of health, in the sense that while the patient has the right to participate in decisions relating to his health care, once such decisions have been reached, he also has an obligation to assume responsibility, commensurate with his capacities, for his well-being. Obviously, it would be unrealistic to expect all patients to be able to exert the discipline necessary to act on their doctor's recommendations. The patient who cannot or will not assume responsibility for his own health care is not abandoned. In such instances, the physician attempts to understand the roots of his patient's noncompliance, and, if feasible, help him to overcome it.

The point is that the physician whose efforts to provide his patients with psychological care based on psychodynamic principles asks questions that differ markedly from those asked by his "humanistic" colleagues, and he gets different answers. His approach is unique in that it reflects a realization that the doctor–patient relationship proceeds on two levels: the manifest and the latent. For example, the physician who is aware of the psychodynamics of hypochondriasis is also aware of the fact that the hypochondriac who complains constantly about his symptoms and "begs" to be cured may, in fact, be "begging" for a relationship with the physician, a relationship he expects to buy and pay for with his suffering. To take away the symptoms of such a patient—the symptoms the patient believes are essential to the maintenance of his relationship with the doctor—would be psychologically inappropriate.

In short, the physician's interventions will succeed only if he has available to him a theoretical substrate enabling him to organize his thinking in regard to psychosocial considerations. From it he can abstract a workable schema for the application of data on human behavior, psychobiological correlations, treatment modalities, etc., that have relevance for the individual patient. Such a substrate would, in addition, promote self-awareness in the physician so that he will be alert not only to those factors that can foster adaptation in his patient, but also to those personality traits within himself that may impede adaptation.

The Creation of an Ecology That Will Facilitate the Incorporation of Psychological Concepts into Medical Practice

It goes without saying that if psychological care is to be effective, the organization and structure of medical practice, and the ambiance of the medical setting, must be conducive to the implementation of its precepts. In such a setting, the patient would be more likely to discuss his psychological and social—as well as his physical—"complaints" with his doctor. In such a setting, the physician and his "normal" medically ill patient may come to regard evaluation of the patient's psychosocial status as a routine medical procedure—no less essential, for example, than taking his blood pressure.

Because the primary care setting exemplifies this ideal, it may be helpful to attempt to summarize briefly the salient features of this form of practice.*

1. The primary care physician is the physician of first contact. He makes the initial assessment of the patient's total condition, psychological as well as physical, and attempts to manage as many of the patient's problems, psychological as well as physical, as possible with minimal use of referral. It has been suggested that by fulfilling these functions the primary care physician reduces the use of hospitals,[7] the length of hospitalization, and even diminishes the use of ambulatory medical facilities.
2. When the patient's physical and/or psychological problems do not lie within his purview, the primary care physician coordinates the services of specialists on the patient's behalf. The need remains, however, for the primary care physician to augment and secure the benefits of the extramural services the patient has received. Thus, even during those periods when

* Other forms of medical practice—family practice, pediatrics, internal medicine—can be similarly characterized. We have selected the primary care physician as our model because these characteristics are regarded as synonymous with primary care medicine.

the patient is not under his direct care, he continues to maintain contact with the patient and his family, and does not relinquish his responsibility for the patient.

3. The three preeminent characteristics of primary care practice —continuity of care, sufficient contact with the patient, and comprehensive care—make the primary care physician an ideal vehicle for the systematic application of core psychological concepts in the medical setting. Nor is the potential effectiveness of the primary care physician in this regard limited to the chronically ill and/or aged. It is now recognized that 50 to 80 percent of all patients seeking medical care suffer from either a primary psychological dysfunction, or a psychological dysfunction secondary to their medical illness.[8] The organization and structure of primary care practice is ideally suited, then, to the accurate diagnosis and effective management of the great majority of medical patients.

IMPEDIMENTS TO THE IMPLEMENTATION OF A MODEL OF PSYCHOLOGICAL MEDICINE

Some of the obstacles to the application in clinical practice of the precepts of psychological care elucidated above were mentioned earlier. They are discussed in further detail below.

Facilitation of the Patient's Adaptation to Chronic Illness

While the physician knows that it is his responsibility to help the patient to adapt to his illness, he is often reluctant to concede that the patient's adaptive capacity will depend, in large measure, on whether the physician himself is able to adapt to the patient. The physician's ambivalence in this regard can be ascribed to his reluctance to explore his own feelings and responses to the patient and his consequent inability to come to terms with these feelings. In that event, the physician's image of himself as the "powerful healer," and, at times, the "worker of miracles," may, paradoxically, be a major obstacle to his capacity to provide effective psychological care for his patient.* Obviously, a feeling of self-confidence is an essential prerequisite for the clinical competence. It is when these feelings of self-confidence do not allow the physician

* The physician's unconscious attitudes vis-à-vis his patients are discussed in some detail by Spikes and Holland.[9]

to explore his psychological responses to the patient, and the extent to which they may be influencing treatment, that they become pernicious. For example, the physician whose overriding goal is to cure a physiological dysfunction may find it difficult to modify this goal when his only alternative is to offer the aged patient psychological support, or help the patient with an irreversible organic mental syndrome to adapt to his disability. If the physician's psychological interventions are then reduced to expressions of kindness, caring, and sympathy, he is likely to become a negative force for adaptation.

The Bio-Psycho-Social Theory of Disease

A major impediment to the incorporation of the bio-psycho-social theory of disease as part of the physician's orientation is his tendency to perceive technological advances and psychological advances as antithetical forces in medicine. The machine is perceived as the "villain in the piece," as posing a threat to the patient's humanness by reducing him to a cipher. Actually, inasmuch as its function is to save, prolong, and improve the quality of life, the machine serves a humanistic function. Clearly, then, the new technological advances and the new insights we have gained into the psychological responses of the medically ill have a common purpose.

The belief that modern medical technology and psychological medicine are incompatible has distorted their relationship. But, more important, it has created a conflict in the physician who tends to regard medical practice in black or white terms, as either scientific or psychological in orientation. Given this perspective, the physician may harbor the conviction that by focusing on the psychological aspects of the patient's condition, he will neglect the physiological aspects of patient care. Thus this misconception becomes a major deterrent to the incorporation of the bio-psycho-social model of disease into medical practice.

The Incorporation of Core Psychological Concepts into Medical Practice

The physician's unconscious fantasies may also be a powerful deterrent to his capacity to apply core psychological knowledge on the patient's behalf.

A corollary of the physician's image of himself as the all-powerful healer is his image of himself as a destructive force. If that fantasy is operative, the physician may be convinced that an attempt to probe the patient's reactions to his illness, beyond his superficial responses, will stir up "dangerous feelings" or precipitate acute psychological distress. In a sense, he likens palpation of the patient's deeper feelings and concerns to palpation of a pheochromocytoma. In short, he may be convinced of his capacity to precipitate acute psychological distress at the worst, and the patient's acute embarrassment or humiliation at the least. In that event, he would understandably be reluctant to move beyond superficial psychological intervention.

Impediments to the application of core psychological principles in medical practice may be rooted in other considerations as well. Despite his psychological orientation, the physician's efforts to explore the patient's psychosocial status may be impeded by an unconscious fear that the patient's revelations will exacerbate his own fears and anxieties with respect to growing old, to diminished cognitive capacity, to failing health, or to being alone. Or, on another level, the physician may be afraid that if he attempts to explore the patient's feelings, he may become the target of the patient's hostility, either because the patient considers such information sacrosanct, or because he equates good medical care with a cold, objective, "scientific" approach.

The Creation of an Ecology that will Foster the Implementation of Psychological Medicine

A possible impediment to the physician's full utilization of the "ideal" ecology provided by the primary care setting is his conviction that once he begins to explore psychological issues in depth, he will be overwhelmed by them and "lose control of the situation." But, just as the psychiatrist feels no compunction about interrupting the patient when his allotted time is up, the physician need feel no compunction about putting a halt to the patient's complaints, to what appears to be an interminable account of his emotional problems. If the doctor has conveyed his interest and concern to the patient, his willingness to talk with him again at their next appointment, then, in all likelihood, the patient will not interpret an interruption as a rejection. In any event, the physician's psychological evaluation of the patient can proceed without fanfare, and over several visits, concurrent with his physical examination. The physician can learn a great deal about the patient by observing his behavior, e.g., his mood, his ability to grasp concepts, his spontaneity, and, most important, his capacity to relate to the doctor.

In addition to the prerequisites listed above, the efficacy of the physician's efforts to provide optimal psychological care for his chronically ill patient depends on the acquisition of certain knowledge and skills. First, he must acquire sufficient knowledge of the psychobiological determinants of adaptation to medical illness. Second, he must be able to elicit significant psychosocial data from the patient. Third, the integration of psychological concepts in medical care is contingent upon the meaningful formulation of these data, and the physician's ability to design a treatment plan that will reflect these data.

The blueprint of a model of psychological medicine is still evolving; our efforts in the chapters that follow represent an attempt to delineate its essential ingredients with greater specificity—and underscore its relevance for the management of the chronically ill.

REFERENCES

1. Lipowski ZJ: Physical illness, the patient and his environment; psychosocial foundations of medicine. In Reiser M (ed): American Handbook of Psychiatry, Vol. 4. New York, Basic Books, 1975, p 3
2. Reiser MF: Changing theoretical concepts in psychosomatic medicine. In Reiser M (ed): American Handbook of Psychiatry, Vol. 4. New York, Basic Books, 1975, p 477
3. Engel GL: The need for a new medical model: a challenge for biomedicine. Science 196:129, 1977
4. Friedman M, Rosenman RH: Association of specific overt behavior patterns with blood and cardiovascular findings. JAMA 169:1286, 1950
5. Stein MJ: Psychosocial response of patients: postmyocardial infarction. American Psychosomatic Meetings, Philadelphia, 1974
6. Cassem NH, Hackett TP: Psychiatric consultation in a coronary care unit. Ann Intern Med 75:9, 1971
7. San Agustin M, Goldfrank L, Matz R, et al: Reorganization of ambulatory health care in an urban municipal hospital—primary care and its impact on hospitalization. Arch Intern Med. 136:1262, 1976.
8. Lipowski ZJ: Review of consultation psychiatry and psychosomatic medicine. II. General principles. Psychosom Med 29(2):153, 1967
9. Spikes J, Holland J: The physician's response to the dying patient. In Strain JJ, Grossman S (eds): Psychological Care of the Medically Ill: A Primer of Liaison Psychiatry. New York, Appleton, 1975, p 138

Chapter 2

The Psychological Determinants of Adaptation to Chronic Illness

Inevitably, the primary care physician will encounter a significant number of patients who, at a particular phase of their chronic illness, or from the outset, present certain patterns of behavior indicative of a failure to adapt to their disability. Among the behaviors that signal maladaptation we would include an excessive dependence on others (which is not physiologically justified), or, conversely, a pseudo-independence; excessive passivity, or conversely, excessive activity (which is medically counterindicated); a diminished sense of sexual identity, or an inappropriate hypersexuality; a preoccupation with self—to the exclusion of all other interests; and, finally, a diminished sense of self-worth. More specific clinical indications of a deficit in the patient's coping mechanisms—e.g., depression, noncompliance, anxiety, sexual and work inhibitions—may be apparent as well.

If only because the patient's inability to adapt to his illness is frequently accompanied by a recurrence or worsening of his physical symptoms, the accurate diagnosis and effective management of his adverse psychological reactions to his illness becomes mandatory. In general, the physician's competence in this regard will depend on his understanding of the psychological origins and development of human behavior. Specifically, he needs to be knowledgable with respect to the four intrapsychic parameters of psychological adaptation to chronic illness: (1) the patient's response to the psychological stress that is universally evoked by medical illness; (2) the extent to which he regresses as a consequence of his illness; (3) the conflicts that are revived by this regression; and (4) the quality of the patient's current object relationships (and, in particular, the doctor–patient relationship).

THE THEORETICAL SUBSTRATE

In many respects, the psychological tasks imposed by medical illness in the adult replicate the psychological tasks imposed on the child at crucial stages in his development. Essentially, all of these tasks center, directly or indirectly, on the child's ability to relate to others, and the way he perceives (and relates to) himself.

In the earliest years of life, the quality of the child's relationships with others, i.e., his object relationships,* is necessarily circumscribed by his biological propensities. Thus, initially he is preoccupied with self; yet, he has no sense of self, and no sense of sexual identity. He is unable to differentiate self from others, and, in particular, from mother—the primary object. More precisely, he assumes a passive stance in regard to mother, on whom he is dependent for survival, and whom he perceives as a need-satisfying object. Only as biological development proceeds, and mental and motor anlage unfold, is the child able to move beyond total involvement with self to a concern for others as well; to differentiate self from others; to assume a more active stance; to achieve greater autonomy; and to perceive the object (mother) not only in terms of her usefulness, but also as a source of love and pleasure, independent of her usefulness. Moreover, his initial psychological asexuality gives way to an awareness of his specific sexual identity.

In summary, then, in the course of normal development, there is a movement (1) from passivity to activity; (2) from dependence to independence; (3) from an ambiguous sense of sexual identity, to a definite sense of sexual identity; (4) from perception of the object as needed, to perception of the object as wanted; and (5) from total involvement with self, to a concern for others as well.

Development proceeds along these tracts simultaneously, rather than consecutively, and not necessarily at the same pace. It is a process that continues throughout one's lifetime, and the individual does not necessarily achieve the same level of maturity in all of these areas. For example, an individual at maturity may be fairly independent, but he may still be excessively self-centered. Furthermore, having achieved a degree of independence, relatively speaking, does not rule out the possi-

* The term *object* is used in the psychoanalytic literature to designate persons and things in the external environment that are of psychological moment for the individual.

bility, under the stress of chronic illness, of a temporary or permanent regression to a more primitive level of functioning. The stresses that give rise to regression (and conflict) are not unique to chronic illness, of course. They are evoked by acute illness and hospitalization as well, and can be clearly demarcated when considered in relation to these life events.

THE CONCEPT OF PSYCHOLOGICAL STRESS

Psychological Stress Evoked by Acute Illness and Hospitalization

Strain and Grossman [1] postulate that all acutely ill, hospitalized patients are vulnerable to eight categories of psychological stress:

The Basic Threat to Self-Esteem and Sense of Intactness (*Narcissistic Integrity*). Sudden illness, hospitalization, and the threat of death challenges the individual's belief that he is indestructible, that he is the master of his destiny.

These events also challenge the infantile fantasy, which may persist in adult life, that our omnipotent parents (and, later, the physician) can ensure our pain-free, pleasurable, and protected existence—and our immortality.

Fear of Strangers. When the patient enters the hospital, he feels that he has put his life into the hands of a group of strangers to whom he has no close personal ties, and who may or may not be competent to assume responsibility for his survival.

This feeling is reminiscent of the fear of strangers which can first be observed in the human infant from the third to the sixth month of life—when the sight of an unfamiliar face produces a startle response, body tension, and tearfulness.

Separation Anxiety. The hospitalized patient experiences anxiety because he is separated from important persons and things—from the environment that provided the support and gratification necessary for his effective functioning and sense of intactness.

This anxiety mimics the anxiety that characterizes the separation–individuation phase of development, which occurs between the ages of six and thirty months. The toddler's ability to separate from his mother is a crucial first step toward the achievement of autonomy. But the individual is always "vulnerable" in this regard; the anxiety surrounding separation may be reactivated, to varying degrees, in later life whenever there is a need to separate from the familiar and confront the unknown.

Fear of Loss of Love and Approval. This stress may be prominent, for example, in the patient who has undergone a mutilating surgical procedure, or in the patient who, because of a debilitating illness, is unable to return to work, and fears that his passive dependence on others may incur the disapproval of his family and friends—and the loss of their esteem.

The fear of loss of love and approval can be observed or inferred from the behavior of the two-year-old, and it persists to varying degrees throughout life. This fear has its onset when the child realizes that his needs may not be gratified automatically by his mother, that their fulfillment is contingent in part upon his ability to please her.

Fear of the Loss of Control of Developmentally Achieved Functions. Severe illness may temporarily undo previously mastered physical and mental functions. Some patients agonize over the transient loss of these functions, and remain convinced, despite assurances to the contrary, that they will never be regained.

Concurrent with his fear of the loss of love and approval, the young child fears the loss of previously achieved physical and mental functions. Specifically, he is aware that his movement from passivity to activity, via the achievement of new skills—standing, walking, talking, etc.—evokes pleasure in his mother. Thus, he equates the loss of these functions with the loss of her love and approval and, carried to its worst possible outcome, the loss of mother herself.

Fear of Loss of or Injury to Body Parts. Once the patient enters the hospital, his body becomes the property of his physicians, to do with what they will. His bodily fluids are drained; he is exposed, probed, and weakened. These routine hospital procedures require the patient to assume a passive-submissive stance vis-à-vis the physician, which may stir up frightening sexual and aggressive fantasies.

Specifically, these fantasies may reactivate the fears of bodily damage that typically arise in the child at about the age of two-and-a-half, and reach their peak when he is five—during the period when he is moving from an ambiguous to a definite sense of sexual identity. This fear of injury to body parts, which is one of the most persistently potent psychological forces in childhood, is readily reactivated in any potentially traumatic situation (either perceived or actual), and particularly by acute illness and hospitalization.

Guilt and Fear of Retaliation. Feelings of guilt and shame which may be revived by physical illness, and the patient's fantasy that illness and hospitalization are punishment for previous "sins" of omission or commission are a major source of psychological stress.

Although he does not identify it as such, the three-year-old child feels ashamed when, for a variety of reasons, he regresses to an earlier stage in his development—when, for example, he loses previously achieved sphincter control, or is unable to control his unacceptable behavior or impulses. Characteristically, when he gets sick, he believes his illness is a consequence of these "sins." Despite the acquisition of logic, intelligence, and experience, the perception of illness and hospitalization as retaliation by a "higher being" for one's transgressions persists in the adult.

Fear of Pain. The fear of pain cuts across all of the stresses listed above. In the vulnerable patient, each of these stresses may compound the basic painful experience, and, conversely, severe pain may increase the magnitude of each of these stresses.

Pain—in the guise of physical discomfort, hunger, or the like—is part of the human condition from birth, and fear of pain is never fully overcome, for once eased, the concern that it may recur remains. The individual copes with pain differently at different stages in his development. The neonate's total organismic reaction to the pain of discomfort or hunger, his demands for immediate relief, and his total dependence on his mother as the source of such relief, give way in the course of normal development to the child's increasing capacity to tolerate discomfort, to his growing ability to separate from mother, to respond favorably to strangers, to be more confident about his ability to control his body, and, in time, to guard his body against injury. Moreover, he is better able to separate mind from body, so that mental pain is less likely to be translated into physical pain.

Although these stresses are present to varying degrees in every medical patient, inevitably they take on different forms at different phases of disease.

Psychological Stress Evoked by Chronic Illness Treated in the Ambulatory Setting

In contrast to the vivid manifestations of stress in the acutely ill, hospitalized patient, the chronically ill ambulatory patient's responses to stress are less likely to emerge in "pure" form. This does not necessarily mean, however, that the intrapsychic experience of stress is attenuated.

For example, the acutely ill, hospitalized patient typically fears that he may not be able to return to work, to sex, that his relationships with others will be altered as a consequence of his illness. But, often, he is able to master the threat these fears pose to his self-esteem in the hospital setting by the use of denial or fantasy. That is, he may deny the severity, or even the existence of his illness, and/or fantasize on a conscious level that his life will be enriched and positively altered by his experience: "Now that they've almost lost me, my family will realize how important I am to them; everyone will appreciate me more now." His acute illness may also reinforce the patient's unconscious feelings of omnipotence: "If I could survive that, I can survive anything." Or, there may be a reduction of stress once the acute stage has passed, and the feelings of guilt and shame that are typically reactivated at the onset of physical illness diminish in intensity. The patient's conviction that his acute illness and hospitalization are punishment for previous "sins" of omission or commission loses potency once it is expanded to include the fantasy that he had paid his "debt."

However, once the patient is discharged from the hospital and must re-enter the community, his capacities are actually put to the test. Now he must demonstrate his ability to perform successfully at work and sex, and to maintain satisfactory interpersonal relationships. Once he is confronted with the reality that his performance in one—or all—of these spheres may be impaired, the defenses (i.e., the use of fantasy and denial) that served him well while he was hospitalized may no longer be adequate. In fact, they may impede his adaptation. To illustrate, for the ambulatory patient who denies, or, more accurately, is unable to accept his limitations, the sheer effort of maintaining a facade of well-being in the face of actual physical disability will, in itself, constitute a chronic stress. And this is particularly true of the patient whose self-esteem is contingent upon his performance, which he believes is essential to retaining the love and approval of others.

Other stresses may diminish in the ambulatory setting for a variety of reasons. For example, the fear of dying and bodily damage may become less potent for the patient who no longer faces a life-threatening situation. As long as his condition remains stable, he may be able to repress these fears.

In other instances, temporal factors serve to diminish the psychological impact of illness. Among the stresses to which the acutely ill patient is vulnerable, we listed the fear of (or actual) loss of control of developmentally achieved functions, which places an immediate burden on the patient's emotional equilibrium. But when the loss of a developmentally achieved function is permanent, the chronicity of the disability may enable the patient to adapt in time to that loss, thereby reducing its psychological impact. Or the loss may occur gradually, over an extended period, permitting the patient to adapt to increasing disability.

Mrs. V., a 73-year-old woman with a chronic organic mental syndrome, secondary to her long-standing obstructive pulmonary emphysema, had been under Dr. J.'s care for 15 years and had managed to function fairly well. Over a 6-month period, however, there was increasing evidence of impaired judgment as well as memory loss. Mrs. V. forgot to take her medication or couldn't remember Dr. J.'s instructions. When she could not remember the name of his nurse—a woman she had known for the past ten years—Dr. J. felt that a formal reexamination of his patient's mental status was indicated. The results showed that Mrs. V.'s cognitive functioning had worsened significantly since her last evaluation.

Because her current symptoms represented a gradual worsening of an existing deficit, Mrs. V. was not particularly upset by her impaired memory. Moreover, she was able to use subterfuge to conceal and thereby adapt to this deficit. Thus, she made excuses for her lapses, and surreptitiously left notes to herself that allowed her to function more efficiently, with the result that the full extent of her memory loss was not apparent to her husband or herself.

The distinctions we have drawn between the psychological stresses experienced by the acutely ill hospitalized patient and those experienced by the chronically ill ambulatory patient have theoretical and clinical relevance. In the final analysis, however, the nature and magnitude of the stresses evoked in the patient by medical illness will not depend solely on the stage of his illness, the setting in which it is treated, or even its nature and severity. The kind of stresses his illness gives rise to and their magnitude will depend, primarily, on the way the illness is experienced intrapsychically by the patient. The present is always evaluated in terms of the past.

THE CONCEPT OF REGRESSION

Illness, which necessitates the curtailment of activity and submission to medical caretakers and procedures, sets in motion the psychological regression that is an innate property of mental life. The ability to follow orders, to let others "take over"—in short, to adopt a dependent life style—may be essential to the patient's survival during the acute stage of his illness. It may be necessary throughout a chronic illness in some patients, or only during periods of exacerbation in others. The point is that regression is not pathological per se; it becomes pathological only when the patient's desire to remain helpless and dependent outweighs the reality of his physical and mental limitations. To illustrate, during the acute stage of his illness, the coronary patient must be carefully monitored with regard to his diet, smoking, physical activities, etc. If he is not able to acquiesce to authority and accept these limitations, he runs the risk of a shorter life span. On the other hand, if he continues to restrict physiologically beneficial activities, such as adequate regular exercise, the physiological as well as the psychological consequences may be just as pernicious.

Implicit in the concept of regression is the notion that the patient who, for valid physiological reasons, returns to a dependent, passive, asexual stance characteristic of earlier stages in his development, will experience alterations in the quality of his relationships with others. It is because of its effect on his interpersonal relationships that regression may become a major source of temporary or permanent conflict primarily for the patient but also for those to whom he must relate: his physician, spouse, children, etc.

THE CONCEPT OF CONFLICT

Conflict exists when the patient's conscious or unconscious thoughts, wishes, or feelings must be repressed because their expression would be unacceptable. It follows then that every "normal" medically ill patient is vulnerable to conflict between his psychosocially dictated need to adopt age- and phase-appropriate behavior and his physiologically dictated need to regress to an earlier mode of behavior, temporarily or permanently, in the service of maintaining physiological homeostasis.*

Every individual, regardless of age, sex, or health status, unconsciously yearns at times to return to the passive, helpless, dependent state of childhood, when he was loved and cared for by mother. With maturity, this yearning conflicts with his fear of passivity; he equates this stance with helplessness, dependency, vulnerability, all of which may signify for him the loss of his vital self, that is, his intellectual,

* It should be noted, parenthetically, that the need to return to earlier modes of behavior, i.e., dependence, passivity, etc., would not be a source of conflict for those patients who welcome the opportunity, provided by their illness, to return to infantile behaviors which they would find unacceptable in the healthy state. In such cases, the illness provides the means for conflict resolution.

physical, and, in particular, his sexual capacities. Consequently, under "normal" circumstances, the individual strives—and is able—to keep his desire to be passive and cared for in check. However, with the onset of illness, there is a resurgence of this desire, which is reinforced by physical realities. The conflict between the desire to remain passive, on the one hand, and the self-condemnation evoked by overt manifestations of passivity, on the other, is then reactivated.

Many patients will be able to keep this conflict in abeyance. For some, however, the demand that they adopt a passive stance, to varying degrees and at intermittent stages of their illness, will have pernicious effects. In these individuals, this conflict may find expression in psychological symptoms—e.g., anxiety or depression—or in behavior that is deleterious to the patient's physiological status. For example, if the patient for whom a sedentary life style is mandatory attempts to ward off his fear of passivity by excessive activity, the physical consequences may be catastrophic.

THE CONCEPT OF OBJECT RELATIONSHIPS

The fourth crucial intrapsychic parameter of the patient's ability to adapt to his illness, the quality of his object relationships, is generally understood, as noted, to refer to the individual's attitude and behavior toward persons and things in the external environment. The term also refers to the individual's capacity to relate to external objects and to the quality of those relationships, and to his conscious and unconscious image of himself. Implicit in this definition is the notion that the way an individual perceives others, together with the way he perceives himself, is the most critical ingredient of behavior.

The individual's capacity to relate to others, and, concomitantly, his ability to differentiate himself from others, will depend primarily on his constitutional endowment and his earliest experiences, which form the "bedrock of mental life."[2] His attitude and behavior toward others (and self) will be shaped by his early life experiences on two levels: His ongoing day-to-day experience with significant people in his environment, and the specific traumatic experiences to which he is exposed—e.g., the chronically rejecting attitude of a parent, the death of a parent or sibling, personal illness, injury, or hospitalization. And, inevitably, the individual's capacity to relate to others—and the quality of his relationships—will be further influenced by subsequent events, and, in particular, the onset of chronic illness. In that event, the most critical ingredient of his behavior may well become his relationship with his physician.

The Doctor–Patient Relationship

It is generally recognized that the stress, regression, and conflict experienced by the chronically ill medical patient will affect his relationship with his doctor. It is less well-recognized that these psychological phenomena may be experienced by the physician as well. A discussion of the components of the doctor–patient relationship must, therefore, include consideration of the psychological determinants of the physician's capacity to adapt to his chronically ill patient.

As is true of the patient, the stresses evoked in the physician by the management of acute illness may differ in form and magnitude from those evoked by the management of chronic illness. Typically, the physician perceives an acute disease as a challenge to his knowledge and skills, and feels optimistic and self-confident because of his potent therapeutic armamentarium. In addition, the day-to-day improvement that commonly occurs in the symptomatology of his acutely ill patient serves as a built-in positive reinforcement for the physician. In contrast, the primary care physician rarely sees day-to-day improvement in the symptomatology of his chronically ill patients. In fact, over a prolonged period of time, he may see day-to-day deterioration, which he is helpless to counteract; in these circumstances the threat to his self-esteem (narcissistic integrity) may constitute a major source of stress.

If the patient's chronic illness follows an erratic course, this too may constitute a source of stress for the physician. With the appearance of long-term complications, and the possibility (or inevitability) of a shorter life span, a new set of subacute stresses is imposed on doctor as well as patient. The patient may become depressed and lose faith in his doctor, with the result that the physician's fear of loss of approval becomes a reality. The patient's day-to-day deterioration, or the erratic course of his disease, serve as constant reminder to the physician of his therapeutic impotence, which, in turn, may evoke other stresses, such as guilt and shame. In addition, if the patient's deterioration is a reminder of his own mortality, this too becomes a prominent source of stress for the physician.

We have advanced the proposition that the regression that occurs in patients with chronic illness may produce a resurgence of past conflicts, particularly those conflicts centering on passivity. We would extend this proposition to apply to the physician as well: The physician's concern about his own passivity may be reactivated by the patient's regressive behavior. And, as is true of the patient, the conflicts which recur in the physician, as well as the stresses and regressive behavior which precipitated the emergence of these conflicts, may find expression in symptom formation—anxiety and depression (and their derivatives, e.g., withdrawal, hostility, etc.)—and in consequent disturbances in his relationship with the patient.

The schema of developmental tracts mentioned earlier * can be elaborated on to enhance our understanding of the doctor–patient relationship, for it permits description of the clinically observable behavioral characteristics that define that relationship.

Passivity—Activity. Passivity, which is an inevitable concomitant of many forms of chronic illness, becomes a source of disturbance in the doctor–patient relationship when the patient's passivity is out of all proportion to his physical disability; when he needs to be loved and cared for on an infantile level; when he appears to be incapable of making a decision on any level; when he is unable to exert any effort on his own behalf.

When the patient's enforced passivity is a source of conflict, such conflict may also provide the basis for disturbances in the doctor–patient relationship if, in an effort to ward off this conflict, the patient assumes a pseudo-active stance, e.g., is unable to take advice or accept a diagnosis, or to place any limitations on his activities, etc.

Dependence—Independence. The chronically ill patient is also expected to depend on his physician to a certain extent. However, his dependency needs may impose a burden on the doctor–patient relationship if they are excessive. For example, such a patient may "over-report" recurrent symptoms, want to know where his doctor is at all times, require constant reassurance, and the like.

Conversely, those patients who cope with their excessive desire to be cared for by affecting a pseudo-independent stance characteristically refuse to surrender any independence, even when their illness demands that they allocate certain functions to others.

Indeterminant—Determinant Sexual State. Patients who suffer from certain types of chronic illness frequently lose all interest in sex, or in making themselves sexually attractive, and the quality of their relationships with others, both male and female, suffers as a result.

Other patients, faced with the same physical problem, may, in

* That is, the movement from passivity to activity; dependence to independence; from an indeterminant to a determinant sexual state; from perception of the object as needed to perception of the object as wanted; and from total involvement with self to a concern for others.

order to reassure themselves of their sexual adequacy, become openly seductive and flirtatious toward the physician, and discuss their sexual fantasies indiscriminately.

Perception of the Object as Needed—Perception of the Object as Wanted. The realities of chronic illness may support the patient's perception of the physician as essential to his survival. This mental state commonly manifests itself in the patient's tendency to cling, to extend his contact with the doctor at every opportunity, to convey a sense of urgency in his communications with the doctor.

On the other hand, the patient who has erected strong defenses against his need for the doctor may perceive him as unnecessary.*

Total Involvement with Self—Concern for Others. The patient who is totally involved with himself automatically assumes that the doctor will be available whenever he wants to see him, that he will be eager to speak with him whenever he phones, and may even expect the physician to call him regularly to inquire as to his status. He assumes, in short, that he is the doctor's primary concern. Moreover, such a patient often feels that the physician will collapse if anything happens to him—that his professional status hinges on the effectiveness with which he manages the patient's illness.

As a defense against total preoccupation with self, the patient may affect a total disregard for self: He does not want to take up too much of the doctor's time, is over-solicitious and overly concerned that he may be bothering the doctor, to the point where he cannot approach the doctor for help even when his demands are clearly appropriate.

The physician's capacity to relate appropriately to patients who manifest such character trait disturbances will depend on the degree to which he has been able to resolve his own conflicts over these issues—e.g., passivity, dependency, egocentricity, hyper- or hyposexuality. For example, if he has not sufficiently resolved his own wishes to perpetuate his early dependent relationships, he may abandon those patients who cast him in the role of the omnipotent, totally involved parent; or he may find it difficult to relate to pseudo-independent patients. Depending on the vicissitudes of his early development, the doctor may react adversely to the passive patient—or, alternatively, he may respond negatively to the pseudo-active patient. If the physician has not resolved his own conflicts

* In many instances, this explains the failure of the coronary patient to take prompt action, i.e., to seek medical help, when he experiences significant symptoms.

around sexuality, he may view the asexual patient as a cipher, and be frightened by the flirtatious, seductive patient.

The physician's inability to resolve his own conflicts surrounding these behaviors may produce analagous distortions in his perception of the patient. If he perceives the patient as needed, i.e., as a source of approval, to the extent that the patient becomes the primary regulator of his self-esteem, his unrealistic expectations with regard to the patient's response to treatment will almost certainly be doomed to disappointment. The physician whose self-involvement finds expression in his need to conduct his medical practice according to rules he has arbitrarily established, and who is not sufficiently flexible to alter these rules (when feasible) to accommodate the specific needs of specific patients, undermines his relationships with his patients.

These responses may have only a minimal effect on the physician's relationships with patients with whom he has only intermittent or acute care contact. Inevitably, however, whether they arise primarily in response to the patient, or originate within the doctor himself, these feeling states will prove damaging (to varying degrees) to his relationships with those patients with whom he has long-term contact—the aged, the chronically ill, and the dying patient.

Prototypes of the Doctor–Patient Relationship. We find it useful to conceive of the doctor–patient relationship, which would subsume both its latent, as well as its manifest characteristics, as falling into one of three categories: concordant, discordant, or fluctuating.

THE CONCORDANT RELATIONSHIP. The patient and doctor may appear to be relating well, feel that they are relating well, and, in fact, have a good relationship. However, they may also have a satisfactory relationship even though it does not appear that way on the surface. That is, a relationship which appears discordant on a manifest level may, nonetheless, be concordant on a deeper level.

> Mrs. W. continues to call her doctor with unnecessary frequency, although he makes no attempt to conceal his irritation with this behavior. In fact, she has been warned by her friends and family that if she continues to provoke him, he may terminate his services.
>
> Actually, this is unlikely. The doctor is relieved when he hears from Mrs. W., who suffers from intractable syncopal episodes which he feels may prove fatal at any time. Similarly, Mrs. W. is relieved when she hears the irritation in his voice because she is convinced that no doctor would express his anger with a patient who was dying.

THE DISCORDANT RELATIONSHIP. The doctor–patient relationship may also be discordant on two levels: The patient and his doctor may not appear to be relating well, and actually have a poor relationship. Or they may appear to have a good relationship, although, in fact, they do not. Judged in terms of their manifest content, these relationships might be described as discordant and concordant, respectively. But in the second instance, where the relationship appears to be concordant (on a manifest level), its true nature may ultimately emerge. In the meantime both doctor and patient are dissatisfied, but incapable of altering their situation.

> Because she held her doctor in high esteem, Mrs. T. made every effort to be a "good"—i.e., compliant—patient. Nevertheless, she sensed his disapproval of her. "I feel he thinks I'm not trying hard enough; he makes me feel guilty."
>
> Dr. L. did indeed feel Mrs. T. wasn't trying hard enough. In general, he tended to look down on patients who lacked moral fiber, i.e., who didn't make a superhuman effort to overcome their deficits. He kept these feelings to himself simply because he felt it would be unprofessional to express his criticism of Mrs. T.
>
> Thus, because Mrs. T. was determined to be a "good" patient, and Dr. L. was determined to repress the annoyance he felt with her, their relationship appeared to be concordant. At base, however, it was clearly discordant, with the result that Mrs. T. saw Dr. L. less and less frequently, and, during her visits to his office, kept her communications to a minimum.

THE FLUCTUATING RELATIONSHIP. Fluctuations occur in the quality of all relationships between individuals. It is logical, therefore, to expect that fluctuations will occur in the quality of the doctor–patient relationship over time: It may be concordant at the outset, and become discordant subsequently, or vice versa. For example, an initially concordant relationship may become discordant as the physical deterioration that accompanies chronic illness intensifies. As his condition worsens, the patient may have less faith in the doctor, or the doctor may be less able to tolerate the patient's growing dependence. On the other hand, the doctor–patient relationship may be discordant at the outset because the doctor is not sufficiently responsive to the patient who, at this stage, is able to maintain his independence. The relationship may improve significantly, however, as the patient's condition worsens and he becomes more dependent on the doctor and values his services more, and as the doctor, in turn, begins to feel more useful.

An initially concordant relationship may also become discordant if the patient's physiological dysfunction gives rise to significant psychological problems which are then superimposed upon his deteriorating physiological state. A cardinal criterion of the doctor's capacity to adapt to his patients is his ability to "ride out" these fluctuations.

> Dr. Y. had been able to maintain a fairly good relationship with Mrs. A. after she underwent a mastectomy, until a lesion appeared in her other breast, requiring its removal. At this point, the patient who had been able to handle her first cancer operation "fell apart." For weeks, she complained tearfully that Dr. Y. had failed her, that his incompetence would cause her to lose everything—her husband, love, admiration, and ultimately life itself.
>
> Initially, Dr. Y. was tolerant of this abuse from his previously cooperative patient; then he became angry and defensive. Finally, he suggested that she transfer to an oncologist, with the result that he was not available to Mrs. A. when she needed his support most, and when she needed someone toward whom she could direct her anger without the fear of abandonment.

Fluctuations may occur even in doctor–patient relationships that have a long history of concordance.

> As Mrs. Q's arthritis worsened, she became increasingly quarrelsome. Nothing her doctor said or did could placate her; her anger seemed out of proportion to the pain and limitations imposed by her illness. Mrs. Q. was simply losing patience with her illness; but her doctor was losing patience with Mrs. Q., whom he had cared for in an atmosphere of mutual trust for fifteen years.

Like Mrs. A., Mrs. Q. displaced her anger at the inalterable progress of her arthritis onto the doctor; and, like Mrs. A., despite her anger, she needed to cling to her doctor at this stage of her illness. Actually, both her need to be angry and her need to cling had occurred in the past in the course of their association, but these behaviors had never occurred simultaneously or with such intensity. When this behavior persisted, her physician was unable to tolerate it. He experienced the continued progress of her illness as evidence of his failure as a physician; he experienced her accusations as a narcissistic wound. Exposed to this combined assault, he responded negatively, as might be expected, to Mrs. Q.'s demands to be supported, reassured, taken care of.

Even the most sensitive and enduring relationships are not immune to such fluctuations.

> Dr. N., who had been Mr. F.'s physician for 10 years, continued to care for him after he developed cancer. Their relationship remained stable until the disease began to metastasize rapidly. As Mr. F., who remained in pain despite large and frequent doses of morphine, de-

teriorated in great distress before his doctor's eyes, both patient and doctor began to lose confidence in each other. Mr. F. complained that Dr. N. was no longer able to help him. Because of their long-term relationship, and because they shared other characteristics in common —they had been childhood friends, were the same age, came from the same neighborhood, etc.—Dr. N. could not tolerate Mr. F.'s distress. Both wondered whether Mr. F. would be better off under the care of a specialist.

In each of the cases described above, the transfer of the patient to another physician presented a possible solution to the discordant doctor–patient relationship. But, in each instance, an attempt to transform the discordant relationship into a concordant one would have been preferable. The onus for this transformation clearly rests with the doctor. Obviously, these patients had regressed to an earlier level of functioning, which was difficult for the doctor to accept. His task might have been easier if he had recognized that the displacement of their anger with "fate" onto him, however inappropriate it appeared, was an expression of their efforts to adapt to their illness. Thus, in the final analysis the transformation of these relationships clearly depended on the physician's ability to adapt to the patient's psychological responses to a particularly difficult phase of his illness. This is not to say that transfer of chronically ill patients is not appropriate under certain conditions. Once the physician is convinced that his efforts to transform a discordant relationship into a concordant one are doomed to failure, for whatever reason, the transfer of the patient to another physician who may be able to establish a more therapeutic relationship with him is in the humanistic tradition.

REFERENCES

1. Strain JJ, Grossman S: Psychological reactions to medical illness and hospitalization. In Strain JJ, Grossman S (eds): Psychological Care of the Medically Ill: A Primer in Liaison Psychiatry. New York, Appleton, 1975, p 23
2. Mahler MS, Pine F, Bergman A: The Psychological Birth of the Human Infant: Symbiosis and Individuation. New York, Basic Books, 1975

Chapter 3

Psychological Dysfunction in the Chronically Ill

The stress, regression, and conflict that arise in response to medical illness produce disparate psychological symptoms which may impede the patient's adaptation to his illness and/or accelerate, exacerbate, or complicate his existing illness by producing new physical symptoms. These psychogenic phenomena may then obstruct the physician's efforts to assess both the psychological and physical status of the patient. Among the symptom complexes most frequently encountered in the chronically ill patient, which reflect the "final common pathway" of the adverse psychological reactions evoked by his illness, we would include character trait disturbances, and specific psychological phenomena, such as anxiety, depression, somatization, conversion reaction, phobia, inhibitions, and psychosis. In addition, we have included in our catalogue two complex psychopathological phenomena, namely, malingering and hypochondriasis, which, although they do not arise in response to the stress, conflict, and regression evoked by chronic illness, pose a major challenge for the physician.

A detailed discussion of these symptoms, in terms of their etiology, multiple, varied manifestations, and differential diagnosis, clearly lies beyond the scope of this book. Nor have we attempted to describe the numerous interview techniques currently used to elicit psychological data from the medical patient. Such techniques have been described at length in the literature over the past several years. Rather, as was true of the preceding chapters, it is our aim in this chapter to provide the physician with a conceptual framework that will enhance his understanding and facilitate his management of psychological issues encountered in primary care practice.

CHARACTER TRAIT DISTURBANCES

Each of the character traits described in the preceding chapter can serve an adaptive function in the physically healthy individual under certain circumstances. But pseudo-independence, excessive activity, hypersexuality, etc., may undermine the physical status of the chronically ill patient.

> Mr. B., the president of a small but profitable manufacturing concern, boasted that he owed his success to the fact that he would not let himself be discouraged by the competition. He enjoyed the challenge of overcoming seemingly insurmountable odds and felt that nothing must be allowed to distract him from the pursuit of his overriding goal —to continue to expand his company, in the face of all obstacles, until it ranked among the biggest in the industry. This philosophy colored his response to his illness, a serious myocardial infarction. He viewed it as a possible "obstacle" to the realization of his ambition, and he wasn't going to let it stop him. In fact, he was determined to work even harder than he had before to make sure that it would not interfere with his master design.

Patients like Mr. B. are commonplace. Typically, they boast that they have "never been sick before this happened." They insist that they know their own body "better than any doctor could," take pride in making their own decisions and in running their own life. Almost invariably, they become management problems. The patient who boasts that he's always on the go, that he never sits still, that he has to be part of the "action," usually finds its difficult to assume the passive stance that may be essential to his survival.

The clinical features of these character traits were described in detail in Chapter 2. In general, their presence can be detected by the excessive quality of the patient's behavior, which is out of keeping with the realities of his current life situation. Since these behaviors often are "part" of the patient, the most the physician can hope to accomplish is to understand and minimize them, and thereby reduce their impact on adaptation and treatment.

In any event, while an assessment of the patient's character permits a global view of his psychological status, it is not sufficient in itself to provide a foundation for adequate psychological care. Such care is contingent upon the physician's awareness and understanding of discrete psychological phenomena as well.

DISCRETE PSYCHOLOGICAL REACTIONS

Anxiety

The only manifestation of anxiety may be the patient's verbal expression, in response to direct questioning, of his concerns and fears. More frequently, however, significant anxiety takes the form of a variety of symptoms, which may be physical and/or psychological. Among the symptoms most frequently encountered in the chronically ill, we would include difficulty in falling asleep, nightmares; restlessness, tremulousness; sweating; dry mouth; pressured speech; frequency of urination; tachycardia, light-headedness, fear of fainting, palpitations; generalized fatigue; vague aches and pains; shortness of breath (especially a sighing respiration); and paresthesias. The patient may also feel fearful, nervous, and panicky for no apparent reason; he may have feelings of impending doom, be convinced that he is "falling apart," and have a constant and excessive need for reassurance.

All of these symptoms must be differentiated from the symptoms of the patient's existing physical illness and from the effects of the medication he is receiving for that illness. They must also be differentiated from the symptoms of an as-yet-undiagnosed physical disease, e.g., an organic mental syndrome.

Depression

Feelings of depression, which are often encountered among acutely ill medical patients, are ubiquitous among the chronically ill. At some point in the course of their illness, chronically ill patients invariably manifest one or several of the symptoms of a depressive reaction: tearfulness; psychomotor retardation (or agitation); sleep difficulty, with early-morning awakening; loss of appetite; feelings of rage at their plight (which are usually suppressed); feelings of helplessness or hopelessness; excessive somatic complaints, e.g., gastrointestinal complaints or constipation.

Despite the frequency with which such symptoms occur, the proper evaluation and management of the depressed chronically ill patient continues to pose a major challenge for the physician. Essentially, the difficulties inherent in these tasks can be ascribed to two factors: First, the chronically ill patient has a real basis for his depression; consequently, the physician may tend to regard such symptoms as the norm, and make no attempt to alleviate them. Second, the accurate diagnosis of depression in the chronically ill is complicated by the fact that this is a broad and ambiguous term that encompasses several different conditions, each with a differing etiology. It is not easy to distinguish among these conditions; their clinical phenomena overlap, and many patients present with mixed pictures. Moreover, diagnosis is further complicated by the fact that medical illness itself can produce many symptoms associated with depression, such as fatigue, anorexia, and weight loss. In an effort to facilitate differential diagnosis, Sachar [1] has identified and described five conditions associated with depressive symptoms:

True Depressive Illness. Broadly speaking, the symptoms typically experienced by such patients can be grouped into "psychological" and "somatic" categories. Psychological symptoms typically include depressed mood; a profound loss of interest (and pleasure) in the environment; feelings of worthlessness or pessimism, with ruminative worrying; and indecisiveness. In addition, such patients frequently experience significant anxiety, suicidal thoughts, and feelings of guilt. True depressive illness can be distinguished from grief reactions by the fact that the patient's psychological concerns are out of proportion to his realistic problems. Moreover, in contrast to grief reactions, feelings of sorrow do not commonly characterize true depressive illness. Conversely, diminished self-esteem is not characteristic of grief reactions.

The most common somatic symptoms encountered in true depression are insomnia, particularly during the middle and end of the night; anorexia; fatigue; psychomotor retardation or agitation; decreased libido; anhedonia; somatic pains, e.g., headaches, backaches, toothaches; autonomic disturbances, such as constipation and dry mouth; and, in some instances, a diurnal variation in symptomatology.

Because the patient with true depressive illness is just as likely to present with somatic symptoms as psychological symptoms, there is a danger that the physician may pursue an organic workup and medical treatment to an excessive degree, or, under the misconception that the patient's physical symptoms are psychogenic, fail to pursue an organic workup and treatment sufficiently.

Grief Reactions. Grief reactions to the stresses evoked by chronic illness are the most common depressive experiences encountered among the medically ill. The physician's first task in such cases is to differentiate between those reactions that are appropriate to the patient's situation and those that are not. For example, a grief reaction in a patient who knows that he has cancer and his prognosis is poor would be regarded as appropriate; in all probability, the doctor would not treat it as he would a classic depression.* If, however, the patient's grief response to his illness is out of proportion to the severity of that illness or to his prognosis, the doctor might justifiably consider the patient's symptoms indicative of a true depressive reaction and treat him by prescribing antidepressants or referring him for psychiatric consultation.

Neurotic Characterological Depressions. Patients who develop "neurotic" depressions in association with their chronic illness have life-long character problems that are intensified by the stress of illness. Typically, such patients are chronically unhappy, masochistic characters, who are filled with self-pity, yet reject any type of reassurance.

Medical Depressions. Certain medical conditions, e.g., endocrine disorders and viral illnesses, may produce psychological symptoms that closely mimic depressive disorders. Patients who have recovered from influenza frequently experience depressed mood, loss of self-esteem, diminished libido, and the like. This syndrome is also common among patients who have experienced infectious mononucleosis and infectious hepatitis. Conversely, a depressive syndrome may be the first sign of a medical illness. Patients who are subsequently discovered to have carcinoma of the pancreas, stomach, or other abdominal organs frequently report fatigue, loss of normal interests, depressed mood, and premonitions of doom at a time when the tumors are silent.

Included among the endocrinopathies associated with specific depressive phenomena, are hyperparathyroidism, Cushing's syndrome, and hypothyroidism, all of which frequently produce depressed mood, pessimism, diminished self-esteem, etc. The precise mechanism by which depression is produced in these conditions is not known. However, the occurrence of this phenomenon points up the importance of differentiating between psychological symptoms that arise in response to an existing illness, and those that are associated with that illness, or prescribed medication, or that presage the impending onset of an as yet undiagnosed physical illness. The task of differential diagnosis in these conditions often presents a major dilemma and may defy the skills not only of the primary care physician but also of the psychiatrist. Indeed, one can speculate that the resolution of these diagnostic dilemmas, such as that exemplified by the case described below, may require an interdisciplinary approach, including the services of the primary care physi-

* In fact, the absence of a grief reaction in such cases should be investigated.

cian, a psychiatrist, psychiatric social worker, endocrinologist, pathologist, etc.

> Mr. W. appeared at his physician's office with all of the classic symptoms of depression—severe anxiety, premonitions of doom, agoraphobia, guilt feelings, apathy, and agitation. In addition, he manifested many of the classic vegetative signs of depression—early morning insomnia, gastrointestinal complaints, and in particular, tenesmus, diurnal variation in symptomotology, tremors, syncopal episodes, leg pain, easy fatigability, anorexia, and weight loss. At first glance this catalogue of symptoms would seem to permit only one diagnosis. The picture was complicated, however, by additional information Dr. M. elicited from Mr. W. Although anorexia and weight loss occur frequently in depression, the fact that Mr. W. had lost 20 pounds over a 3-week period, and in conjunction with this weight loss had experienced tenesmus and abdominal pain, mandated an immediate physiological workup of the patient.

Drug-Induced Depressions. Several medications are believed to provoke depressive reactions. For instance, it has been reported that as many as 15 percent of patients receiving reserpine for hypertension experience significant depressive phenomena, and that a significant number of true depressive illnesses are included among these responses. Aldomet can provoke mild depressive phenomena. Both estrogens and progesterone have been implicated in depression. Valium may exert a mild depressive effect; and transient depressive states, ranging from mild to severe, are common after withdrawal from amphetamines and other stimulant drugs.

In summary, for empirical purposes, the symptoms that characterize depressive reactions can be grouped, with greater specificity, under the following broad categories:

1. Vegetative or somatic symptoms (e.g., diminished libido, change in appetite, sleep disturbances, disturbance in GI functioning)
2. Disturbances in attitudes and feelings (e.g., loss of self-esteem, feelings of helplessness and hopelessness, somatic delusions, suicidal ideation, and diurnal variations in symptoms)
3. Alterations in appearance (agitation, tearfulness, psychomotor retardation)

If there is marked evidence of current dysfunction (as opposed to the patient's premorbid state) in the majority of these categories, there is a strong possibility that patient suffers from a true depressive reaction. The presence of a specific constellation—severe loss of appetite, insomnia, lowered self-esteem, inability to function, pessimism, anhedonia, and frank suicidal wishes—mandates emergency intervention. As a general rule, this group of patients should be referred for psychiatric consultation.

It is important, however, for the physician to identify the presence of depression in any of its forms; his ability to provide effective medical management may well hinge on his capacity to do so. For example, prescribing Maalox for the patient who complains of a gastrointestinal disturbance that, in fact, is due to a depressive reaction will not help the patient. Further, the failure to accurately diagnose a depressive reaction, and to provide appropriate treatment may well lead to the worsening of physical symptoms—which may have life-threatening consequences.

Somatization

The somatization process discussed here is not necessarily associated with a major psychiatric disorder; it is a common psychological phenomenon. More specifically, this process occurs when feelings are discharged, without conscious awareness, via the body, and especially along the tracts of the autonomic nervous system.* Vasovagal phenomena frequently accompany affective arousal: feelings of uneasiness or embarrassment may be expressed directly by increased heart rate, blushing, diaphoresis, tachypnea, etc. Since these physical symptoms do not differ from "pure" physical symptoms, somatization may impede the accurate diagnosis of physiological events.

Conversion Reaction

In conversion reactions, affects are not experienced consciously, but are "converted" into physical symptoms (most often in organs or parts of the body mainly under voluntary control). These physical symptoms serve to minimize the conscious impact of psychological affects produced by consciously unacceptable sexual or aggressive impulses.

A diagnosis of conversion reaction is contingent upon the presence of four specific clinical features:

* A more technical definition of somatization appears in the psychiatric literature. It is defined in one such work as ". . . the tendency to react to stimuli . . . with physical rather than psychic manifestations. The infant reacts to painful stimulation with a host of somatic responses. With progressive maturation, however, somatic responses to stimuli are replaced by action or thought processes. . . ." [2]

1. The symptom has symbolic significance. It represents the expression of prohibited sexual or aggressive impulses, and as such, serves as the resolution of an unconscious conflict.
2. The patient's affective reaction is not in keeping with the symptom ("la belle indifférence").
3. The symptom is not associated with primary physiological structural change.
4. The symptom does not conform to known anatomical and/or physiological patterns, e.g., hemi-anesthesia or stocking and glove peristhesias.

Mr. W., 39 years old, had long-standing rheumatic heart disease, which did not interfere appreciably with his ability to function professionally or socially. It had to be watched, however, for he did experience fatigue, discomfort, and some chest pain for brief periods from time to time. After one of these episodes, Dr. M. suggested that Mr. W. consider surgery for the repair of his damaged mitral valve. Such an operation would eliminate his current symptoms. Moreover, it would, in all probability, prove necessary eventually since there was some initial evidence of decompensation. It might be prudent, therefore, to undergo surgery at this stage of his life. Although Mr. W. did not reject this suggestion out of hand, he was not enthusiastic about it. However, he ultimately yielded to the combined urging of his physician and his family.

Surgery was uneventful; yet, contrary to all expectations, instead of feeling stronger, Mr. W. complained of overwhelming feelings of weakness and an immobilized right arm. These symptoms, which, surprisingly, did not seem to bother the patient, persisted, although a review of the physical findings showed that there was no physiological basis for this response.

Only after lengthy discussions with his patient, over time, did it become evident to Dr. M. that Mr. W. had deeply resented his insistence and the "demands" by his family that he undergo surgery. Mr. W. felt unconsciously that he had been forced to submit, against his wishes, to an unnecessary and potentially life-threatening procedure. Apparently, he had not been consciously aware of his rage at the perpetrators of this "injustice." Rather than punch the doctor in the nose, he expressed his anger via his physical symptoms.

Phobia

Although the phobic patient consciously recognizes that no immediate danger exists, he continues to experience fears that have no basis in reality about the status of his body and/or mind. Medical patients who suffer from a phobia may be afraid to venture into the street to visit their physician—even when such a visit is essential, i.e., there has been an exacerbation of their illness or they are in pain.

Mr. G. had suffered from asthma for ten years. In the last five years his physician had been able to bring it under control. Yet, Mr. G. continued to function on the premise that an attack was imminent: He was unable to leave his home to go to his office, never accepted social invitations, and even stopped going to Sunday Mass. In fact, Mr. G.'s phobia became progressively severe, to the degree that despite his concern with his health, he was ultimately unable to travel to his doctor's office.

Inhibitions

The inhibited patient, like the phobic patient, fears the full expression of his physiological or psychological potential. However, as opposed to phobia, psychological inhibitions limit certain behaviors, but do not preclude them.

Mr. B., a 30-year-old single man, had been hospitalized for a perforated ulcer, and had made a satisfactory recovery. Nevertheless, six months after his hospital discharge, he was still working only three days a week. Actually, his physician had given him permission to return to full employment three months earlier. He was afraid to follow these new instructions, however, because he was convinced that he would "get another bleed" if he acted precipitously.

Psychoses

Patients with a developing or fixed psychotic process may harbor the delusion that a part of their body is defective, that they are suffering from a physical disability, or that some aspect of their perception has been altered—e.g., seeing, hearing, feeling—secondary to an organic process.

A 79-year-old woman, suffering from a psychotic depression following the loss of her husband, to whom she had been married for 51 years, was convinced she had a cancer that was obstructing her bowels, despite her doctor's assurances to the contrary. In fact, she had been constipated for three weeks as a consequence of her depressive reaction.

Malingering

Strictly defined, malingering is the persistent, planned simulation of medical symptoms for a gainful purpose.[3]* Thus, the patient may feign symptoms in order to obtain pecuniary gains through insurance claims or disability benefits, to avoid assigned duties, etc. It is this secondary gain feature of malingering which has commanded the most attention—and is responsible for the tendency of many physicians to erroneously equate malingering with unremediable anti-social behavior.

It is less well recognized that malingering serves an important intrapsychic function as well. Via malingering, the patient is able to express his "unacceptable" feelings, i.e., anxiety, aggression, and sexual impulses; to gratify his unconscious longing for special treatment; and to get the punishment he feels he deserves for fantasized or real guilt. In other words, the malingerer has the same impulses, conflicts, and anxieties as the normal or neurotic human being. It is the way he copes with these impulses, conflicts, and anxieties that sets him apart. Both the normal individual and the neurotic employ intrapsychic processes (repression and symptom formation, respectively) to resolve their internal problems. The malingerer, who has not progressed beyond a fairly primitive level of ego development, is able to make only partial use of intrapsychic processes. Consequently, he must employ extrapsychic processes—cheating, lying, and the manipulation and exploitation of individuals and situations—not only because of the benefits he derives from these behaviors, but because they enable partial solution of pressing internal issues.

Hypochondriasis

Hypochondriasis is a chronic condition characterized by the individual's preoccupation with his body, and his unshakeable conviction that he has a physical illness. Typically, he presents vague somatic complaints that are markedly exaggerated in relation to physical findings. Nor can his symptoms be alleviated by traditional treatment.

As a general rule, the hypochondriac has an extremely limited social life. Usually, his relationships with others are fraught with difficulty. There is a consequent tendency among these patients to with-

* It should be noted, however, that the patient does not usually resort to self-mutilation or deliberately expose himself to bodily harm to produce symptoms. Thus, malingering stands apart from the Munchausen Syndrome, in which the patient may expose himself to life-threatening medical procedures.

draw from the outside world; the body becomes a substitute for interpersonal relationships. Another striking feature of hypochondriasis is the apparent satisfaction the patient takes in his long history of suffering. He relishes the conviction that he has been let down by others and takes pride in his self-image as "victim." Yet, he appears to be completely oblivious to the fact that by his constant complaints he is making others suffer. Difficulties in his object relationships, his angry feelings, and a need to be cared for, are all ascribed by the hypochondriac to his poor health.[4] Illness and suffering are the means by which he maintains gratifying (albeit ambivalent) relationships. Thus, in contrast to the malingerer, the hypochondriac actually experiences medical symptoms, but like the malingerer, his suffering provides important primary gain. Via his suffering, the hypochondriac is able to express his unacceptable dependency needs and anger without loss of self-esteem, for the hypochondriac's belief that his illness really does exist protects his self-esteem. Unlike the malingerer, he does not consciously attempt to deceive anyone.

The preceding description of the psychological symptomatology encountered in primary care practice raises several questions: The first of these refers to the complexity of differential diagnosis. Anxiety can be mistaken for depression, and, if it takes the form of an excessive concern with bodily function, for hypochondriasis. Inhibition can be mistaken for malingering; a grief response or a medically induced depression can be mistaken for a true depression. Concomitantly, the physician must distinguish between symptoms that arise from psychological factors, as opposed to psychological symptoms that are a consequence of pathophysiological processes. The patient with an organic mental syndrome may present with all of the symptoms described above, as well as a variety of distinctive mental symptoms, such as impaired judgment or memory. Thus, the presence of these symptoms mandates their differential diagnosis, via procedures discussed in detail below (Chapter 5), designed to enable detection of this syndrome.

Once the patient's symptom has been identified definitively as a pure psychological symptom, the physician turns to the question of whether the management of this symptom lies within his purview. Inasmuch as malingering and hypochondriasis have their roots in the early experiences of life, their elimination does not lie within the domain of the primary care physician. Rather, he can best focus his energy on the modification of the response these diagnoses evoke in him. However, the physician will be able, in most instances, to manage the psychological symptoms that arise in response to medical illness, and, in fact, is in an ideal position to do so. Nevertheless, he must also recognize that referral of some patients for psychiatric consultation may be indicated. Patients who are severely depressed and/or suicidal; patients with a phobia who do not respond to reassurance, behavior modification, or limited psychotherapy; and some patients with conversion reactions which are not self-limiting, would be appropriate candidates for psychiatric referral.

MANAGEMENT

The psychological symptoms described above can be treated by a variety of therapeutic modalities, including psychopharmacology, reassurance and support, behavior modification, family intervention, and environmental manipulation. All these modalities have been described skillfully and in great detail in the literature. In any event, the recapitulation of these modalities is not relevant to our thesis. In contrast to these treatment techniques—which have as their goal the reduction of specific, manifest psychological symptoms—we believe that the patient's psychological needs might be better served if the physician also addresses himself to the sources of these psychological dysfunctions, to the stresses, conflicts, and regression universally evoked by chronic illness. We proceed on the premise that the reduction of manifest psychological symptoms, in itself, cannot ensure long-term adaptation to chronic illness. Such adaptation can best be achieved via reduction of the factors that gave rise to these symptoms, that prevent the development of a disease-compatible life style and the formation of a viable doctor–patient relationship. Moreover, we hold the conviction that such long-term adaptation will depend on the reduction of adverse psychological responses to chronic illness in the doctor as well as the patient.

The Reduction of Psychological Stress

Reduction of the psychological stresses evoked by chronic illness begins with the physician's awareness that each of these stresses constitutes a normal reaction to chronic illness, and that they are operative to a greater or lesser extent even when there is no overt evidence of discomfort.

When they are viewed from this perspective, the management of these stresses can be reduced to a rather simple formula: The blow dealt by chronic illness to the patient's narcissistic integrity can be diminished by overt or covert reassurances that changes in his body have not diminished his importance as a person. The fear of strangers and separation anxiety obviously will occur frequently among patients who are candidates for institutionalization (i.e., admission to a hospital, a short-term acute care setting, or nursing home). These responses can be lessened in this population by the physician's efforts to encourage the patient's family and friends to maintain contact with him, and to support him, and, where possible, by the doctor's participation in his care. Although family members may help to lessen the patient's fear of loss of love and approval, the physician's explicit and implicit approval of the patient, despite his disability, may give the family's reassurances currency. By the same token, the physician's approval may be the most potent antidote to the family's rejection of the patient. The physician can best reduce the patient's fear of injury to body parts or loss of control of developmentally achieved functions, whether physical or mental, by helping the patient undo the equation that dominates his thinking that loss of bodily function equals loss of masculinity (or feminity). The seventh stress evoked by chronic illness, guilt and the perception of illness as a retaliation for past transgressions, can be undone by the physician's deliberate efforts to elicit the patient's injurious fantasies, and put them to rest by his unequivocal statements to the effect, for example, that the dissolution of a marriage does not cause emphysema or that having an abortion does not lead to breast cancer.* The final, and perhaps most prominent source of psychological stress in the medically ill—the fear of unbearable, unending, and intractable pain—which must be borne alone—can be diminished by the physician's assurance that should the patient experience such pain, he will be with him and try, to the best of his ability, to eliminate it, or, at least, make the pain tolerable.

The reduction of maladaptive behavior occurs automatically as a consequence of the reduction of these stresses and of the conflicts and regression they give rise to.

The Reduction of Conflict and Regression

As we have said, the nature and magnitude of the patient's response to these stresses will depend on what his illness means to him, which, in turn, will depend on the success with which he has coped with core

* In some instances where the relationship between "transgression" and medical disease does exist, e.g., alcoholism and pancreatitis or sexual promiscuity and gonorrhea, the patient's feeling of guilt is understandable. If the physician unwittingly conveys his disapproval to these patients, he may further intensify their guilt feelings, thereby magnifying their stress, regression, and conflict.

developmental conflicts to date. If the patient coped successfully with his conflicts surrounding passivity and dependence in the past, his illness is less likely to cause a major resurgence of these conflicts. He is less likely then to perceive his illness and the demands it imposes for passivity, dependence, and even loss of functions as an overwhelming threat to his narcissistic integrity. The patient who has been able to cope successfully with conflicts surrounding dependence is less likely to experience overwhelming separation anxiety or fear of strangers. The patient who has been able to resolve conflicts surrounding sexual identity is less likely to experience an inordinate fear of loss of developmentally achieved functions.

The reduction of conflict, therefore, becomes a major thrust of the physician's therapeutic efforts. To this end, the physician attempts first to elicit and then to correct the patient's misconceptions with regard to the limitations imposed by his illness and the altered self-image produced by these misconceptions, and thereby keep his regressive tendencies to a minimum.

> Mr. D., an obese tool and die maker, had been forced to retire at the age of 48 because of chronic and progressive rheumatoid arthritis. His enforced passivity, as a consequence of his illness, had affected every aspect of his concept of self. Thus Mr. D., who had formerly been an independent, aggressive individual who made his own decisions, now felt that he was totally dependent on the largess of others. His perception of himself as a virile male was dissipated; he was totally preoccupied with his pain, with his deformed fingers, and his prognosis. As further evidence of his regression, his perception of his wife as wanted, loved, and cherished was eradicated by his stronger need to experience her as his caretaker.

The physician's task, in this case, was to induce Mr. D. to view the limits imposed by his disability more realistically. Although he could no longer function as a tool and die maker, he was not useless, nor was his survival dependent on the nurturing of others. Furthermore, the physician emphasized that Mr. D.'s deformity need not restrict his sexual activities. He was no less a man because he needed help at times, and this help was provided by his wife. The physician also touched on Mr. D.'s attitude toward his wife, which he correctly surmised had given rise to some feelings of guilt. A total preoccupation with one's self, at times, and at this phase of Mr. D.'s illness was normal; there was no need for him to feel guilty on this score. Also, an overriding concern with having one's needs fulfilled when one was unable to fend completely for oneself was equally understandable.

The physician then restructured his relationship with the patient to reinforce these injunctions, and, at the same time, to reduce the impact of the conflicts Mr. D. was experiencing. Thus the physician attempted to actively foster Mr. D.'s independence (admittedly on a minor scale) by enlisting his cooperation in the treatment plan: Specifically, doctor and patient decided together when Mr. D. should take his medication, when he should exercise, how much he should try to do, what kind of activity he should engage in, and how often he should come to the doctor. Finally, the doctor discussed Mr. D.'s illness with him openly and frankly; and he was informed of the purpose of the medication he took, the benefits of his prescribed exercises, and the need for dietary restraint. As Mr. D.'s conflicts diminished, his tendency to regress to more primitive behaviors diminished as well. Furthermore, there was a concomitant reduction of his manifest symptoms, i.e., his grief response and his sexual inhibitions.

CLINICAL CORRELATIONS

The two cases presented below demonstrate in greater detail the clinical application of psychological medicine in the primary care setting.

Case 1

The first case illustrates the vicissitudes of long-term management of the psychological stresses imposed on the patient during the acute phase of her illness and hospitalization, and as she moved to the chronic phase of illness in an ambulatory setting. We have attempted to highlight the identification and management of character trait disturbances and discrete psychological symptoms, as well as the stress, conflict, and regression which underlie these phenomena, with special emphasis on their consequences for the doctor–patient relationship.

Mrs. G., a 67-year-old former model, married, and with two adult children, was admitted to the hospital for diagnosis of a suspected retroperitonial mass. After diagnostic mesenteric angiography, the patient suffered a left lower leg paralysis, a post-operative psychosis, cardiac arrest, and bilateral weakness and pain—eventually chronic—in both lower extremities.

During her acute illness, Mrs. G. was extremely passive, helpless, dependent, and self-centered, and constantly demanded that Dr. X. restore her ability to walk and make her well again, "like I was before the tests." She was overtly hostile toward the staff and hospital. However, although she constantly berated Dr. X. for "butchering her," * Mrs. G. clung to him and behaved as though he had no other patients. Moreover, she was grateful to Dr. X for helping her to take her first postoperative steps, and for encouraging her to return home to be with her family. Only Dr. X. cared about what happened to her, only he could protect her from all the "bad" people who surrounded her, only he could be trusted.

Dr. X. was able to accept Mrs. G.'s demands, complaints, passivity, excessive dependency, and self-centeredness, because he recognized that she had been through a major ordeal. He also felt that a doctor should "tolerate" the demands of a critically ill patient; and, despite her behavior, he genuinely liked her.

Mrs. G. was sent home with a walker, pain medication, and a homemaker, and was followed in the ambulatory clinic by Dr. X, who saw her weekly over a period of eight months. During this period, Dr. X.'s initial tolerance of her behavior gave way to annoyance and impatience and, finally, to anger. He was provoked, in particular, by Mrs. G.'s refusal to give up the homemaker—whose services were provided at public expense—despite his efforts to persuade her that these services were no longer required, that she could—and should—do more for herself. At each clinic visit, Dr. X. was forced to listen to a recitation of Mrs. G.'s complaints: "I just came in for tests, and look at me now. Nothing works right. If my husband didn't need me, I would end it all." This account was interspersed with a stream of accusations leveled against the surgeon who had damaged her and who, instead of abjectly pleading for her forgiveness, ". . . had the nerve to tell me I should be grateful because he saved my life by cardiac resuscitation."

Formulation

STRESS, REGRESSION, AND CONFLICT. Mrs. G. experienced all of the psychological stresses which are universally evoked by acute illness and hospitalization: loss of self-esteem and a sense of intactness (narcissistic integrity); fear of strangers; separation anxiety; fear of the loss of love and approval, and of the loss of control of developmentally achieved functions; fear of the loss of, or injury to body parts (fear of dying); guilt and shame; and the fear of pain. However, with the assistance of an empathetic doctor she felt she could trust, Mrs. G. was able, during the acute phase of her illness, to maintain adequate defenses against these stresses. Moreover, she was able to regress adequately in the service

* Dr. X. was not directly involved in the administration of the diagnostic procedure. Nevertheless, in Mrs. G.'s eyes, he was guilty by virtue of his association with the surgeon who had done the angiography and with the hospital.

of recovery from the medical crisis which had necessitated her prolonged hospitalization. Finally, during this initial phase of her illness, Mrs. G. had access to her feelings and fantasies, and was able to communicate her needs to her physician, Dr. X. In short, Mrs. G. was generally able to fulfill the prerequisites for successful adaptation to acute illness and hospitalization.

However, once she had been discharged from the hospital and was being seen on an ambulatory basis, her capacity to adapt diminished significantly. During the chronic phase of her illness, the stresses Mrs. G. had experienced initially were intensified—and she was less able to defend against them. The regressive behavior, which had served an adaptive function in the acute phase of her illness, persisted in the chronic phase, but at this point it was out of keeping with the reality of her physical impairment. These stresses and regressive behavior, in turn, produced a resurgence of intense conflicts in Mrs. G., which centered primarily on passivity, sexual identity, and egocentricity.

MANIFEST PSYCHOLOGICAL SYMPTOMS. Some of the stresses and conflicts Mrs. G. experienced during the chronic phase of her illness were observable; others were operative on an unconscious level. In any event, their existence could be inferred from Mrs. G.'s manifest psychological symptoms, and from alterations in the quality of her relationship with Dr. X.

Specifically, Mrs. G. showed many of the classic symptoms of a depressive reaction: a depressed mood, incomplete grief response, a pessimistic outlook, internalized rage, and suicidal thoughts. Moreover, as is typical of such patients, Mrs. G.—who had previously been a model and had always taken great pride in her appearance—now neglected herself and seemed less attractive with every clinic visit. In addition, she experienced significant anxiety: She was anxious about leaving the house, afraid she would collapse on the street, and could not be left alone. Finally, there was an exaggeration of certain of Mrs. G.'s life-long personality traits, e.g., a chronic dissatisfaction with her present lot and a tendency to ruminate about and idealize the past.

OBJECT RELATIONSHIPS. The passive, dependent stance Mrs. G. had adopted toward Dr. X. while she was hospitalized persisted and became even more pronounced in the ambulatory setting. Although Mrs. G. was no longer critically ill, she retained the homemaker and insisted that she must accompany her to the clinic. She also continued to demand Dr. X.'s exclusive attention, and to behave as though she were dependent on him for her survival. Predictably and understandably, after listening to seemingly endless recitations of Mrs. G.'s physical symptoms week after week for months on end, and after responding to her frequent "urgent" telephone messages, Dr. X. began to lose patience.

> She won't try to help herself. She just complains, and doesn't hear anything I say. A few weeks ago when I told her to take her dress off so I could examine her, she screamed for the homemaker to do it. I got mad then and yelled at Mrs. G. to try to do something for herself. I admit I lost control, and I feel very guilty about it. But, frankly, at times, I feel sadistic toward her. I can't stand her endless diatribes against the surgeon either. When is she going to realize that what's done is done? I see so many patients who are much worse off than Mrs. G. She's furious with the hospital because they want to take away her homemaker, but she really doesn't need her. I can't even feel much sympathy for Mrs. G. now.

Dr. X. had entered the relationship eight months earlier with an earnest desire to help his patient; Mrs. G. reported to the clinic faithfully every week with what appeared on the surface to be an equally earnest wish to be helped. Initially, their relationship had been a concordant one, and both patient and doctor wanted it to continue in the ambulatory setting. But once the patient had recovered from the acute phase of her illness and entered the convalescent and chronic illness phase, the doctor–patient relationship entered a new phase as well. What had once been a concordant relationship now became a discordant one.

Management. Mrs. G.'s anger with her surgeon was understandable, and in giving her license to ventilate that anger, Dr. X. was acting in her best interests. However, his failure to set limits in time on such expressions was neither in the patient's nor his own best interests. For by permitting Mrs. G. to "nurse" her rage, he fostered her preoccupation with her physical plight, which led, in turn, to the intensification of the psychological stresses and conflicts she experienced, her regressive behaviors, and, of course, her manifest psychological symptoms. Moreover, his failure to call a halt to Mrs. G.'s provocative behavior meant that he had to cope with the feelings of anger and guilt it evoked in him.

Dr. X. and Mrs. G. might have maintained their concordant relationship during the chronic phase of her illness if he had clarified her physical status, explained the diagnostic procedure she had undergone, and its rationale, and, above all, emphasized that the disability she had suffered as a consequence of that procedure was not unique. In addition, Dr. X. might have been more comfortable with Mrs. G., and she might have been able to achieve a more successful adaptation to her chronic illness, if he had explored the roots of her psychological symptoms instead of continuing to tolerate them on the surface, while, at the same time attempting to control his anger with her. Thus, for example, Dr. X. might have learned on further inquiry that Mrs. G. was so reluctant to give up the services of the homemaker because she was afraid that she might have another cardiac episode when she was alone and helpless. Despite her anger with the surgeon, the fact that he had been available to give her cardiac resuscitation when she needed it remained a vivid memory. Direct reassurance on this point might have alleviated Mrs. G.'s anxiety significantly. If Dr. X. had made it plain to Mrs. G. that he considered her excessive dependence inappropriate to her physical status, she might have interpreted this as evidence that he did not consider her critically ill. She might then have been willing to give up the homemaker, and it might also have served to diminish her passivity and her excessive dependence on Dr. X.

Complex clinical data such as that presented above are not always readily available to the primary care physician. When cases present complicated diagnostic or management problems, it is appropriate for the primary care physician to consult with a psychiatrist in order to clarify his understanding of the patient's behavior. In any event, this case clearly illustrates why tolerance of endless complaints and regressive behavior coupled with "blind" reassurance, that is, reassurance which is not based on the physician's awareness of the nature of the psychological stresses the patient is experiencing, are antithetical to psychological medicine. However well-intentioned, such attitudes on the part of the physician may impair the quality of the doctor–patient relationship, and, as in the case of Mrs. G., impede adaptation to chronic illness.

Case 2

The second case selected to demonstrate the complexities inherent in the management of psychological reactions to chronic illness highlights the importance of the patient's characteristic manner of relating to others as a determinant of her mode of adaptation to illness.

> Mrs. M., a 58-year-old married woman with three children, suffered from diabetes of 25 years' duration. In the past 5 years, the disease had accelerated to the point where she was totally blind, had lost sensation in her fingertips and toes, and was experiencing increasing renal failure. In short, the realities of her chronic illness justified her dependence on her physician and her family at several levels, and, in

fact, made such dependence mandatory. However, Mrs. M. had been an extremely self-reliant person all her life, and prided herself, above all, on her ability to take care of herself and her family. Consequently, she had attempted to cope with her growing sense of helplessness by maintaining a pseudo-independent stance and resisting all attempts to provide her with the assistance she obviously required. As a result, in the course of her effort to perform her "normal" household duties, she had had several rather serious "accidents" secondary to her blindness and paresthesias: e.g., falls and burns.

Mrs. M.'s pseudo-independent stance adversely affected her psychological status as well. Her inability to accept help from others had led to the progressive alienation of her doctor, family, and friends who, on the one hand, didn't know what to do about her, and, on the other, expected too much of her. Finally, in desperation, Mrs. M. described her predicament to her physician, Dr. D.:

"I've been terribly depressed. I feel as though I'm just falling apart, piece by piece. Sometimes, I wish I were dead. Once I stopped taking my insulin, and now I only eat to feed my insulin. When the photocoagulation treatments didn't help, I felt there was no sense in going on. The loss of my sight has had a terrible effect on me. I'm a very independent person. I can't ask people to do things for me. I was always so handy; now, I'm a lump. I still try to cook, straighten up, rinse out my things, and maybe I could manage if my family would cooperate. But, the other night, I ran into a cupboard door, and my son and husband told me to look where I was going. I've lost contact with my friends, too. I can't go out to meet them, and I'm ashamed to ask them to visit me because my son and my husband are two of the biggest slobs in the world. My house is such a mess. I've dropped lots of hints, but no one offers to help. If I just had a little help from someone, I'm sure I could manage. My biggest concern is that I don't have anyone to talk to. If a friend or someone in my family would come to visit for only one hour a week—just to sit and talk with me—I would feel better. But now my family and friends don't even call me anymore. Out of sight, out of mind. And I certainly wouldn't call them. I feel I've been abandoned by everyone."

Formulation

STRESS, REGRESSION, AND CONFLICT. Not surprisingly, Mrs. M.'s previous adaptation to her illness was undermined when she had to cope with its long-term complications: blindness, paresthesias, and increasing renal failure. Nor is it surprising that these events—and, in particular, the loss of her sight—evoked all of the psychological stresses.

These stresses might have been reduced, to some degree, had Mrs. M. been able to regress, in the service of physical—and psychological—adaptation. As opposed to Mrs. G., whose regressive behavior was out of keeping with the reality of her physical disability, regressive behavior in Mrs. M.'s case was clearly justified. However, Mrs. M.'s characteristic mode of conflict resolution, that is, her efforts to ward off conflicts centering on dependency or passivity by adopting a pseudo-independent or pseudo-active stance, for example, inhibited any tendency toward adopting a more disease-compatible life style.

MANIFEST SYMPTOMS. Mrs. M.'s most prominent psychological symptom was an overwhelming grief reaction to her progressive physical deterioration, which had led to suicidal thoughts, and even an abortive attempt to kill herself (her decision on one occasion to stop taking her insulin).

OBJECT RELATIONSHIPS. The stresses and conflicts Mrs. M. experienced can best be understood if they are viewed in the context of her mode of relating to her doctor, family, and friends. Mrs. M. had always been an extremely independent woman, who derived a great sense of satisfaction from her ability to "take care" of those close to her. Thus, despite her progressive blindness, she attempted to maintain her traditional role as the perfect housewife, as a mother figure, and, in fact, communicated her desire for things to stay the same to her family and friends. Indeed, she was quite adamant on this point: "I don't want any special consideration because I'm blind." By adopting this stance, she was able to deny her tragic disability—not only to herself but also to her family. Her family deferred to her wish to be regarded as normal, and expected her to be able to function as she had in the past. Having taken this position, she could not retreat, even when she realized it was untenable. She could not ask anybody to take care of her (physically or psychologically), and her family and friends felt she would resent any efforts they made to force such care on her. Her independence, which had previously served her so well, was maladaptive in light of her deteriorating physical condition. Mrs. M. felt the only independent act she was still capable of was suicide, "but I don't have the courage for that."

Management. Mrs. M.'s expression of suicidal thoughts alerted Dr. D., who, like her family, had been misled by her pseudo-independence, to the seriousness of her psychological predicament and the need for his immediate intervention. Mrs. M.'s "confession" was a consequence of his determination to get to the root of her problem.

After he talked with her, Dr. D. made several specific recommendations. To begin with, he encouraged her to tell her family she needed their support and encouragement; that she needed to talk with them about her situation, and to discuss certain changes in their life style. Mrs. M. was also encouraged to call her friends and married children, to invite them to visit her, and, at the same time, ask that arrangements be made so that she could visit them.

Dr. D. also realized that, in all probability, Mrs. M. would not follow this advice unless she understood the rationale on which it was based. Accordingly, he explained that by striving to maintain her independence, she had invited the neglect and abandonment she now found so painful. Her family and friends were unconsciously supporting her own need to maintain the illusion that she was her old self, that is, they were responding to her unspoken wishes. Mrs. M. accepted Dr. D.'s interpretation and was amazed at the irrationality of her behavior: "What a stupid thing to do. You're absolutely right. I keep taking over when they try to help, and even tell them to stop treating me as though I were an invalid, as though I wasn't good for anything anymore."

On the other hand, there was a risk inherent in encouraging Mrs. M. to assume a passive, dependent stance. If she were forced to adopt this alien behavior, she might experience a fall in self-esteem. It was essential, therefore, that Dr. D. take steps to prevent this possibility. He did so by emphasizing the fact that despite the loss of her eyesight and despite her limited capacity to function, her personality and strength would preserve her image as caretaker in the family.

Finally, Dr. D. recognized, correctly, that it was not enough to encourage Mrs. M. to talk with her family. He felt that it was also important to counsel her family, to explain the double message she was sending, and convince them that it was crucial for them to treat her more appropriately—in keeping with the limitations imposed by her illness.

REFERENCES

1. Sachar EJ: Evaluating depression in the medical patient. In Strain JJ, Grossman S (eds): Psychological Care of the Medically Ill: A Primer in Liaison Psychiatry. New York, Appleton, 1975, p 64
2. Moore B, Fine B: Glossary of Psychoanalytic Terms and Concepts, 2nd ed. New York, The American Psychoanalytic Association, 1968
3. Eissler KR: Malingering. In Muensterberger WGJ (ed): Psychoanalysis and Culture. New York, International Universities Press, 1951, p 218
4. Altman N: Hypochondriasis. In Strain JJ, Grossman S (eds): Psychological Care of the Medically Ill: A Primer in Liaison Psychiatry. New York, Appleton, 1975, p 76

Part II

Selected Clinical Issues

Chapter 4

Problems in Diagnosis and Prognosis and Related Issues

Up to this point, we have described broad psychological concepts and procedures that can influence the practice of primary care medicine. We turn now to the application of these concepts to selected clinical issues that typically pose major problems for the physician.

Clinical competence in medical practice hinges on diagnostic skill, which subsumes the ability to detect the presence of physical disease, to identify the specific nature of that disease, and to predict its course and outcome. And, by the same token, clinical competence hinges on the physician's ability to resolve the dilemmas inherent in these procedures. Psychological issues enter into the problems posed by diagnosis and prognosis at each phase of these processes. The purpose of this chapter is to inquire into the nature of these psychological issues and offer guidelines for their management.

Our discussion begins, logically, with an overview of the difficulties posed by diagnosis and prognosis. For schematic purposes, these can be organized under three categories: (1) misdiagnosis, (2) lack of diagnosis, and (3) diagnostic ambiguity that stems from the presence of multiple and interacting diseases. We turn then to the problems that arise in conjunction with psychological diagnosis, per se, in the medical setting; to the physician's response to diagnosis; and, finally, to informed consent to and communication of diagnosis, which, although they are intrinsic to the diagnostic process, have not been studied sufficiently from a psychological point of view.

As is true of every aspect of medical practice, diagnostic procedures have been significantly affected in the past several decades by the technological revolution and the emergent bio-psycho-social theory of disease. A brief discussion of the implications of these developments for diagnosis and prognosis can serve as an appropriate preamble to a more detailed discussion of the dilemmas that confront the physician in these areas.

The problems posed by diagnosis have been eased by the development of sophisticated devices and procedures, e.g., computers, scanners, arteriography, and telemetry. However, these procedures do not, in themselves, guarantee diagnostic accuracy; nor have they eliminated the problem of the undiagnosed disease. In fact, the technological and scientific revolutions have complicated the task of diagnosis in many respects, and created new dilemmas for the physician.

In earlier times, diagnoses were necessarily formulated in broad terms, so that a diagnosis such as "consumption," for example, encompassed a host of chest-related diseases and conditions. We are now able to identify many diseases of the chest: lung cancer, the pneumonias, congestive heart failure, asthma, emphysema, etc. However, these diagnoses are still not sufficiently specific in many instances, for we have also become aware of the heterogenity of disease.[1] Thus, while the availability of elegant diagnostic techniques may allow for a more accurate diagnosis of asthma and its differentiation from emphysema, the physician cannot always determine with certainty the specific form of asthma the patient is suffering from. Nor can he always predict the course of the disease or its outcome. The issue of heterogenity emerges even more vividly with respect to ulcerative colitis. We now know that ulcerative colitis can take several forms, each with a different course and prognosis. One form, Crohn's disease of the colon, is now considered a separate disease altogether. To cite another example, until recently a high serum pepsinogen blood level was regarded as the most important predisposing factor to peptic ulcer disease. We now know as a consequence of major advances in research that there are many different kinds of serum pepsinogen, only some of which place the individual at risk for peptic ulcer disease.

The penultimate example of the diagnostic confusion and anxiety that have been created by the technological revolution is the controversy currently surrounding the diagnosis of death itself. We are now able, through highly sophisticated machinery, to determine brain death, or cardiac death. But when is the patient truly dead? Does he cease to exist when his brain no longer functions? Or is the criterion of death the cessation of heartbeat? Or are both essential to the verdict of death?

In some diseases, the uncertainty as to prognosis has been heightened as a consequence of recent technological and scientific advances. Thus, while a diagnosis of breast cancer can usually be made with greater certainty, predictions as to the course and outcome of the disease have become more uncertain owing to our greater knowledge of prognostic factors (e.g., lymph node involvement), and the development of new, as yet insufficiently validated, treatment procedures (e.g., triple chemotherapy, high-powered cobalt bombs, and sophisticated surgical techniques).

Diagnosis and prognosis have been further complicated by our growing knowledge of the relationship between mind and body. It is now widely conceded that psychological stress may find expression in somatic symptoms, and vice versa. We know too that the patient's psychological reactions to his illness may influence its course to a large extent. Clearly, then, medical diagnosis and prognosis must be based not only on evaluation of the patient's biological status, but also on evaluation of his psychosocial status.

CURRENT PROBLEMS IN DIAGNOSIS AND PROGNOSIS

Current problems in diagnosis and prognosis were delineated earlier as consisting of misdiagnosis; lack of diagnosis; diagnostic ambiguity; and one other diagnostic issue which resists specific categorization, namely, the formulation of a psychological diagnosis in the medical setting. These problems may, in turn, result from, or give rise to premature diagnosis, as well as over- or under-diagnosis.

Misdiagnosis

The frequency with which errors in medical diagnosis occur have been well publicized in the professional literature.[2-4] But such errors are inevitable, given the state of the art. Perhaps the most pernicious element of this phenomenon is the inability of physician and patient alike to accept errors in diagnosis as a reality of medical practice. The quality of even the most concordant doctor–patient relationship may fluctuate or become discordant if the doctor errs in diagnosis, however minor his error may be. In a great number of patients, misdiagnosis leads to doctor-shopping, a loss of faith in or overt anger with the doctor, and the inevitable deterioration of the doctor–patient relationship.

Several technical explanations for diagnostic error have been advanced in the literature. First, misdiagnosis may be due to incomplete or isolated laboratory findings, errors in the laboratory findings reported, and/or an error in the use of sophisticated technological equipment for the acquisition of data.[5] At the same time, laboratory findings which are accurate in themselves may nonetheless be a source of diagnostic error if they are not properly interpreted. For example, a laboratory finding of an elevated serum uric acid (hyperuricemia), which is frequently the basis for the diagnosis of gout, may not be idiopathic but may occur as a response to psychosocial stress.[6] In any event, recent investigations have shown that only a minority of patients with hyperuricemia suffer from gout; [7] they are more likely to suffer from osteoarthrosis, which is not etiologically related to the plasma uric acid level.

Secondly, errors in diagnosis can be ascribed to the physician who, under pressure from his patient, the patient's family, third-party payees, his colleagues, and/or himself to make a diagnosis, does so prematurely—that is, without having accumulated sufficient data. Meador [8] has emphasized the dangers inherent in this situation and cited as a possible consequence the emergence of the phenomenon of "nondisease." He points out that in some instances, the presence of signs and symptoms, and even abnormal laboratory findings, do not justify a diagnosis of a specific disease state. The patient's clinical picture may not fit an established syndrome. Or his clinical picture may resemble that of an established syndrome, but the signs and symptoms detected or presented, and even abnormal laboratory findings, may not be sufficient quantitatively or qualitatively to warrant a diagnosis of that particular syndrome.

In short, under pressure from one or several of the sources described above, the physician may diagnose an illness on the basis of findings which, while they are unusual, are not necessarily pathological. Simple cardiac murmurs have been diagnosed prematurely as mitral stenosis; endocrine diseases are frequently diagnosed solely on the basis of clinical observation—and diagnostic error is especially high in these syndromes; any medical or laboratory value subject to a lower and upper limit of normal can lead to an erroneous diagnosis of hypothyroidism, anemia, hypertension, etc. The fact that an individual over the age of 60 shows degenerative changes in the cervical and lumbar spine does not automatically justify a diagnosis of osteoarthrosis of the spinal column.[9] And when a finding of degenerative changes in the cervical and lumbar spine is accompanied by the finding of an elevated erythrocyte sedimentation rate, the danger of an erroneous diagnosis becomes even greater: Simple osteoarthrosis may then become rheumatoid arthritis. Drug reactions can also produce a diagnosis of "nondisease." Drug toxicity and toxicity due to drug interactions are relatively common, and the resultant symptomatology can mimic other diseases. A diagnosis of disease on the basis of symptoms or laboratory findings that appear to be abnormal but that are, in fact, within normal limits for the population at large (or are average for a given racial group, or for individuals at a certain age) may lead to exhaustive, unnecessary, and expensive investigations.

There is, of course, another side of the coin. Diagnostic error may be the result of insufficient investigation. For example, Britton [2] found that errors in diagnosis occurred most frequently in patients over 70 years of age. There are several possible explanations for this phenomenon. First, such patients frequently suffer from multiple ailments which complicates the task of diagnosis. Second, these patients have a limited physiological response to stress, which may cloud the issue of diagnosis. The absence of signs and symptoms of pathophysiological processes cannot, in such cases, be interpreted as evidence of the absence of disease.[10] Third, elderly patients are less likely to provide a complete medical history. Fourth, and most important, physicians who regard physical deterioration as synonymous with aging may not pursue diagnostic issues sufficiently in the elderly.

Lack of Diagnosis

The physician's admitted inability to arrive at a diagnosis is certainly preferable to a premature—and erroneous—diagnosis, or to over- or underdiagnosis. Viewed in this light, such a "failing" would be considered an indication of clinical competence. This parameter of clinical competence is rarely rewarded, however. The patient who seeks medical help makes three demands on his doctor: He wants (at least on a conscious level) to be told what is wrong with him; how long his symptoms will last; and what can be done about them. The physician's inability to arrive at a definitive diagnosis promptly is as inevitable as are diagnostic errors. If he and his patient were better able to accept this fact, they would avoid the adverse psychological sequelae of this contingency. Instead, if the doctor cannot arrive at a definitive diagnosis within a reasonable period of time, the patient and his family are likely to feel that he has failed to fulfill the most basic of their expectations. On a deeper level, the doctor's inability to arrive at a definitive diagnosis, or his uncertainty about the course and severity of the patient's illness, may evoke acute psychological stress in the patient, for this uncertainty may stimulate fantasies about his illness and his body.* In fact, since the patient usually "anticipates the worst," the stresses that arise from fantasized illness may be even more acute. Lack of diagnosis may also set the stage for conflict. Many patients who feel "obligated" to maintain a relationship with the physician pending his ability to reach a diagnosis may view their stance vis-à-vis the doctor as dependent, passive, and helpless.

The stresses the physician experiences as a result of his inability to arrive at a diagnosis may be equal to those experienced by the patient. Although, on an intellectual level, he accepts his limitations in this regard, his narcissism, his feeling of being in control, and his professional self-esteem may all be threatened when a diagnosis remains elusive. If this situation persists, the physician may eventually cope with his inability to arrive at a definitive diagnosis initially by endlessly repeating consultations and tests, and by eventually missing or cancelling appointments with the patient. It is at this point that the physician is most liable to solve his problems by making a premature diagnosis, over- or underdiagnosis, or by the formulation of a psychological rather than a physical diagnosis, and vice versa. On the patient's side, as with misdiagnosis, an inability to concede the physician's fallibility may lead to doctor-shopping, demands for additional (and, at times, unnecessary) diagnostic and therapeutic procedures, and, once again, to the deterioration of the doctor–patient relationship.

Diagnostic Ambiguity: Multiple and Interacting Diseases

When more than one illness exists in the patient, the diagnostic problems in each of the categories discussed are, of course, compounded, particularly in the following situations: (1) when physical diseases find expression in psychological symptoms, or vice versa; (2) when symptom complexes appear to be incompatible; (3) when the patient develops diseases related but not identical to his original disease; and (4) when one disease that is strikingly evident preempts a coexisting and more serious, but less visible, disease.

The first of these contingencies, the manifestation of physical disease via psychological symptomatology, or vice versa, has been ob-

* The eight psychological stresses discussed in an earlier chapter—e.g., fear or loss of function, loss of love, etc., which diagnosed illness gives rise to may also arise as a consequence of the lack of a diagnosis.

served by Leeman [11] in the busy emergency room of a general hospital. In this setting, the tendency of physicians to regard patients as either having physiological or functional disease based on their initial impressions of the patient's manifest symptomatology have often led to inaccurate diagnosis and improper treatment.

Often under the pressure to make a diagnosis—and to make one quickly—the physician is overzealous in his use of psychological diagnosis. For example, carbon monoxide intoxication may present with psychiatric symptoms, and as a result the underlying physiological dysfunction may be overlooked.[12] The symptoms of insulinoma often lead to its diagnosis as a neurological or psychiatric disorder.[13] Cancer of the pancreas frequently presents as depression; anxiety can be a symptom of hyperthyroidism; paranoia can be a symptom of a brain tumor. The point is that the physician needs to be alert to the fact that manifest psychological symptoms do not obviate the need for a physical examination and evaluation. Neurological disorders, such as psychomotor dysfunction and petit mal or grand mal epilepsy, frequently present with signs and symptoms that are usually associated with psychological disorders.[14] Finally, there is a related issue that needs to be emphasized in this connection: The physician's suspicion that the patient's physical complaints are caused by psychological stress is not sufficient in itself to justify a psychological diagnosis. Such a diagnosis should be made only on the basis of positive psychological findings, the absence of positive physiological findings, and, perhaps, psychiatric consultation.

Diagnosis may also be complicated when coexisting symptom complexes appear to be incompatible—when, for example, a patient with low blood pressure also presents with central nervous system signs and symptoms that are not due primarily to cerebrovascular disease. This might occur, for example, if the patient suffers, in addition, from hypoxia or hypercapnea, secondary to chronic lung disease.

There are many examples of the third contingency—the existence of several related, but not identical diseases. Thus, multiple endocrine insufficiencies may coexist or develop with time. For instance, Addison's disease, when caused by idiopathic atrophy of the adrenal cortex, may be associated with other endocrine abnormalities. Primary hypothyroidism, hypogonadism, and adrenal insufficiency can exist concurrently as a manifestation of pituitary insufficiency, as, for example, occurs in Sheehan's syndrome or pituitary adenoma. Or these symptoms can develop with normal pituitary functions, as a consequence of multiple primary endocrine gland insufficiencies.

Finally, one disease that is strikingly apparent, such as a dermatological disease, may preempt a co-existing, and less visible, yet more serious, disease. Of a total of 100 patients seen by Kossard et al,[15] who suffered from a dermatological disease, one out of three were subsequently found to have a previously undiagnosed internal disease.

PSYCHOLOGICAL DIAGNOSIS IN THE MEDICAL SETTING

To an increasing extent, patients are bringing their psychological problems to the doctor. It has recently been reported that emotional disorders rank second among the minor illnesses for which patients seek the help of the primary care physician in a given year; that severe depression ranks second among the acute major illnesses; and that chronic mental illness ranks second among the chronic illnesses.[16]

These statistics point up the need for the physician to develop some expertise in the evaluation of problems that are purely psychological. The importance of diagnostic accuracy is underscored by sociocultural factors. Once a diagnosis of addiction, homosexuality, schizophrenia, hypochondriasis, malingering, etc., is entered on the patient's chart, it becomes a matter of record and all too frequently may thwart the patient's future efforts to obtain employment, get security clearance, or even obtain adequate medical care. The inequities that may ensue for the patient (and the doctor) when psychological diagnosis is not fully understood or is made frivolously emerge with particular clarity in malingering and hypochondriasis. These syndromes were defined and described in the preceding chapter of this book. In the following discussion, we will focus on the clinical implications of these diagnoses.

Malingering

Once malingering is suspected, the doctor tends to immediately confront the patient with his suspicions and attempt to "unmask" him. Typically, he expresses his anger by referring the patient to a psychiatrist. Such action inevitably forces the patient to flee, and deprives the physician of a unique opportunity to gain some insight into the mentality of the patient and the factors that compel him to engage in such bizarre behavior. The doctor's response is understandable. He is angry because he has been deceived and made a fool of; and he wants to bring the patient, whom he perceives as a psychopath, to justice. But in all probability, by branding the patient a malingerer and conveying to the patient that he regards him as such, he forces the patient's exodus.

In so doing, the physician does the patient a serious injustice: If such a diagnosis is entered on the patient's chart, he may be deprived of the care he requires when he develops a medical illness.

At the least it is incumbent upon the physician to determine whether the patient's aberrant behavior is a symptom of another disease—an organic mental syndrome, schizophrenia, etc. Ideally, the physician will attempt to establish an open relationship with the patient, one that can be tolerated by both because the physician does not try to hide his honest confusion and bewilderment, and his desire to find out why the patient behaves as he does.

Hypochondriasis

When the physical workup fails to produce significant findings, the hypochondriac typically responds to the "good news" with anger and an insistence on further procedures. At this point, the doctor–patient relationship becomes mutually hostile. Smith [17] provided a concise and accurate description of the quality of this relationship: The patient accuses the doctor of being incapable or incompetent to diagnose his condition, or relieve his suffering; the doctor, directly or indirectly, accuses the patient of feigning his symptoms, or being emotionally disturbed. The doctor cannot convince the patient that he doesn't need to be seen as frequently. Moreover, efforts to refer such patients to a psychiatrist are rarely followed up.* The hypochondriac will not be swayed from his conviction of illness and his right to be seen by a medical doctor; if he is rejected by one physician, he will find another.

Clearly, the hypochondriac will tax the patience of the busy physician, who is concerned about his patients who are "really" sick. But the illness of the hypochondriac is no less real, and it requires special clinical skills. The appropriate approach to such patients is a supportive one—a sustaining one. Specifically, the physician sees the patient on a regular basis, regardless of his medical status. Although he sets appropriate limits on the patient's behavior, so that he will be able to maintain a therapeutic attitude toward the patient, he does not challenge the patient's symptoms; he tolerates his endless repetitive complaints. For early attempts to promote insight, or to use confrontation to induce such patients to give up their symptoms or to recognize the psychological origins of their physical complaints, are doomed to failure.

* We do not mean to imply that the psychiatrist is an ideal solution. On the contrary the hypochondriac is the bête noire of the psychiatrist as well.

The primary care approach, which can accommodate these concepts, may provide the only viable setting for the management of these patients.

THE PHYSICIAN'S RESPONSE TO DIAGNOSIS

An important determinant of the patient's response to diagnosis is his tendency to link diagnosis and prognosis. For example, despite the fact that several forms of cancer are now known to respond to available treatment procedures, and the prognosis for other forms is more optimistic than it once was, such a diagnosis is still equated with death by many patients, who then develop psychological reactions to their illness. In some physicians, too, a diagnosis of cancer and other illnesses, in which major advances have been made, continues to cause therapeutic nihilism. For instance, as a consequence of advances in our knowledge of the etiology of alcoholism, and the development of new treatment techniques, this disease has been mastered by a significant number of patients. Yet, such patients are still regarded as "hopeless" and untreatable in some quarters. Moreover, the physician's response to the patient's diagnosis, which is inevitably conveyed to the patient, will, in many instances, adversely affect the patient's attitude toward his illness and his prognosis; the physician's response to the patient's diagnosis has more influence than is generally recognized on the patient's ability to adapt to his illness.

Maladaptive responses may also arise in the physician when there is a lack of diagnosis, or when his findings are inconclusive. The physician may be reluctant or unable to communicate his "failure." The nature and intensity of the doctor's response to this contingency will, of course, depend on the degree to which his need to think of himself as the omnipotent healer governs his day-to-day practice of medicine. When the need to present himself as infallible is a prepotent factor in his modus operandi, the prospect of admitting that he's "stumped" becomes insupportable. The possible sequelae of this attitude have been referred to throughout this chapter. Briefly, the physician may then cope with this stress by making a diagnosis prematurely; by diagnosing an illness when, in fact, none exists ("nondisease"); by ascribing physical symptoms to psychological causes, without first ruling out the possibility of physical disease or confirming the presence of psychological disease; by continuing to subject the patient to exhaustive (and exhausting) diagnostic tests and procedures, even when his clinical judgment tells him that, more than likely, these procedures will be inconclusive; and, finally, by abandoning the patient.

Psychological issues are preeminent at times in the course of many illnesses. The physician's task in this situation is to "shift gears" when necessary, and view the patient as having a psychological rather than a primarily physiological problem. For example, we have seen that the coronary patient who has fully recovered physically from the acute phase of his illness may be psychologically impaired during the convalescent phase, as evidenced by his inability to work or engage in sexual activity because he is afraid that the exertion required may precipitate another attack. It may also be useful for the doctor to think of the patient as a psychological problem when all diagnostic possibilities have been exhausted. For within that diagnostic frame of reference, he may feel that even though he can't diagnose the patient's illness, he can help him to adapt to that situation. The physician may then be less angry with himself for his diagnostic impotence and feel less need to withdraw from and abandon the patient whom he perceives as "evidence" of that impotence.

INFORMED CONSENT

At times, of course, laboratory tests and/or technical procedures that are painful, risk-laden, and time-consuming are nonetheless essential to assure diagnostic accuracy. The physician's diagnostic skills will count for naught if he is unable to persuade his patient to undergo such procedures. Within the past decade, a new "code" of medical ethics has evolved that requires (1) that the physician obtain the patient's consent to any procedures used to arrive at a diagnosis and (2) that he inform the patient of the nature, outcome, and possible side-effects of any treatment procedure that is recommended. The law further stipulates that, provided he is mentally competent, the patient has the right, on the basis of such information to refuse to consent to treatment. Finally, the concept that every patient has the right to know his diagnosis and prognosis, although not yet enacted into law, continues to gain currency in our society. These trends have created new dilemmas for the physician.

Some of the problems that stem from the issue of consent (to both diagnostic and treatment procedures) are self-evident. The physician is enjoined by the Hippocratic oath to do nothing that will harm the patient. However, he is enjoined by law to obtain the patient's fully informed consent to a painful, life-threatening diagnostic or therapeutic procedure. And in fulfilling his legal obligation to tell all, the physician frequently imposes an acute and painful psychological stress on the patient as evidenced in the following consent form to a bone marrow transplant.

It is my understanding that I have advanced leukemia, for which I have received many chemotherapeutic agents as well as X-ray therapy. The chances of my responding to any further conventional therapy for any prolonged period are extremely remote and, when I no longer respond, my chances for survival become virtually nil. There is a chance of responding with a prolonged remission if I receive a bone marrow transplant using my [brother], who is immunologically compatible, as a source of marrow.

I will be isolated in a germ-free environment, and will undergo treatment with extremely high doses of cyclophosphamide, total body irradiation (TBI), procarbazine, and antithymocyte serum (ATS). This preparatory treatment is necessary both to destroy the leukemia cells and to suppress my immune system so as to enable me to accept the donated marrow. When this initial preparation is completed, bone marrow obtained from my brother will be given as an intravenous infusion. It is hoped that this infusion of bone marrow will reconstitute my marrow.

The risks of this procedure to me are extreme. The preparatory therapy is probably lethal unless the transplant succeeds, since any remaining normal marrow which I have will have been destroyed. There is also a chance that the leukemia will recur. Even if a successful graft does occur, there is a significant risk of the graft reacting against me despite careful matching of me and my [brother]. This is called graft-versus-host disease (GVHD). This disease may vary in intensity from minimal to severe, but, if severe, it may be lethal. Another medication, methotrexate, will be given posttransplant in an attempt to mitigate this problem. Methotrexate can cause lung, liver, and intestinal damage. ATS may also be of help in treating established graft-versus-host disease.

Even if all goes well, my immune system will not function fully for 6 to 12 months. During this time, I will have to be watched carefully for the development of infection.

The long range effects of TBI include probable sterility, almost certain cataracts (vision being adequate using contact lenses after surgery), and an increased risk of developing tumors. Cyclophosphamide may cause temporary hair loss and gastrointestinal upset, as well as bladder bleeding which rarely leads to permanent bladder damage. Cyclophosphamide will also contribute to the problem of sterility. Other long-term effects of high dose cyclophosphamide are largely unknown. Procarbazine may cause gastrointestinal upset as well as drowsiness, and muscle and joint pains. ATS is produced in rabbits and can cause rapidly fatal allergic reactions, nephritis, and serum sickness.

Using this procedure both in Seattle and in Boston, there is an approximately 30 percent chance of success. On the other hand, the alternative is conventional chemotherapy with virtually no chance for long-term survival. This bone marrow transplantation represents an attempt to achieve a longstanding remission. All of the doctors involved agree that a transplantation attempt should be made, despite the grave risks involved.

Accordingly, I consent to the procedure to the extent that I am legally competent to do so.[18]*

Thus the question arises whether the patient can psychologically assimilate the fact that quite apart from the side-effects and complications that may occur, he has only one chance in three of surviving the bone marrow transplant which currently offers his only hope.

* This form was published in Psychosom Med 38:439, 1976.

Even when the doctor is completely candid, and presents all the known data regarding the risks and complications that may occur with anesthesia, drugs, surgical procedures, etc., the patient may not remember that he has been so informed. Robinson and Merav,[19] in a unique project undertaken at Montefiore Hospital and Medical Center, studied open heart surgery patients four to six months after the operation had been performed to ascertain the extent to which they recalled having given their informed consent to such surgery. Although they acknowledged that they had understood the doctor's comments at the time, all the patients interviewed failed to remember large segments of the material presented. Many denied that they had ever been informed of about 50 percent of the items. In fact, however, their consents, which had been recorded on audio cassettes, clearly demonstrated that they had been so informed. Thus, the possibility that the patients didn't remember what they had been told because they had not been adequately informed must be ruled out. There is a second possibility, that a normal decay in memory over a 4-6 month period accounted to some extent for this phenomenon.

Actually, there are two more plausible explanations (which have not yet been validated) for the memory deficiency Robinson and Merav observed: (1) Having made the decision to undergo a life-saving surgical procedure, these patients may not have been able to "hear" anything which might have tempted them to alter that decision,* or (2) having survived the operation, they may have repressed and suppressed many issues surrounding the traumatic consent experience. In any event, if the findings from this study can be generalized to apply to other patient populations, this study may have important implications for the issue of informed consent. We would speculate that the information a patient receives regarding the risks entailed in a life-saving diagnostic or therapeutic procedure is only one determinant of his final decision to undergo or forego that procedure. Such a decision will also depend on his relationship with his physician and the way the physician communicates his diagnosis and prognosis.

THE COMMUNICATION OF DIAGNOSIS

In a sense, the issue of communication transcends the dilemmas posed by diagnosis per se. To illustrate, if the physician is unable to arrive at a diagnosis, he is faced with the challenge of communicating his

* The question arises as to whether the same findings would have emerged from a study of patients whose consent was required for a less serious surgical procedure.

inability to identify the patient's disease in a manner that will foster the patient's acceptance of the lack of diagnosis; so that the patient will not be overwhelmed by his fantasies; and the concordant doctor–patient relationship can be preserved.

Most physicians know from experience that their impression that psychological factors play an important role in the patient's complaints should be communicated with caution. If the physician arrives at a psychological rather than a physiological diagnosis, he must be prepared for the possibility that the patient may *not* be relieved to know that there is nothing physically wrong with him, that it's "all in his mind." Even in this age of enlightenment, many patients feel stigmatized by the doctor's suggestion that they may be "nervous," emotionally upset, or under strain, rather than physically ill. And, of course, we have seen that nothing will be accomplished by the physician's insistence that the hypochondriac's symptoms are a figment of his imagination.

Particularly difficult problems attend the communication of the diagnosis of a degenerative disease. If the patient is experiencing diminished mental and/or physical competence, the doctor must make him or his family aware of these deficits, for they may mandate certain major changes in the patient's life style. He may, for example, have to give up his life's work, stop driving a car, accept residential placement.

The stresses inherent in the communication of a catastrophic diagnosis are self-evident. Under this rubric we would include diagnoses perceived by the patient as catastrophic because they involve the loss of or damage to a particularly valued body part. For instance, a diagnosis of arthritis would be perceived as catastrophic by a concert pianist; an Olympic skater would react similarly to the need for a leg amputation. The dilemmas that confront the physician in such situations center on the management of the patient's reaction to the communication of his diagnosis.

But the physician's task becomes infinitely more complex when it involves the communication of a diagnosis that is equated with death. Such a communication may be as stressful for the physician as it is for the patient: He may attempt to cope with these stresses by deceiving the patient with respect to his prognosis. Thus, the physician may hold out false hopes; or, if the stress becomes overwhelming, he may simply abandon the patient psychologically. That is, he may go to any lengths to avoid talking with the patient and his family; and when confrontation cannot be avoided, he may use medical double-talk to skirt the issues of diagnosis and prognosis. In other instances, there is an understandable tendency to overwhelm the patient, infantalize him, and foster dependency. This latter approach, though well-intentioned, may be as deleterious as abandonment for the patient who needs to rely on his own resources to come to terms with the catastrophe that has befallen him.

Briefly, the physician must decide in such cases, on the basis of his knowledge of the patient's psychological makeup, whether he should be informed of his diagnosis, when he should be told, how much he should be told, and who should tell him. The physician cannot make these decisions independent of the patient's family and their feelings, which in this matter may conflict with his own views. For example, the family may not want the patient informed of pessimistic findings, or the physician may feel that his diagnosis and prognosis should be withheld from the patient.

In some instances, the doctor's decision not to tell may take precedence over the family's feeling that such concealment would be deceitful—to the detriment of both the patient and his family.

> When Mr. M.'s wife became ill, he was advised by her doctor not to tell her she had cancer. The doctor felt she "couldn't take it." Although in the 31 years they had been married, the M.'s had always been open with each other, Mr. M. was able to keep that secret from his wife for six years—until she died.
>
> But Mr. M.'s constant need to dissemble placed a great burden on him, and, more importantly, it caused a rift in the couple's relationship, so that, at the end, they lost the closeness and the feeling of mutual support which had made their marriage unique.

Conversely, the doctor may feel that the patient should be told, the family may disagree, and the doctor may abide by their wishes. Again, as illustrated below, this decision may have deleterious consequences for the patient, his family, and the physician himself.

> Dr. G. was convinced that Mr. F. was strong enough to "take" the news that he had cancer. His reasoning, based on his long-term contact with Mr. F., proceeded from his evaluation of his patient as an independent, active, autonomous individual who characteristically assumed a dominant role in business and in family life. These traits would seem to argue for openness with the patient. Mr. F's family felt, however, that he should be able to live out the rest of his life without the shadow of death constantly hanging over him. Dr. G. was understandably influenced by the demands of this distraught family.
>
> Because efforts to dissemble are never completely successful, and because Mr. F. was an intelligent, insightful man, he recognized early on that something was awry. With minimal persistence, he was able to elicit the information from his family that he had cancer. Predictably, Mr. F. was hurt by their lack of faith in him. His response

to his physician was even more extreme. He felt betrayed by Dr. G. In fact, he felt that their previously concordant relationship, which he thought had been based on mutual understanding and trust, had been a sham.

Actually, there is no way of predicting with certainty that patients who appear on the surface to be independent and autonomous will be able to handle a catastrophic diagnosis with equanimity. The physician must be able to differentiate between the patient's request to be told and to know, and his latent unconscious wishes in this regard. A demand to be told "the worst" may, on a deeper level, be a plea for reassurance. This distinction cannot be made on the basis of intuition. Only an understanding—made possible by long-term doctor–patient contact—of the patient's psychological, social, and cultural makeup, will enable the physician to determine what and how much the patient should be told about his physical status. On the basis of this understanding, the physician may be able to guide the family so that they can adopt an appropriate approach to this sensitive issue.

REFERENCES

1. Weiner H: Psychobiology and Human Disease. New York, Elsevier, 1977, p 14
2. Britton M: Diagnostic errors discovered at autopsy. Acta Med Scand 196: 203, 1974
3. Gruver RH, Freis ED: A study of diagnostic errors. Ann Int Med 47: 108, 1957
4. Heasman MA, Lipworth L: Accuracy of certification of cause of death. London, Her Majesty's Stationery Office, 1966
5. Bell C, Talal N, Schur PH: Antibodies to DNA in patients with rheumatoid arthritis and juvenile rheumatoid arthritis. Arthritis Rheum 18:535, 1975
6. Weiner H, Hart S: Promising interactions between medicine and psychiatry. In Arieti S (ed): American Handbook of Psychiatry. New York, Basic Books, 1974
7. Fessel UJ: Seminar on Rheumatoid Arthritis I–275, 1972
8. Meador CK: The art and science of nondisease. New Eng J Med 272: 92, 1965
9. Hart DF: The importance of nondisease. Practitioner 211:193, 1973
10. Eisenberg J: Problems of the so-called geriatric gastrointestinal diseases. Fortschr Med 93: 1216, 1975
11. Leeman CP: Diagnostic errors in emergency room medicine: Physical illness in patients labelled "psychiatric" and vice versa. J Psychiatr Med 6: 533, 1975

12. Jefferson JF: Subtle neuropsychiatric sequelae of carbon monoxide intoxication: two case reports. Am J. Psychiatry 133: 961, 1976
13. Service FJ, Dale AF, Elvaback LF, Jiang NS: Insulinoma: Clinical and diagnostic features of 60 consecutive cases. Mayo Clin Proc 51: 417, 1976
14. Lawall J: Psychiatric presentation of seizure disorders. Am J Psychiatry 133: 321, 1976
15. Kossard S, Paver K, Doyle J, Krivanekj J: Dermatology in hospital practice. Med. J. Aust 2:486, 1976
16. Rogers DE: The challenge of primary care. In Knowles JH (ed): Doing Better and Feeling Worse. New York, WW Norton, 1977, p 81
17. Smith JA: Hypochondriasis: symptom or entity. Psychosomatics 11:413, 1970
18. Brown HN, Kelly MJ: Stages of bone marrow transplant: psychiatric perspective. Psychosom Med 38:439, 1976
19. Robinson G, Merav A: Informed consent: recall by patients tested postoperatively. Ann Thoracic Surg 22: 209, 1976

Chapter 5

The Organic Mental Syndromes

The organic mental syndromes are among the pathophysiological disorders most frequently encountered in the chronically ill.* Yet, their accurate diagnosis is fraught with difficulty for a number of reasons: Among these we would include the misconceptions which continue to surround organicity; the problem their assessment presents in the context of routine primary care practice; and the obstacles that are felt to preclude their effective management. At times these difficulties are exacerbated by the response the illness, its assessment, and management may evoke in the physician.

DEFINITION

The organic mental syndromes occur as a consequence of the effect of pathological physical processes on the structure or metabolism of the brain. For purposes of diagnostic classification, these syndromes can be divided into two major categories: (1) transient disturbances of

* The organic mental syndromes are correctly identified by the physician as pathophysiological disorders. At times, however, the mental and behavioral symptoms manifested by these patients as a consequence of pathological physical processes become a predominant consideration. The physician may then deal with the organic mental syndrome as though it were a psychological disorder, to the degree that he may feel that its management lies within the domain of the psychiatrist.

cerebral metabolism that produce acute, reversible syndromes referred to as *delirium,* and (2) disturbances in which structural damage occurs and neurons are destroyed—e.g., tumor, cerebral vascular accidents, trauma, demyelinating diseases, degenerative diseases such as Alzheimer's or Pick's disease, and presenile dementia—that produce chronic and irreversible syndromes which are referred to as *dementia.**

Delirium is present in most patients with severe anemia, fever, peripheral circulatory collapse, cardiac arrest, congestive heart failure, respiratory failure, pulmonary insufficiency, hepatic or renal insufficiency, acidosis or alkalosis, electrolyte imbalance, or infection. It is also present in patients suffering from the effects of many different drugs, and from the effects on the central nervous system of almost every phenomenon, including sensory deprivation, that produces a disturbance in physiological homeostasis. When these conditions remain uncorrected, patients who suffer from reversible mental syndromes (delirium) at the outset may subsequently develop irreversible brain damage (dementia). Thus, the same etiological agent may produce temporary or permanent brain damage.

A third variation of the organic mental syndrome occurs when an acute organic syndrome is superimposed upon an existing chronic syndrome. Here, too, the existence of the acute syndrome—which inevitably exacerbates the chronic syndrome or becomes a chronic process in and of itself—frequently remains undetected.[3]

CLINICAL FEATURES

Regardless of the nature of the pathological process that precipitated the organic mental syndrome, and regardless of whether that syndrome is reversible or irreversible, the physical stresses that damage the structure of the higher center of the brain, or interfere with cerebral metabolism, characteristically produce deficits in the patient's mental functioning.

The nature of these deficits may vary considerably. The only clin-

* Neurologists and some internists do not subscribe to this classification, which is employed by most psychiatrists. For example, many neurologists believe that some forms of dementia are reversible. The terms *sub-acute amnestic confusional state* [1] and *acute confusional state* [2] represent attempts on the part of psychiatrists to update their current classification, so that it will accurately reflect the indeterminant clinical pictures these syndromes often present. The problems of nomenclature lie beyond the scope of this discussion. Rather, our purpose is to classify these syndromes in a manner that will facilitate the presentation of data regarding their detection and management.

ical feature of an organic mental syndrome may be the patient's subjective feeling that he is not himself. Or the physical processes that interfere with brain function may alter a host of specific mental functions: relationship to reality, memory, intellectual capacity, judgment, perception, level of consciousness, attention, comprehension, capacity for abstract thought, ability to synthesize, use of language, and capacity for self-evaluation. Deficits in mental functioning may also find expression in a variety of other behavioral disturbances: impaired motor control, lack of impulse control, and inability to control mood or feeling states.

The clinical features of organicity may include symptoms that extend beyond these cardinal signs. Among such symptoms are apathy, weakness, excessive fatigue, subdued affect, etc., which may be characteristic of delirium and dementia alike, yet, as a rule, are not routinely associated with organicity. Diagnosis may also be complicated by the chaotic behaviors these patients may manifest, e.g., acute agitation, disorganized and uncontrolled emotional and motor discharge. These symptoms may be so bizarre that the physician feels overwhelmed and presses for the patient's referral to a psychiatrist. Furthermore, regression may take place, allowing for a more primitive moral and ethical code. That is, there may be a breakthrough of heretofore-repressed sexual and aggressive impulses. Typically, the functions that are most complex, and developed last, are the most vulnerable to early disruption, while the more primitive functions are the most enduring. Finally, the hallmark of the organic syndrome is its fluctuating features in both the acute and chronic forms. Changes occur from moment to moment and day to day, and gradual changes occur over weeks or months.

The way in which the patient adapts to these deficits in mental functioning will depend on the nature and course of the illness that precipitated the organic mental syndrome, the nature and severity of the deficits produced by the syndrome, and the patient's premorbid character style and personality. A further determinant of the patient's coping ability is the speed with which the lesion develops. When the onset of an organic lesion is acute, the patient is given very little time to make an adjustment to the mental deficits it produces. When there has not been sufficient time for a defensive adaptation to occur, the patient may be vulnerable to a "catastrophic reaction"—that is, a disorderly, defective performance, with anxiety, agitation, irritability, and/or depression. In contrast, slowly developing (chronic) lesions enable gradual adaptation. Consequently, although the patient with a chronic mental syndrome may sustain enormous deficits in mental functioning, he may be better able to adapt to them.

In summary, there is a constant interaction between the organic dysfunction and the patient's psychological functioning. But, in addition, both of these processes—the organic and the psychological—may adversely affect the patient's physiological status, and vice versa. For example, a bout of congestive heart failure may cause an organic mental syndrome that will adversely affect the patient's psychological functioning. Psychological symptoms (anxiety, agitation, hyperkinetic motor discharge) may then produce further impairment of cardiac function, which, in turn, will worsen his organic mental syndrome. And if this vicious circle is not interrupted, the sequence of events may have a fatal outcome.

All of the phenomena mentioned above are diagnostically significant. But perhaps the central clinical feature of the organic mental syndromes is the difficulty such patients universally and inevitably experience in their capacity to relate to others, and, in particular, in their capacity to form an adaptive alliance with their physician which would allow him to become their "natural ally" in the pursuit of recovery or the achievement of a degree of adaptation to their illness.

The definition of organicity and the description of the clinical features of this syndrome were intended to serve as background material for the discussion that follows of the difficulties that frequently impede the accurate diagnosis and effective management of these patients, and the formation of a viable doctor–patient relationship.

DIAGNOSIS

There are several major obstacles to the accurate diagnosis of organicity. Many of the clinical features described above are not immediately visible. Nor is the physician's intuition an adequate diagnostic tool. Detection of an organic mental syndrome may only be possible through the administration of a systematic, structured mental status examination. However, there are many difficulties inherent in the utilization of the standard mental status examination, which remains the primary diagnostic tool for detection of the presence of these lesions, identification of the extent of the patient's cognitive deficit, and evaluation of the significance of the deficit in terms of the patient's life style. Many physicians have not been adequately trained in the administration and interpretation of the findings elicited. Yet these skills are essential to the accuracy and full utilization of these findings.

Admittedly, the administration of the standard mental status examination is time-consuming and cumbersome. Nor can these objections be eliminated by administering isolated parts of the examination, which may not be sufficiently sensitive for the diagnostic task. For example, Talland [4] found that even patients with severe Korsakoff's psychosis performed adequately on that part of the standard examination designed to test memory by requiring the patient to repeat a series of digits forward (digit span). It is our impression that busy physicians working in an ambulatory setting often limit their mental status examination to checking the patient's orientation to time, place, and person, thus using in isolation three of the least sensitive indicators of organic mental syndromes. Better, more sensitive and discriminating neuropsychological mental status examinations that entail the use of miscellaneous testing objects exist; but, by and large, they remain unused in the medical setting because they require too much time to administer and evaluate, and considerable skill to interpret, which, of course, detracts from their usefulness as a routine screening procedure.

In any event, the standard mental status examination may not be sufficiently sensitive to discriminate between functional and organic pathological processes. On the one hand, depression, anxiety, and catastrophic reactions frequently occur in the brain-damaged patient. On the other, the disruption of short-term memory, a central feature of organicity, can also occur in an anxious, depressed, but organically intact patient.[5] The task of differentiating between a functional disorder and an organic mental syndrome in such cases may pose a major diagnostic problem.

Furthermore, the standard examination may not make adequate provision for the possibility that test findings may be contaminated by other variables, apart from the affects already mentioned. For example, the patient's score will be affected by his level of intelligence, education, verbal skills, and his ability to comprehend the English language. More subtle sources of contamination exist as well. If the patient gets the impression from the content of a question that the physician thinks he is crazy, stupid, or uneducated, he may try to conceal his symptoms, in which event his responses to subsequent questions may be guarded or incomplete. Similarly, a patient may not volunteer the information that he has hallucinations (a frequent symptom of organic dysfunction), not because he wants to conceal the fact, but because he considers this experience normal.

Finally, apart from the defects inherent in the structure of the standard mental status examination, failure to take into account the essential nature of organic dysfunction may detract from the accuracy of diagnosis. As Shands [6] has pointed out, the fluctuating nature of the symptoms of organicity mandates serial evaluations of the patient's mental status.

A brief 30-item mental status questionnaire—the Cognitive Capacity Screening Examination (Fig. 2)—designed to correct some of the deficiencies of the standard mental status examination, and thereby facilitate the prompt diagnosis of a diffuse organic mental syndrome, i.e., delirium, in patients with medical illness was developed recently by Jacobs, Bernhard, Del Gado, and Strain.[7] In addition, questions were formulated which require performance of an interposed task,* which elicits undetected deficits by imposing enhanced cognitive stress. This task can be used in much the same way an exercise test is used to uncover previously unrecognized cardiac dysfunction.

With regard to the practical aspects of the test, the authors felt it was essential to limit the amount of time required for its administration to approximately five minutes. The test form includes instructions for its use and scoring. Further, and most important, in an attempt to help physicians to focus on the physiological basis of the organic mental syndrome, the form would direct the physician, in the event of a low score, to assume the presence of organic (rather than functional) pathology and to review the patient's vital physiological data.

Although a low score on this questionnaire does not, in itself, substantiate a diagnosis of organic mental syndrome, it does identify patients with diminished cognitive capacity. This deficit may arise, in turn, from one or a combination of factors: an organic mental syndrome, mental retardation, low level of intelligence, minimal education, cultural deprivation, impaired English language comprehension, poor hearing, and so forth. In practice, it is relatively easy to differentiate those patients who score low on the questionnaire because of diffuse organic dysfunction from those patients who score low as a result of defective hearing, cultural deprivation, and so forth. In any case, the prompt identification of cognitive deficits, whatever their source, is critical to good patient care. If a patient does not know how to add or subtract as a result of limited intelligence or poor education, he may not be able to medicate himself without danger. Most physicians assume that patients have these skills, and few patients will readily acknowledge their absence. Partially deaf or amnesiac patients will frequently nod their heads in agreement, rather than admit to themselves or their doctor that their hearing or memory is failing.

* For example, the patient is told to remember four digits, to count to 10 out loud, and then repeat the four digits.

Examiner ________ Date ____

Instructions: Check items answered correctly. Write incorrect or unusual answers in space provided. If necessary, urge patient once to complete task.

Introduction to patient: "I would like to ask you a few questions. Some you will find very easy and others may be very hard. Just do your best."

1) What day of the week is this? ____
2) What month? ____
3) What day of month? ____
4) What year? ____
5) What place is this? ____
6) Repeat the numbers 8 7 2. ____
7) Say them backwards. ____
8) Repeat these numbers 6 3 7 1. ____
9) Listen to these numbers 6 9 4. Count 1 through 10 out loud, then repeat 6 9 4. (Help if needed. Then use numbers 5 7 3). ____
10) Listen to these numbers 8 1 4 3. Count 1 through 10 out loud, then repeat 8 1 4 3. ____
11) Beginning with Sunday, say the days of the week backwards. ____
12) 9 + 3 is ____
13) Add 6 (to the previous answer or "to 12"). ____
14) Take away 5 ("from 18"). Repeat these words after me and remember them. I will ask for them later: HAT, CAR, TREE, TWENTY-SIX. ____
15) The opposite of fast is slow. The opposite of up is ____
16) The opposite of large is ____
17) The opposite of hard is ____
18) An orange and a banana are both fruits. Red and blue are both ____
19) A penny and a dime are both ____
20) What were those words I asked you to remember? (HAT) ____
21) (CAR) ____
22) (TREE) ____
23) (TWENTY-SIX) ____
24) Take away 7 from 100, then take away 7 from what is left and keep going: 100 - 7 is ____
25) Minus 7 ____
26) Minus 7 (write down answers; check correct subtraction of 7) ____
27) Minus 7 ____
28) Minus 7 ____
29) Minus 7 ____
30) Minus 7 ____

TOTAL CORRECT (maximum score = 30) ____

Patient's occupation (previous, if not employed) ____ Education ____ Age ____

Estimated intelligence (based on education occupation, and history, not on test score):

Below average, Average, Above average ____

Patient was: Cooperative ____ Uncooperative ____ Depressed ____ Lethargic ____ Other ____

Medical diagnosis: ____

IF PATIENT'S SCORE IS LESS THAN 20, THE EXISTENCE OF DIMINISHED COGNITIVE CAPACITY IS PRESENT. THEREFORE, AN ORGANIC MENTAL SYNDROME SHOULD BE SUSPECTED AND THE FOLLOWING INFORMATION OBTAINED.

Temp.	____	BUN	____
B.P	____	Glu	____
Hct	____	Po_2	____
Na	____	Pco_2	____
K	____		
Cl	____		
Co_2	____		
EEG	____		
ECG	____		

Endocrine dysfunction? ____
T_3, T_4, Ca, P, etc.

History of previous psychiatric difficulty ____

Drugs: ____

Steroids? L-Dopa? Amphetamines? Tranquilizers? Digitalis?

Focal neurological signs: ____

DIAGNOSIS: ____

FIGURE 2

Cognitive capacity screening examination. (Adapted from Jacobs, Bernhard, Delgado, and Strain: Ann Int Med 86:40, 1977)

This screening device has the further advantage that it appears to be relatively immune to contamination by disturbances of mood, i.e., anxiety and/or depression. On the other hand, it is not without its limitations. As mentioned above, it does not identify an organic mental syndrome, per se; nor does it identify focal lesions, e.g., epilepsy, abscess, tumors, etc.* Therefore, further workup of the patient who does not register cognitive deficits but who continues to manifest symptoms of a neurological disorder becomes mandatory.

Whatever their limitations, the routine use of some structured diagnostic aid would seem advisable. The findings derived from such a screening device may be the only clue to the presence of an ongoing physical illness. For example, a disordered sensorium may be the single clinical indication of an electrolyte imbalance, which, if not suspected, confirmed by laboratory findings, and treated, may lead to death. This device, or one like it, can facilitate differential diagnosis as well. If the physician fails to recognize that the patient's anxiety and aberrant behavior are secondary to an organic mental syndrome, he may, in his eagerness to "do something" for the patient, prescribe unnecessary and/or inappropriate psychological treatment and possibly harmful medical treatment. Supportive psychotherapy, unnecessary surgery, instituting an inappropriate drug regimen all impose further delays in the diagnosis of an organic mental syndrome.

The routine assessment of the patient's mental status is particularly important for chronically ill patients who are at high risk for an organic mental syndrome, either because of their illness, or because of the

* A recent study was undertaken to further evaluate the Cognitive Capacity Screening Examination (CCSE).[8] Cognitive deficits detected by the CCSE were compared to those elicited in patients admitted to a neurological service. In this study the CCSE correctly identified 73 percent of patients who had demonstrable cognitive deficits on neurological evaluation. It did not, however, identify all of the cases of dementia and patients with limited intellectual deficits. Specifically, it did not identify some patients with cognitive deficits associated with major cerebral pathology. The significant incidence (15 percent) of false-negative results in this follow-up study stemmed, in part, from the arbitrary distinction made originally between cognitive deficits caused by focal lesions and those caused by diffuse cerebral dysfunction. Focal lesions in certain areas produce aphasia, constructional apraxia, or other discrete intellectual deficits. Destruction of cerebral tissue in any area may create intellectual impairment in proportion to the mass of tissue damaged. Therefore, large or critically situated focal lesions can lead to diffuse dysfunction, e.g., hydrocephalus, massive edema, and seizures, which are associated with either dementia or delirium. It is our impression that false-negative results also occurred because the CCSE did not include tests of language, judgment, or fund of knowledge (which are a routine part of the neurological screening device), and because its results were based on an arbitrary fixed "cut off" score. Correction of these defects would increase the high yield (73 percent) of this device.

kind of medication they are receiving, and for the aged because of the frequency with which cognitive changes occur in that population.* In these instances, the routine administration of such an examination provides the physician with a useful, permanent record of the patient's cognitive functioning which can serve as a baseline for future diagnostic reference.

MANAGEMENT

Management of the patient with an organic mental syndrome requires a two-pronged approach. The patient's organic dysfunction requires prompt intervention, where feasible; and the psychological and behavioral aspects of his dysfunction require psychological intervention, where feasible.

In most cases, the physician's decision as to the main thrust of management will be determined by individual patient considerations. It is generally felt that extremely agitated patients should be offered immediate symptomatic relief—which can be accomplished by the use of psychotropic medication. However, the precipitous use of sedatives or tranquilizers may confuse the clinical picture, or even increase the severity of the mental syndrome. For example, these drugs may alter the state of consciousness, and thereby obscure the diagnosis and course of a subdural hematoma. On the other hand, there are times when the patient's symptomatic behavior must be controlled immediately, by whatever means available, as a life-saving measure.

> When Mrs. O., a 52-year-old alcoholic, was brought to her physician's office, she was febrile, tachypnic, diaphoretic, and had a tachycardia of 120. In addition, she manifested the classic clinical features of an organic mental syndrome, as a consequence of delirium tremens: She was hallucinatory, extremely anxious, and so combative that she had to be physically restrained. Because of a recent myocardial infarction, Mrs. O.'s behavior was considered life-threatening, and psychopharmacological intervention was mandatory.

In other cases, reversal of the physiological process that produced the organic syndrome will effect a remission of its psychological sequelae once organic integrity has been restored. Often this approach

* The incidence of organic mental syndromes in the aged is also due to the frequency with which drugs are administered to this population.

is sufficient when the patient's behavior is neither disruptive nor a potential source of physiological stress.

> Although Mrs. L. was extremely passive and compliant, Dr. J.'s initial impression was that she was suffering from a psychosis. The patient's orientation, memory, and judgment were impaired; she was withdrawn; and she talked in a gibberish reminiscent of the "word salad" that is a classic symptom of schizophrenia.
>
> However, on reviewing the patient's records, Dr. J. noted that she had lost 60 pounds over an eight-month period. Moreover, she looked dehydrated and was febrile. When he did blood studies, the findings showed that she had a hematocrit of 41, a normal WBC, a sodium of 105, and a chloride of 69. Dr. J. hospitalized Mrs. L. and within 24 hours after fluid and electrolyte replacement were begun, the patient was alert and oriented, and her "schizophrenic" symptoms had disappeared.

If Dr. J. had focused on Mrs. L.'s psychological behavior, her already critical physiological condition would have become even more serious. Instead, he correctly initiated treatment of the pathophysiological process underlying her psychological deficit with the expectation—which also proved correct—that this intervention would eliminate her "psychological" dysfunction.

When the patient's organic syndrome is irreversible, ideally, the physician will attempt to provide psychosocial and psychopharmacological interventions that will maximize his remaining resources. These efforts must extend beyond modification of the patient's aberrant behavior. The fact that the underlying organic deficit cannot be corrected and normal mental functioning restored, does not rule out the possibility that many such patients can be helped to adjust to their deficits in mental and intellectual functioning. The primary care physician is in an ideal position to help the patient to achieve long-term adaptation to his organic deficits. Specifically, he can help the patient to use his intact capacities to compensate for his losses. He can also attempt to manipulate the patient's environment, e.g., he can enlist the cooperation of the family in achieving this treatment goal.

> Mrs. R. had a history of arteriosclerotic heart disease, hypertension, and congestive heart failure. These had caused occasional dizziness, confusion, and memory lapses, but were kept under control by digitalis, diuretics, and anti-hypertensive agents. When she was brought to the doctor's office for her most recent check-up, however, it was clear

that her chronic mental syndrome had worsened. Moreover, while she had been able to cope with these deficits in the past, this time the realization that she had forgotten her own name precipitated a panic. Dr. F. suspected that digitalis toxicity might be contributing to her altered mental state, and his suspicion was confirmed.

A few days later, when Mrs. R. had responded to anti-anxiety medication and her digitalis toxicity cleared, and when, as a consequence of these events, her mental status had improved somewhat, Dr. F. attempted to find out why Mrs. R. had taken an excessive amount of digitalis. Specifically, he wanted to find out whether this had been precipitated by general confusion that could be associated with organicity. In the course of his discussion with family members, he learned that one of Mrs. R.'s daughters had died since he had seen the patient last, and that this event had given rise to feelings of deep despair, helplessness, hopelessness—and some confusion.

Thus, the treatment approach for Mrs. R. was clearly defined. Haldol was used to treat her behavioral disturbance (anxiety and panic), and the acute cognitive concomitants of her organic dysfunction were alleviated by monitoring her ingestion of digitalis and anti-hypertensive agents. It was then necessary to turn to Mrs. R.'s psychological problem—her inability to cope with her bereavement.

To begin with, Mrs. R. was encouraged by Dr. F. to ventilate her anger and hurt over the loss of her daughter. In the course of her discussions with Dr. F., she was able to verbalize her feelings of bewilderment: What would happen to her if she were left alone, if she outlived her family? Would she lose her mind completely eventually? Mrs. R.'s concern was justified. Despite the fact that she was beginning to recover from her acute organic syndrome, she still suffered significant organic impairment as a result of her chronic, irreversible syndrome. Yet, she had not lost the capacity to relate to others and her desire to be self-sufficient.

Mrs. R. was clearly not a candidate for a wheelchair; nor, at this point, need she spend the rest of her life in a nursing home, cut off from all outside activities. She followed Dr. F.'s suggestion that she participate in a senior citizens' group, and this involvement helped to mitigate the loneliness and sense of abandonment she experienced after her daughter's death. Furthermore, her occasional memory lapses and episodes of confusion became less important once she had established an alliance with a group who tended to be interested in her past experiences rather than her present deficits.

Thus, it becomes clear that the physician has the potential capacity to provide psychological care for many patients with chronic organic mental syndromes. However, the extent to which he is able to draw on this capacity depends first and foremost on his response to the patient.

THE PHYSICIAN'S RESPONSE TO THE ORGANIC PATIENT

The physician's response to the organic patient is in large measure a product of deficits in his medical education and clinical training. As a consequence of these deficits, certain misconceptions regarding these syndromes have flourished. For example, the doctor's clinical experience may support his view of the organic mental syndromes as diseases of the aging and terminally ill and his view of both delirium and dementia as "hopeless." Many patients with organic mental syndromes are aged, without families, and often express the wish to die. Moreover, these syndromes frequently do accompany terminal illness. But the view of organicity as a disease of old age may contaminate the physician's clinical observations. For instance, if the patient is elderly, and any of the clinical features listed above are present, the doctor may be biased toward a diagnosis of chronic mental syndrome, which may or may not be accurate. If the patient is relatively young, and manifests these same symptoms, the physician may be biased toward a diagnosis of a functional disorder, which may or may not be accurate. In fact, there is irrefutable medical evidence that both delirium and dementia can, and do, occur at any age and with many illnesses. If it is detected promptly, delirium almost always responds to treatment. Admittedly, there are limits to what can be done for the patient with dementia, but the physician who has a preconceived notion that any therapeutic effort on behalf of this patient group would be futile may not reach these limits.

A second misconception that exists in regard to the organic mental syndromes is that the organic patient has greater control over his behavior than he actually does. It is an interesting paradox that whereas the physician would be unlikely to get angry at a patient whose kidney did not function normally, he may resent the organic patient who does not behave "appropriately." In short, he accepts the fact that the patient cannot control his kidney output, but finds it difficult to accept the fact that the patient cannot control his brain output (i.e., his behavior), at least to some extent.

An accurate assessment of brain function would depend, therefore, on the physician's ability to switch hierarchal levels from the physical to the psychological. The physician routinely employs a wide variety of physiological techniques—neurological examinations, skull films, lumbar punctures, brain scan, arteriography, etc.—to assess brain function. However, the brain, as opposed to other body organs, has two distinct functions: psychological and physiological. Furthermore, within the psychological sector, there are two distinct categories of function—thinking states and feeling states. The physician needs to accumulate information regarding both categories—the patient's cognitive functioning (e.g., intellectual capacity, memory, judgment, in short, his capacity to cope with daily life), and his affective status (e.g., anxiety and depression and their derivatives).

The physician's quest for such information may be complicated by prosaic clinical issues. Although physical examinations necessarily require a degree of cooperation from the patient, by and large he assumes a passive stance and the physician plays the active role. This applies to the assessment of the brain's physiological function as well. However, an examination of the brain's psychological function requires the cooperation and active participation of the patient.

In addition to the aforementioned factors, the physician's reluctance to undertake the routine task of assessing his patient's mental functioning may have deeper psychological roots. Specifically, he may be reluctant to expose his patient to a test that he perceives as upsetting and potentially embarrassing, to a test that will evoke anxiety and self-condemnation in his patient. In short, the physician believes unconsciously that he has the capacity to hurt the patient and is afraid that such an assessment will be destructive. Consequently, he tends, instead, to favor superficial exploration of his patient's mental life and capacities with probes that lack depth, breadth, and sufficient specificity to elicit disguised deficits—or to avoid an assessment of the patient's mental status altogether.

The doctor's aversion to assessment of the patient's mental status may also stem from a need to protect himself against threats to his fantasies of omnipotence. The patient who may have an organic mental syndrome forces the physician to confront his clinical limitations (his inability to cure dementia). But such a patient also forces the doctor to confront the broader issue of his own vulnerability, his own mortality, and the inevitable eventual diminution of his own intellectual vigor. As is true of the physician who must examine the end-state cancer patient, the patient who has suffered a debilitating stroke, or the patient whose rheumatic heart no longer responds to therapeutic agents, the physician who examines the patient's mental status runs the risk of experiencing these universal human fears and self-doubts on a conscious level.

The physician's unconscious adverse response to the organic patient may be reinforced by the quality of the doctor–patient relationship. As mentioned earlier, the patient whose brain functioning has been impaired may manifest violent, irrational behavior, so disruptive as to make his management extremely difficult. Or the patient's behavior disorder may take another form: He may be apathetic or unable to remember what he's just been told. These behaviors may compromise the doctor–patient relationship because such a patient will be unable to follow the physician's directions, recognize his efforts to be helpful as such, or convey gratitude to the doctor in any manner. These behaviors are likely to evoke resentment, and a wish to withdraw from the patient in even the most dedicated physician. Impairment of brain functioning, then, may interfere with the patient's management via the deleterious effects of these syndromes on the doctor–patient relationship. If the physician is receptive toward the patient, regardless of his resistance to the administration of a mental status examination, regardless of his unconscious tendency to identify with such patients, regardless of the quality of his relationship with the patient, he is more likely to use his potential therapeutic capacities to full effectiveness.

REFERENCES

1. Kral VA: Confusional states. In Howells JG (ed): Modern Perspectives in the Psychiatry of Old Age. New York, Brunner/Mazel, 1975, p 356
2. Lipowski ZJ: Delirium, clouding of consciousness and confusion. J Nerv Ment Dis 145:227, 1967.
3. Simon A, Kahan RB: Acute brain syndromes in geriatric patients. Psych Res Repo 16:8, 1963
4. Talland GA: Deranged Memory: A Psychonomic Study of the Amnesic Syndrome. New York, Academic, 1965
5. Mattis S: Mental status examination for organic mental syndrome in the elderly patient. In Bellak L, Karasu TB (eds): Geriatric Psychiatry. New York, Grune, 1976, p 77
6. Shands H: An outline of the process of recovery from severe trauma. Arch Neurol 13: 403, 1955
7. Jacobs J, Bernhard M, Del Gado A, Strain J: Screening for organic mental syndromes in the medically ill. Ann Int Med 86: 40, 1977
8. Kaufman D, Weinberger M, Strain J, Jacobs J: Screening the neurological patient for organicity. In preparation

Chapter 6

Noncompliance

Just as specific clinical issues precipitated the move to primary care, others have surfaced as a consequence of this development. Noncompliance has always been an issue in medicine, but the primary care physician, by virtue of his long-term, continuing contact with his patients, is in a unique position to identify and deal with this problem. Recent studies reveal that one-quarter to one-half of the patients seen in this setting fail to comply, in one way or another, with their prescribed medical regimen.* The implications of this finding—not only in terms of the course and outcome of the patient's illness, but also for the doctor–

This chapter is based on the Alpha Omega Alpha Lecture, delivered at Hahneman Medical College, Philadelphia, Pa., February, 1977. In its original form, the paper was published in the *Pharos* of Alpha Omega Alpha, Summer 1978.

* This finding requires further elaboration on two counts. First, it should be emphasized at the outset that the term noncompliance was used in these studies (and is used throughout this chapter) to refer to patients who have been informed of the necessity for an established medical regimen, and who have full confidence in their physician's judgment in this regard, but fail nonetheless to follow his recommendations. In contrast, those patients who consciously choose not to comply with their physician's prescriptions because they question his judgment, because they believe, rightly or wrongly, that the protocol he has recommended is too radical, or, alternatively, too conservative, would not, strictly speaking, be described as noncompliant.

Second, the validity of the research design that yielded this exceptional finding is, of course, open to challenge. It is not our purpose in this chapter to discuss the methodological problems inherent in establishing noncompliance. However, this issue, which may be of primary importance for the physician, merits brief comment. As Feinstein [1] has pointed out, compliance or noncompliance with a medical regimen usually occurs in circumstances where it cannot be directly patient relationship—are staggering. Clearly, then, this clinical issue merits investigation that must extend beyond the recognition of noncompliance as an aberrant behavior. Our purpose in this chapter is to illuminate its possible origins, to alert the physician to its clinical implications, and, finally, to enhance his ability to formulate an effective plan for its management.

Strictly defined within the framework of medical practice, noncompliance refers to an inability or abject refusal on the part of the patient (for conscious or unconscious reasons) to comply with the medical regimen prescribed by his physician, or to continue in treatment. Frequently, the patient is aware that his refusal to comply with "doctor's orders" may adversely affect the course and outcome of his illness; that such behavior may delay his recovery; that by refusing to follow the doctor's instructions, and thereby arousing his anger, he risks abandonment by his physician. Yet, despite his awareness of its possible consequences, he persists in this behavior.

PATHOGENESIS

Psychological and sociocultural factors are often interdependent; for purposes of clarity, however, the role of these pathogenetic agents in noncompliance will be discussed separately.

---

observed by the physician. The frequency with which it occurs depends, too often, on whether the patient decides to report it. Thus in an era that emphasizes the value of "hard data," data on noncompliance is, by and large, considered to be extremely "soft."

Three methods are currently used to determine noncompliance: The first, which is clearly the "most scientific," involves the measurement of the presence of a prescribed drug (or one of its metabolic products) in the patient's urine. A second involves dosage unit counts; specifically, at each visit the patient is given a fixed number of doses of a prescribed drug in a container that is returned at the next visit. The defects in both of these techniques are obvious: The urine test may not indicate whether the drug was taken in the prescribed manner; and perhaps more important it would not indicate whether the patient has complied with other aspects of the prescribed treatment regimen. The pill count method is even less reliable. The patient may forget to bring the container with him, he may dispose of the pills in a variety of ways, and of course he may not take the pills as prescribed. It is Feinstein's opinion, and we would agree, that the best way to evaluate compliance is by the interview technique. Of course, this approach has its own defects. The accuracy of the information elicited in the interview depends on the patient's "recall and reliability, and also on the skill of the interviewer." [1] When the attitude of the physician is punitive, the patient may feel the need to distort information. Nevertheless, despite these potential pitfalls, the interview technique is often the optimal source of compliance data. But data derived from one of the other two "objective" techniques described above is usually added to verify the patient's reliability in the interview setting.

Sociocultural Factors

A variety of propositions have been advanced by authors who interpret noncompliance in terms of the patient's sociocultural background and his manifest response to illness. For example, it has been suggested that there is a correlation between noncompliance or poor compliance with the medical regimen and dropping out of treatment and the patient's lower social, cultural, and economic status. Noncompliance has also been attributed to the patient's fear of his medication, per se, or to his first-hand experience of the adverse side-effects of a prescribed medication. A third hypothesis states that patients are noncompliant because they do not have sufficient knowledge about their illness; because the reasons the medical regimen has been prescribed have not been sufficiently explained, and the harmful effects of lack of treatment have not been sufficiently emphasized or are not understood by the patient. Finally, as Baekeland and Lundwall [2] have pointed out, a sense of well being, despite clinical findings, may also be a contributant to noncompliance.

Obviously, a patient's health status, as well as his social, cultural, and economic status, may all be linked to noncompliance. If, for example, there is a language barrier and the patient is unable to understand the physician and to convey his lack of understanding, he will not be able to comply with the physician's verbal instructions. If he cannot read English, he will not be able to follow written dosage directions on a prescription bottle. If the patient cannot afford medication, he will not have prescriptions filled. If he comes from a culture that eschews the services of physicians in favor of faith healers, family remedies, etc., and saw the physician only when all else had failed, he may not even return for a second visit, let alone follow a prolonged medical regimen.

If the prescribed medical regimen causes painful, frightening, or unusual body reactions, or if the patient has been alerted to the possibility that such side-effects may occur—by the doctor, pharmacist, or a friend—he will be understandably reluctant to comply with that regimen. The patient who doesn't understand why he should take a particular pill four times a day, how the pill "works," and how it will make him better, may not take that pill. Or if the patient remains unconvinced of the efficacy of the doctor's regimen, even if he is given this information, he may not comply with that regimen.

Clearly, these hypotheses, which have been widely publicized, have relevance for our understanding of noncompliance; but they cannot fully explain this phenomenon in the individual patient. The search for a clinically useful explanation of noncompliance must proceed on a deeper, psychological level.

Psychological Factors

At the outset, the physician must rule out the possibility that noncompliance exists as a symptom of another psychological, psychophysiological, or physical process. Among the psychological conditions that may find expression in noncompliance, we would include depression, psychotic states, phobic conditions, and obsessional preoccupations. Noncompliance may also be a manifestation of apathy, inertia, helplessness and hopelessness, or a suicidal wish (all of which are classic symptoms of depression).

> Mrs. K., a 69-year-old widow, had been seen by the same physician for many years for severe atherosclerotic heart disease. The patient had lived by herself for thirteen years and had been reasonably content, and her physical complaints had been relatively minor. In the past year, however, she had become increasingly isolated, to the degree that her only visitor had been her son.
>
> The rather dramatic change in Mrs. K.'s life style in that year had been accompanied by certain changes in her physical status. Eight months earlier, she was hospitalized with a large anterior-wall myocardial infarction, complicated by ventricular fibrillation, and later by complete heart block, requiring insertion of a pacemaker. She subsequently developed congestive heart failure and was started on digitalis and diuretics, and there was some improvement in her physical status. But she found it increasingly difficult to leave her apartment, even to come to the doctor's office. Moreover, when Mrs. K. ran out of her medications, she did not bother to refill them. When the physician asked why she wasn't taking her pills, she said, "What's the use?" He then learned of her anorexia and insomnia and her growing feelings of apathy and hopelessness.

In the psychotic patient, noncompliance may stem from the patient's delusion that he *must* not comply or he will "lose" himself and his body, or the delusion that God has told him to disregard the dictates of his doctor, that all medicines are poison. The paranoid patient who is suspicious of the motives of his physician—or any physician—may not be willing to comply with a prescribed medical regimen. The obsessional patient may be so filled with self-doubt that he cannot be decisive enough to follow a treatment plan. ("Should I take the medicine?" "Did I give the doctor the right history?" "Did he examine me thoroughly enough?" Does he have me confused with another patient?") Such obsessional thinking may result in rigidity, ritualism, confusion, forgetting, and disbelief, all of which may lead to noncompliant behavior.

Noncompliance may also be a manifestation of certain pathophysiological processes: e.g., the confusional states that may follow the ingestion of psychotropic drugs (such as Valium, even in small doses), antihypertensive agents, and chemotherapeutic medications. The organic mental syndromes may result in noncompliant behavior, as a consequence of the impaired memory and cognition, faulty judgment, or extreme distractibility and agitation that are characteristic clinical features of these syndromes.

> Mrs. G., who had suffered from diabetes mellitus (adult onset type), which had been managed successfully for 25 years, was operated on for the removal of a cataract. A few days after her release from the hospital, she became confused and disoriented, and told her daughter she no longer needed to take insulin or watch her diet—that her surgery had been a success.

The patient's capacity to comply with a medical regimen may also be compromised by physical phenomena, such as severe pain or extreme fatigue, deafness or impaired vision. Once these possibilities have been excluded, the physician can explore the origins of noncompliance in greater depth.

Among the psychological factors that may be implicated in the pathogenesis of noncompliance as a discrete behavioral phenomenon, we would include psychological stress, the patient's need to suffer, and the physician's contribution—and response—to noncompliance.

Psychological Stress. Noncompliant behavior may arise as a consequence of the stresses evoked by medical illness.* For example, if the illness has revived conflicts centering on dependency, the patient may attempt to deal with the resurgence of early dependency wishes by adopting a noncompliant, pseudo-independent posture in relationship to his physician. Such a patient, who can function only if he sees himself as totally self-reliant, is convinced that he can get well without the doctor's "help." Similarly, if the stress evoked by illness revives conflicts centering on passivity, noncompliance may provide the means by which the patient can maintain his autonomy and preserve his self-esteem.

In the clinical example presented below, noncompliance represented an attempt on the part of the patients to cope with their fears of becoming dependent, passive, and submissive.

> Mr. and Mrs. M. were elderly, lived alone, and were fiercely independent. Both arrived at their doctor's office with a low-grade fever.

* This is especially true in the aged.

> Their chest X-rays were negative and their complete blood counts were consistent with a flu-like syndrome. Mrs. M. also had chronic symptoms of congestive heart failure. Mr. M., in addition to his fever, complained of a chronic lateral malleolar ulcer, and was given erythromycin and told to administer soaks. Because of the unavailability of hospital beds, their physician agreed to allow the couple to go home with the proviso that they arrange for a 24-hour home attendant.
>
> Although they agreed to this condition initially, once the M.'s had left the doctor's office, they decided they were capable of fending for themselves. However, the next day, Mrs. M.'s temperature was even higher. Mr. M. did not take his erythromycin; moreover, he was unable to dress his wound himself, and his wife was too weak to do it for him. Although both were frustrated and angry at themselves, and at their doctor, they were adamant in their refusal to get a home attendant.

Finally, noncompliance may provide a vehicle for the denial of illness. Briefly, the patient attempts to deny the existence of his illness, and this illusion is strengthened by his avoidance of the medical regimen. Or he may go beyond passive denial to engage in counterphobic behavior; that is, he may actively court physical disaster in an attempt to master his anxiety concerning illness and dying. For example, this would be true of the hemophiliac who, despite his doctor's warnings and his own experience, continues to ride his motorcycle.

The Need to Suffer. Another explanation for noncompliance—and one which is not sufficiently understood—is the patient's need to suffer. Man is traditionally depicted as driven by two overriding desires: the avoidance of pain and the achievement of pleasure. In striking contrast to this popular view of human behavior, the patient who needs to suffer deliberately seeks mental or physical pain (possibly via noncompliance) as a source of unconscious pleasure.*

Defined in terms of their general pattern of behavior, typically these patients are pessimistic, feel put upon, manifest a negative attitude toward persons and things, and, paradoxically, can feel displeasure in good fortune. The way they perceive, understand, and deal with the world around them is tinged by their unconscious need to feel "victimized." It is not surprising, given this orientation, that their life style is characterized by recurrent humiliations, felt hurts, disappointments, and remembered transgressions. At the same time, they experience

* Obviously, the patient who needs to suffer has many psychological features in common with the masochist.

major disturbances in their relationships with others. For their contrariness, obstinance, constant complaining, chronic dissatisfaction, and martyrdom all take on an accusatory ring that antagonizes, aggravates, and alienates the important people in their environment.

ONTOGENESIS. Several explanations have been advanced for the origins of the need to suffer. For one, exposure to overwhelming psychological trauma at critical stages of the child's development—specifically, prolonged separation and/or physical trauma or illness—may result in an exaggerated fear of loss of love and/or abandonment.

The child who, as a consequence of his early experiences, is vulnerable to the fear of abandonment, may attempt to cope with this fear by deliberately provoking punishment from his parents as a means of gaining their attention and ensuring their interest. In so doing, he creates the illusion that he can control his parents—and his fate. When such a relationship continues over time, the child may become convinced that he is most loved when he suffers most. Suffering may then be used as a form of blackmail: He learns that his parents are most responsive when he appears to be unhappy, when he is experiencing physical discomfort or pain, and, most important, when they are made to feel that they are responsible for his plight, that they have failed, somehow, to fulfill their obligations as parents. Thus, the child not only makes himself suffer, he also makes his parents suffer, which serves an important purpose: When the child makes others suffer, he provokes their wrath, and is made to suffer in turn.

Second, this behavior may have its roots in the quality of the child's relationship with his parents. If a child is criticized constantly, or if he is treated in a cruel, humiliating, and rejecting manner, in later life he may come to believe that he doesn't deserve any better.[2] He may treat himself badly and expect similar treatment from others, or provoke others to treat him in a cruel and rejecting manner.

Third, the need to suffer may derive from sustained feelings of guilt. The young child is under great pressure from his conscience to follow the dictates of his parents and society. When parental prohibitions are excessively harsh or unrealistic, their violation produces overwhelming feelings of guilt, which lay the groundwork for the need to suffer.

CLINICAL IMPLICATIONS. With illness, there is a tendency toward a resurgence of the infantile attitudes and perceptions that governed the child's early relationship with his parents. When the need to suffer was a prominent feature of that relationship, it will be operative in the adult patient's attitude toward his illness and in his perception of and relationship with the physician. This attitude and perception may find expression in noncompliance. By being noncompliant, he gains the physician's attention and interest, which, paradoxically, diminishes his fear of abandonment. If he learned early in life that he is loved most when he suffers most, noncompliance may provide him with a royal road toward suffering. At the same time, even while he is experiencing the physical discomfort and pain caused by his noncompliance, he attempts to convince the physician that the responsibility is the physician's; that he has failed to fulfill his clinical obligation. Furthermore, he provokes the physician via his noncompliance with the unconscious hope that the physician will take "revenge." The functions that the need to suffer served in the context of the parent–child relationship are extant in the context of the doctor–patient relationship.

Thus, such a patient may refuse to adhere to a treatment regimen of demonstrated efficacy or manifest a "negative therapeutic reaction," i.e., react with hostilty to the doctor's reassurance that his chronic illness can be stabilized; or discount the possible benefits of any remission. Inevitably, these behaviors give rise to disappointment, disgust, and frustration in the physician who may then respond, understandably, with anger and rejection: "How can Mr. F. be so damn ungrateful?" "To hell with him, he's going to bitch regardless of what I do." "Let him suffer—that's what he wants anyway."

We have said that by refusing to comply with the prescribed treatment regimen, the patient is able to fulfill his need to suffer. At the same time, his noncompliance enables him to maintain control over the physician by depriving him of his most precious possession—his therapeutic potency.[3] In short, the physician falls into the patient's "trap" when he responds with annoyance and rejection to his behavior, for in so doing, he fulfills the patient's wishes. The patient is then convinced that it is the doctor who is the difficult one, that he is, once again, the helpless "victim." Actually, both the patient and his doctor are victims.

Clinical Examples. The two cases described below demonstrate various manifestations of noncompliance.

> Mrs. T., the 54-year-old mother of three grown children, suffered from severe rheumatoid arthritis. As soon as she was admitted to the doctor's office, she began to cry (she would rather die than suffer this way); she continued to wail intermittently throughout the examination, and afterward. The physician, when he could interrupt her tirade, asked whether the medication he

had prescribed had helped at all. Mrs. T. then admitted that she had stopped taking her medication. She could not understand why she should have to take three kinds of medicine, and do those painful exercises. She had sacrificed too much and worked too hard to bear such a burden. In any event, they probably wouldn't do her any good. Dr. G. tried to reason with her. She had just begun to take the medicine and do the exercises; it was too soon to judge their effectiveness. He knew she was in pain, but he hoped that if she followed the regimen, there would be some improvement in time.

Mrs. T. then changed her tactics: Dr. G. was not really interested in her. How could she be sure that a doctor who didn't care about her would prescribe the right pills? As her totally unfounded allusions to his medical competence became less subtle, Dr. G. found Mrs. T. increasingly hard to take. As time went on and there was no indication that she was willing to comply with his instructions, he found that he was trying to make her visits as brief as possible, and was no longer really listening to what she was saying.

The specific origins of Mrs. T.'s need to suffer are obscure; however, her behavior and its sequelae are typical of such patients. Mrs. T. cherished and nourished her self-image as a "victim." She saw herself as a cripple, bemoaned her fate, and complained incessantly that nobody cared what happened to her. Yet Mrs. T. refused to take her medication as prescribed, although she had been told repeatedly that compliance with this regimen might alleviate her symptomatology. And, as a further consequence of her noncompliance, Mrs. T.'s fantasized hurts and rejections began to take on a semblance of reality: Her behavior led to the progressive withdrawal of her physician and her family. Her physician was increasingly less able to tolerate her behavior, and her family found her obstinancy, selfishness, and self-centeredness unbearable. As is typical in such cases, Mrs. T. was unable to recognize that her noncompliance had contributed to—and even created—her problems in her relationships with her family and physician. Instead, she perceived their attitude as "evidence" that she was being treated unfairly.

Noncompliance as an expression of the need to suffer may also take the form of a failure on the part of the patient to seek medical care, even when such care is imperative. Mr. M. suffered in "silence" in an attempt to expiate his intense feelings of guilt.

When Mr. M.'s father, with whom he had a close relationship, died of a heart attack, his older brother became a surrogate father. In fact, Mr. M.'s relationship with his brother was an am-

> bivalent one. Although Mr. M. felt his brother was superior, and admired him, he was also jealous of his superiority, and harbored a great deal of hostility toward this brother.
>
> It is not surprising, then, that when his brother (like his father) died suddenly from a heart attack, Mr. M. was overwhelmed by guilt feelings. Mr. M. was then warned by his own doctor, who was aware of the family history, to notify him immediately of any symptoms of coronary heart disease. Ironically, three months later, Mr. M. was awakened early in the morning by crushing and unremitting chest pain. But, paradoxically, Mr. M., whose outstanding virtue was not his stoicism, felt that he could endure this pain.

Mr. M.'s inability to comply with the injunction laid down by his own doctor may have been motivated to some extent by denial, but there is also a strong possibility that his noncompliance was due to the guilt feelings he harbored for having survived his father and, in particular, his brother.

THE DOCTOR'S CONTRIBUTION AND RESPONSE TO NONCOMPLIANCE

A discordant doctor–patient relationship has been described in the literature as a major source of noncompliance.[4] Specifically, the physician's contribution to noncompliance is considered to lie in his failure to explain the nature of his disease and the rationale for the medical regimen to the patient, and/or his failure to inquire routinely as to the efficacy of prescribed medication—and even whether the patient is taking such medication. When the patient does not comply with a prescribed medical regimen because he does not have sufficient knowledge of his disease or the treatment plan, essentially his noncompliance is caused by deficits in the doctor–patient relationship. On the one hand, the patient is unable to ask the doctor the right questions; on the other hand, the doctor is unable to sense the patient's need for certain answers and, at times, for the repetition of information that may have particular significance for the patient. The point has also been made that many physicians fail to take the patient's life style into consideration in formulating a particular treatment plan. Recommendations that the patient alter life-long habits—e.g., smoking, or behavioral patterns involving excessive activity—are notoriously difficult to implement. It has also been suggested that some physicians do not take the essential precaution of making certain that their instructions are fully understood.

All of these behaviors may be interpreted by the patient as indicating that the physician attaches little value or importance to his prescription. This interpretation may, in our opinion, be a major contributant to noncompliance.

> Mr. P., a 71-year-old overweight patient, had a 22-year history of adult-onset diabetes, complicated by hypertension and arteriosclerotic heart disease. His physician, Dr. B., had prescribed a regimen of Orinase (1.5 grams in the morning and 1.0 gram in the afternoon). In addition, he recommended a 1500 calorie diet and suggested that Mr. P. consult with a dietitian, who would advise him in this regard. Mr. P. took his Orinase faithfully. However, although he consulted the dietitian on one occasion, he made no changes in his eating patterns. Consequently, laboratory tests continued to reveal elevated blood sugar and positive urine fractionals.
>
> Discouraged by Mr. P.'s lack of progress, Dr. B. accused him of failing to comply with his instructions. The patient then clarified his specific area of noncompliance and explained that he felt that Dr. B. did not consider diet control important. If it were important, Dr. B. would have asked him about his eating behavior; subsequently he would have reviewed the prescribed diet with him; and just as he asked him regularly about whether he was taking his Orinase and monitoring his urine fractionals, he would have asked whether he was keeping to his diet.

Two important conclusions emerge from this vignette. First, the physician must give sufficient reinforcement to his prescriptions if he wishes to avoid noncompliance. Second, the physician cannot automatically assume that his noncompliant patient is deliberately being difficult, defiant, or obstinate just to make trouble for him. Nor can he jump to the conclusion that the patient's aberrant behavior has a psychological or physiological basis. Unless he recognizes that he too may have contributed to the patient's noncompliance, he will be unable to alter this behavior. In any event, the physician's negative response to noncompliance—his initial anger with the patient, then indifference, and finally rejection—may detract from his attempts to identify and, if possible, to remove the source of the patient's noncompliance—or, at the least, adapt to the patient's aberrant behavior.

A major determinant of the physician's negative response to the noncompliant patient is his fantasy of omnipotence. The physician who believes that he alone has the power to restore the patient to health, or, at the least, to bring about symptom relief, may be infuriated by the patient who deliberately thwarts his efforts to "cure" him. The physician's fantasies of omnipotence may, in fact, be a determinant of the patient's noncompliance. For example, the physician who needs to keep his patients dependent in order to achieve unrealistic therapeutic goals may drive the patient away. The deleterious effects of these fantasies are even greater if they prevent the physician from identifying the noncompliant patient as such. The physician may be convinced that he is transmitting specific, unchallengeable, irrefutable directions to his patient. The patient, however, may hear these orders quite differently: He may interpret them as "suggestions" from the doctor and feel that the decision to act on them or not is his to make.

The hostility the patient's noncompliance evokes in the physician is problematic for another reason as well. The physician feels impatient and angry with the patient, but he tries to repress these feelings, for he views his impatience and anger as inappropriate and unprofessional. If this conflict cannot be resolved, the doctor may become immobilized, or decide that he no longer wants to be "involved" in the patient's care.

MANAGEMENT

The primary care physician is uniquely qualified to take on the challenge of noncompliance at every level. Because he screens the patient initially, he can detect the presence of noncompliance early in ths course of treatment and make a tentative judgment as to its source.* Since he follows the patient over time, he can check on the accuracy of his initial diagnostic impression and, if indicated, formulate a more valid explanation for the patient's noncompliant behavior. At the same time, in the course of his contact with the patient, he can simultaneously reinforce his treatment plan and attempt to attenuate the factors that are contributing to the patient's noncompliance.

The appropriate management of noncompliance when it occurs secondary to sociocultural or economic factors is self-evident. If, for example, the patient's noncompliance is a consequence of his inability to understand English, arrangements might be made for a family mem-

* Certain cases of noncompliance elude etiological classification. Some patients, despite repeated attempts, cannot comply with a treatment regimen for psychological or physiological reasons which cannot be identified. The management of such patients must take another form. Active intervention is called for when the super-obese patient cannot adhere to a diet, or when the patient with chronic renal disease refuses to go on renal dialysis. A jejuno-ileal bypass may ultimately be the treatment of choice for some massively obese patients. A renal transplant may ultimately be the treatment of choice for those end-stage renal patients who refuse dialysis.

ber to interpret the physician's instructions. When the patient's noncompliance is related to his low socioeconomic status, it may be eliminated by a less expensive and complicated treatment plan. Or noncompliance may be eliminated if an attempt is made to coordinate the treatment plan with the patient's daily routine. For example, very busy people might tend to omit medications during the day, but have been found to be reliable adherents to early morning and bed-time prescriptions.

The physician also needs to be aware of the possibility that the influence of important persons in the patient's environment may constitute a destructive force in terms of compliance. Therefore, whenever this issue arises, the physician would do well to inquire into the possibility that the patient's attempts to comply with his treatment plan are being undermined by family members or friends.

When noncompliance is a symptom of another psychopathological process—e.g., depression, psychosis, obsessional thinking, paranoia, excessive anxiety, etc.—the physician should treat the "primary lesion" via drugs, psychological intervention, or, in some cases, psychiatric referral. If the physician has the impression that the patient's behavior is due to the psychological stresses that are normally and universally precipitated by medical illness, he might find it helpful to adopt the therapeutic approach outlined in Chapter 3.

As opposed to noncompliance that is due to sociocultural factors, or occurs secondary to a psychiatric disorder, or is a consequence of psychological stress, noncompliance caused by the patient's need to suffer presents major management problems for the physician. In all probability, the physician will not be able to effect any basic change in the patient's attitude. Rather, the effective management of this group hinges on the physician's ability to temper both the patient's behavior and his own adverse response to such behavior—in short, to adapt to the patient. Within this framework, the doctor's "stance" can be defined with greater specificity.

First, the expectation that physiological improvement and the attention of a kindly, sympathetic, noncritical doctor will eliminate the patient's need to suffer, and will enhance his compliance with the treatment regimen, is misguided. Moreover, to hold out the prospect of a diminution of physical suffering as a consequence of compliance will only intensify the patient's anxiety—and his aberrant behavior.

Second, the doctor's attempts to introduce the element of reality into the patient's view of his condition will not necessarily alter his negative and pessimistic orientation. The physician who attempts to change the patient's orientation does not understand that the patient's ability to have a relationship based on suffering enables him to maintain psychological homeostasis.

Third, a therapeutic attitude vis-à-vis such patients would be analogous to that of the parent who must deal reasonably with a sulky, stubborn, provocative child.[2] If the parent is wise and does not allow himself to become overly involved emotionally with the child's behavior, he will not be excessively upset or disturbed by such behavior, but remain calmly observant and understanding, however seductive the child's efforts to provoke him may be. The physician's relatively limited contact with, and emotional investment in, the patient who needs to suffer should make this affectively neutral stance at least as feasible for him as it is for the parent.

At the same time, although we have stressed the need for the doctor to tolerate such behavior, certain limits should be set in terms of his own response. The physician is not required to become the patient's victim. He is not required to tolerate the patient's noncompliance in silence, without at least calling it to his attention. He is not required to calmly accept the patient's accusations that he is incompetent, when the patient's failure to improve is clearly the result of his noncompliance.

Finally, the maintenance of an on-going doctor–patient relationship over an extended period of time, a relationship that will not crumble in the face of the patient's repetitive, monotonous expressions of dissatisfaction with his lot in life, that will withstand his refusal to comply with the medical regimen, is the single most important aspect of management.

REFERENCES

1. Feinstein AR: Biostatisical problems in 'compliance bias.' Clin Pharm Therapeut 16: 846, 1975
2. Baekeland F, Lundwall L: Dropping out of treatment: a critical review. Psychological Bull 82:738, 1975
3. Brenner C: The masochistic character: genesis and treatment. J Am Psychoanalytic Assoc 7:197, 1959
4. Altman N: Hypochondriasis. In Strain JJ, Grossman S (eds): Psychological Care of the Medically Ill: A Primer in Liaison Psychiatry. New York, Appleton, 1975, p 76

Chapter 7

The Aged Patient

In 1970, only 5 percent of the aged in this country lived in institutions;[1] the bulk of the medical care for this population was provided in the ambulatory setting, or during hospitalization for acute conditions. Today, two-thirds of the patients seen in the ambulatory setting are over 65 years of age, and 70 percent of all acute hospital, medical, and surgical beds are occupied by the aged. Fifty-two percent of the amount of money allocated for health care by government agencies is now spent on the elderly.[1] Yet, it is universally acknowledged that the medical services, and particularly the psychological care, provided for this population are grossly inadequate.

We believe the defects in existing services can be attributed to several factors: a lack of sufficient knowledge of the aging process; insufficient funds for research and development, and the clinical application of such knowledge; and the physician's negativistic attitude toward the aged. Our focus here is on the amelioration of the third problem, that is, the need to modify the physician's attitude toward the aged. It is our intention in this chapter to trace the origins of this adverse attitude; to present certain core data that may facilitate its modification; and, finally, to set forth guidelines for the psychosocial management of the elderly that should facilitate adoption of a more therapeutically useful approach to this patient population.

The physician's deleterious attitude toward the aged patient is frequently ascribed to our system of medical education and training, which attaches minimal importance to instruction in the diagnosis and treatment of the aged.* The curricula of most medical schools include few courses in geriatric medicine that would provide the student with a basic understanding of the normal aging process, so that he might view older patients in proper perspective. Nor is he likely to acquire such understanding once he begins his clinical training. During his internship, the physician's contact with the aged is necessarily limited to those patients who suffer from acute and/or chronic illness of sufficient severity to warrant their hospitalization. Consequently, during this crucial period, when the new doctor is in the process of developing the professional orientation that will determine the form and quality of his future medical practice, he equates aging with death, with irreversible, progressive disability, intractable symptoms—and with therapeutic hopelessness and helplessness. And, on the psychological side, he comes to associate aging with child-like behavior (dependence, querulousness); senility (memory loss, confusion, acute agitation, or, conversely, apathy and inertia); lack of judgment; and with psychiatric symptoms such as depression, rigidity, and "disengagement." It is not surprising, then, that the house staff generally regards caring for the elderly on the acute medical ward as one of the more burdensome tasks imposed by training. Concurrently, in the course of his training, the doctor is exposed to certain social stereotypes of the aged. Typically, elderly patients are perceived as senile or at the least mentally incapacitated, ineducable, and asexual. These physiological, psychological, and social myths and misconceptions persist and lay the foundation for the neglect and indifference that so often characterize current medical attitudes toward the aged.

The existence of these myths and misconceptions has prompted gerontologists, recruited from various scientific disciplines, to hypothesize that improved medical care for the aged is contingent upon the availability of reliable information about the normal aging process. Presumably, once the physician corrects the misconceptions he harbors concerning the biological events he currently views as inevitable concomitants of the aging process he will be able to view his ambulatory aged patients more objectively and treat them more effectively. Obviously, this hypothesis has merit. But more importantly, perhaps, he must overcome his long-standing psychological, social, and cultural prejudices toward this group sufficiently to be able to assimilate and apply such knowledge. In short, he must be able to adapt to this

* This has been confirmed by recent research findings.[2] Of the primary care physicians in private practice who responded to a questionnaire designed to elicit attitudes toward the elderly, 70 percent indicated that they had had no formal training in geriatric medicine during their medical education.

patient population and their diffuse physical complaints. Such adaptation depends, in turn, on the physician's awareness of the conscious and unconscious responses the aged patient typically evokes in him.

Our efforts to foster such adaptation in the physician logically begin with a summary of data accumulated by gerontologists on the normal aging process that refute the most widely held myths and misconceptions concerning the physiological, psychological, and social characteristics of the aged.*

Physical and Psychological Characteristics of the Aging Process: An Overview

Three findings have crucial implications for our understanding of the physical characteristics of the aging process. First, in normal aging, an important alteration occurs in immunoglobulin concentration, as well as a marked increase in its variability. Specifically, Weiner [4] has pointed out that there is provocative evidence

> that a number of basic immunological and physiological mechanisms may alter during maturation and with aging. Some immunoglobulins produced in the young appear to be highly specific to an antigen. . . . [With] aging, changes occur in the synthesis . . . of these immunoglobulins, resulting in a diminution of the tendency to react with only specific antigens. As a result, broad spectrum antibodies are produced and a range of cross-reactions with several chemically similar antigens may take place. . . .

In addition, age-dependent changes in the regulation of heart rate, as well as the regulation of renal function and related maturational patterns of the circadian output of the pituitary gland have been described.[4] Specifically, the loss of reserve has been cited as a preeminent characteristic of the aging process.[5] For example, between the ages of 25 and 65, the individual's cardiac output at rest is decreased by 30 to 40 percent, on the average. At the same time, a decrease occurs in kidney function; the glomerular filtration rate falls approximately 46 percent, and the renal plasma flow falls 56 percent between the ages of 20 and 90. Researchers have identified a similar decline in cerebral blood flow. Third, symptoms may take a different form in the old.[6] While, typically, the younger hyperthyroid patient is hyperactive, the aged individual with hyperthyroidism may be apathetic. The aged patient with tuberculosis may present no signs or symptoms of the disease. In the

* Many institutions are investigating the normal aging process (in ambulatory subjects). However, for this discussion, with some exceptions, we have drawn on the data presented in a particular series of studies, i.e., the study published by the Center for the Study of Aging and Human Development at Duke University.[3]

aged, coronary heart disease may require differential diagnosis. The patient may not present with chest pain but, instead, appear confused and disoriented, raising the possibility that he may have had a stroke. Even appendicitis, when it occurs in the aged, may present a diagnostic dilemma, for it may occur without the characteristic tenderness at McBurney's point.

These findings suggest that the frequency with which disease (both physiological and psychological) occurs among the aged—and, in particular, the nature of these diseases—may be related to the biological changes that accompany aging, which then result in a diminution of the individual's capacity to adapt to his physical (as well as his psychological and social) environment.[4]

Gerontological studies have been extended to include investigations of the relationship between the anatomical changes that occur with aging, and pharmokinetics, i.e., the absorption, distribution, metabolism, receptor state activity, and elimination of psychotropic drugs. For example, an identical dose of diazepam, administered to both elderly and younger patients, will result in lower blood concentration and longer blood half-life in the elderly,[7] which probably occurs secondary to their decreased capacity for drug absorption, metabolism, and drug elimination.[8] The replacement of lean body mass by fat, which usually occurs with advancing age,[9] also affects drug distribution and further increases the retention of lipid-soluble psychotropic drugs. Clinical investigations have yielded data that suggest the presence of absorption difficulties in older people.[8] However, alternative routes of delivery, such as liquid concentrate or parenteral administration, may alter drug action. Age-related alterations in receptor sensitivity can result in changes in drug activity. Frolkis and his co-workers[10] have demonstrated conclusively that the aged are more sensitive to neurotransmitters; from 20 to 50 percent less of this substance is required to initiate an end-organ response in the aged. Finally, in addition to suffering the more common side-effects,[11] the elderly are especially susceptible to particular psychopharmacological agents described below.

Physiological data that challenge the stereotype of the aged as mentally incapacitated (if not senile) and asexual have also emerged from recent gerontological studies. Although EEG occipital frequencies do tend to decline with age, by and large, individuals between the ages of 60 and 69 show only slight cognitive decline, e.g., mild impairment of memory, and difficulty in comprehension or concentration. And, for the most part, they are able to compensate adequately for these difficulties. Cognitive decline does increase between the ages of 70 and 79; etiological factors, such as microstructural changes in brain tissue—

i.e., plaques and neurofibrillary tangles, associated with senile dementia—may be implicated.

There is considerable variability among the aged with respect to reaction time (which is frequently viewed as a parameter of mental capacity). As a general rule, the aged have slower reactions than younger persons, both in terms of premotor and motor times. However, the number of correct responses is similar for both groups. Moreover, the normal aged can improve their reaction time with practice.

Contrary to the widespread belief that old people are asexual, sex continues to play an important role in the life of the normal aged person. Nor are the elderly excessively preoccupied with death, imminent incapacitating illness, and/or mental deterioration, as is commonly believed. Furthermore, as opposed to the stereotype of the elderly individual as a chronic complainer, the authors of the study cited throughout this chapter[3] found that the majority of the aged in their sample were fairly realistic in evaluating their health, and tended to be consistent, over time, in their self-assessment. (It should be noted, however, that self-rated health is an important determinant of satisfaction with life in the elderly; this may account for the finding that occasionally the aged tend to overestimate the state of their health.) As further evidence of their ability to adapt to old age, while elderly individuals tend to avoid taking risks unnecessarily, their cautiousness is no greater than that of younger people when they are confronted with a situation that demands that some risk be taken.

Myths and misconceptions regarding psychological morbidity in the aged have been rejected by such research findings as well. While over half of the elderly in the Duke sample[3] had definite psychological symptoms, in most cases these did not lead to significant psychological morbidity. Only 13 percent of the general population showed significant psychosocial dysfunction secondary to emotional problems.

In summary, although inevitable changes in physical functioning occur in the elderly, findings derived from recent gerontological studies show that these changes in themselves are not indicative of the presence of pathology; they only represent the decrement of a vast physiological reserve. Illness may intervene only when additional exogenous stress is imposed on a compromised physiological system.[5] However, such pathological reactions, when they do occur, are not necessarily irreversible. Health and physical functioning can and do improve in some older persons, just as they do in younger persons. Again, although intellectual impairment and aging have long been regarded as synonymous, the findings derived from recent longitudinal studies indicate that "such impairment is not as predictable as was thought, and may not occur at all in respect to certain mental functions until shortly before death." [7]

One must also be impressed by the number of normal aged individuals who are able to maintain fairly stable levels of social and psychological functioning. This tends to refute the disengagement theory, which states that decline and withdrawal in the elderly are biologically determined, and, therefore, typical, inevitable, and normal.[12] These findings point up the need for the physician to recognize that his intervention (or nonintervention) must be based on a realistic assessment of the physical, mental, and psychological status of the individual patient, regardless of the patient's age. At the same time, however, he must recognize that the aged patient has certain physical, mental, and psychological areas of vulnerability.

THE PSYCHOLOGICAL PROBLEMS OF THE AGED, THEIR DIAGNOSIS AND MANAGEMENT

Almost without exception, the aged must cope with the loss of love and/or important persons in their environment, as well as with changes in their social and work status, and consequent changes in their self-image and in the way they are perceived by others. These changes and losses all impose severe stress on the individual, who may have little opportunity to form new relationships, to develop a new career, who may not have the resources to retain his former status in the community. Thus, the older individual is often expected to relinquish important roles that contributed to his sense of intactness. The psychological reactions these life events evoke—increased dependency, regression, feeling of helplessness and hopelessness—may contribute to the development of the psychological dysfunctions that occur most frequently in the aged, namely, depression, hypochondriasis, and organicity.

Depression

As opposed to younger people, depression is more prevalent among the elderly,* who are vulnerable to all forms of this disorder, as described

* The etiology of depression in the aged is not fully understood. Biological changes associated with the aging process, including alterations in the immune system, may account for the higher incidence of depression in the elderly. Or depression may be more prevalent among the aged because they lack the psychological resilience that would enable them to deal with the vicissitudes of life.

in Chapter 3. However, the aged patient is particularly apt to experience a grief response, which, if it persists, may become a reactive depression. With respect to the factors that may contribute to the development of these syndromes, the aged do not differ significantly from younger patients.[13] But, the contributing factors—loss of one's loved ones, loss of self-esteem, declining bodily function, altered social role, or decreased financial security—are more visible in the elderly. Nevertheless, the elderly depressed patient may not conform to the physician's preconceived notion of the depressed individual. He is less likely to verbalize his feelings of despair, and more apt to assume the "beaten" expression that accords with the physical stereotype of the aged individual. The depressed elderly patient is more preoccupied with his physical than with his psychological symptoms. This is not to say that he is unaware of his feelings of despair, hopelessness, and despondency. But he tends to focus on the physical expression of his depression—his feelings of apathy, fatigue, weakness, or his vague somatic complaints and sleep disturbance,* rather than its ideational components.

When these complaints persist and the physician can find no somatic basis for them, he may then diagnose the patient's condition as hypochondriasis. The diagnosis of depression may be further complicated if the aged patient also manifests symptoms that are commonly associated with organicity—if, for example, his disturbance in mood is accompanied by diminished cognitive capacity, confusion, and disorientation. The point is that preconceived and erroneous notions held by the physician with regard to the aging process may prevent him from pursuing symptoms suggestive of depression. His failure to do so may place the patient at risk for physiological complications (dehydration, malnutrition), and adverse psychological sequelae (growing apathy, anhedonia, and suicide). Of these psychological sequelae, suicide carries the greatest immediate risk.

THE SUICIDAL PATIENT. In direct contrast to younger people, in whom the number of suicide attempts greatly exceeds the number of com-

* It is an interesting paradox that while, in general, there is a tendency among physicians to underestimate the incidence of depression in the aged, the presence of sleep disturbance (a classic symptom of all forms of depression) is, at times, regarded as diagnostically significant, when, in fact, it may be a norm of behavior in this patient population. In the aged, there is little deep sleep (Stage 4) and very little REM (rapid eye movement) sleep. Two or three awakenings occur per night, during which the aged person may get up, go to the bathroom, then easily return to sleep. For an older person to sleep 8 hours at a stretch runs counter to the normal pattern for this age group. Moreover, daytime catnaps from ½ to 1½ hours in duration are also normal variants in the elderly.

pleted suicides, in the aged the number of completed suicides approximates the number of attempts.[13–16] In fact, the rate of completed suicides in the aged is twice as high as it is among younger persons. Because the methods used become increasingly violent with age, the possibility of success is further enhanced.

Contrary to popular belief, the aged rarely arrive at a rational decision to commit suicide as an alternative to tolerating the pain and indignity of a prolonged terminal illness.[17] Rather, in the great majority of cases, there is a positive correlation between suicide and psychosocial stress. Studies show that suicide in the aged is precipitated most frequently by the loss of a loved one. The suicide rate is alarmingly high among aged widows and widowers in the first year following the death of a spouse, and even higher among those persons who are recently divorced or separated.[18,19] In fact, the aged individual remains particularly vulnerable to suicide for a five-year period following the loss, for whatever reason, of a loved one. The data are impressive: In the first four years following the loss of a spouse, the risk of death among the bereaved aged from suicide exceeds the suicide rate at any other life epoch.[18, 19] Furthermore, the rate of suicide among the elderly bereaved is three times higher for those who then must live alone, i.e., who experience social as well as emotional isolation.[20]

Other statistical data regarding the incidence of suicide among the aged have relevance for the psychological assessment of this population as well. First, the suicide rate is higher among those persons with high (rather than low) socioeconomic status. Second, the rate of successful suicides in the elderly male is twelve times greater than the rate of successful suicides in the elderly female.[21] Third, suicide occurs more frequently among divorced men than divorced women. Fourth, the risk of suicide is higher among those persons who drink excessively and/or present evidence of organicity, and, in particular, impaired judgment. Finally, from 20 to 65 percent of all aged persons who eventually commit suicide successfully have a history of previous suicide attempts.[20]

These data emphasize the need for the physician to be alert to the signs of an impending suicidal crisis. Among these are increased agitation; growing despondency about a physical disability; the patient's increased preoccupation with his physical status; expressions of the fear of dying (which, as noted above, are not typical of the normal aged); unusual fatigue and/or apathy; signs of confusion. And these prodomata will, of course, take on additional significance when the patient has suffered a recent loss. Even the anticipation of separation from a loved one may be a major source of depression in the aged.

Treatment. The primary care physician may perform several different functions on behalf of his elderly depressed patient who suffers from medical and drug-induced depression, grief response, and reactive depression. The treatment of depression secondary to medical illness or drug use will, of course, require the elimination of these physiological precipitants.

The elimination of the emotional precipitants of a grief response or a reactive depression may be more difficult. Many elderly patients are confronted with an unending series of crises, along with a diminishing social network. Yet, even in this seemingly insoluble situation, the physician can attempt to minimize the patient's feelings of helplessness, hopelessness, and isolation. The doctor–patient relationship can be an important source of psychosocial support for the patient: The physician can help the bereaved patient to deal with his loss by giving him an opportunity to ventilate his anger, guilt, his fears about the future. It has been our experience that the aged benefit from such attempts at crisis intervention. At times, the doctor should encourage the patient to continue to work and to follow avocational pursuits when possible as a means of strengthening his self-esteem. The patient should also be encouraged to explore other areas of interest, and to utilize and even expand his social network more fully in order to counteract the losses that inevitably accompany aging. The elderly are usually responsive to such supportive efforts and to environmental manipulations that help them to adapt to their changing status. But the doctor's efforts to induce his aged patient to continue to participate in life to the full may, paradoxically, diminish the patient's self-esteem. In some cases, when the patient is no longer physically or psychologically capable of pursuing certain activities, the doctor will then have the more painful task of persuading him to abandon them. Great tact and sensitivity are required to encourage the elderly patient to "retire" if he is no longer capable of doing his job, or to stop driving a car if it is obvious that he no longer possesses the necessary skills. Yet, the physician's ability to persuade the patient to give up these activities is essential if he is to minimize the feelings of failure they inevitably and repeatedly give rise to.

Antidepressive medication must be used with caution in the elderly. The psychotropic drugs used most frequently in the treatment of depression in this population are the tricyclics, the monoamine oxidase inhibitors, and stimulants. Of these the monoamine inhibitors are least suitable because of their capacity to produce both hypotensive and hypertensive episodes in the elderly patient whose cardiovascular system is already compromised. Clinical claims of the efficacy of the tricyclics require further validation, particularly in light of their possible side-effects. Elderly patients on tricyclics are at risk for cardiac toxicity, hypotensive episodes,* acute glaucoma, urinary retention, and acute organic mental syndromes. Although stimulants, such as methylphenidate and d-amphetamine, have been used successfully for brief periods in the treatment of mild depression in the elderly, their extended use may produce adverse reactions, such as excessive weight loss, tachycardia, hypertension, the production or exacerbation of paranoid symptoms, and anxiety.

The special hazards associated with the use of antidepressants in the geriatric population have been summarized elsewhere in the literature as follows. [22]

1. Severe toxicity may occur at "ordinary dosages," i.e., 75 to 150 mg a day.† For example, amitryptyline HCL (Elavil) may be effective in doses of 10 mg and produce toxic reactions at 25 mg.
2. Aged patients are more vulnerable to hypersensitivity reactions (e.g., dermatological reactions, agranulocytosis, anemias) to psychopharmacological agents.
3. In this population, which has a heightened susceptibility to cardiovascular and cerebrovascular insufficiencies, psychotropic drugs may lead to congestive heart failure, myocardial infarction, cerebrovascular accidents, syncopal, hypertensive, and hypotensive episodes.
4. Paradoxical reactions to drugs often occur in this age group (e.g., barbiturates may cause agitation, disorientation, and aggressive behavior).
5. Long-term side-effects of drugs (such as tardive dyskinesias and pigmentary skin and ocular deposits) are common in the aged.
6. The administration of drugs to geriatric patients may complicate or precipitate the appearance of organic disease (e.g., prostatic hypertrophy, angle-closure glaucoma, diabetes).
7. Finally, in aged patients receiving other drugs at the same time, there is an increased risk of synergistic or potentiating effects.

When a patient's grief response is protracted, when his reactive depression is prolonged or particularly severe, when he suffers from an

* In the elderly, a hypotensive episode, due to monoamine inhibitors or tricyclics, can result in a broken hip, which often has fatal sequelae.

† However, the dosage must be sufficient to achieve therapeutic results. An error can be made on either side.

endogenous ("true") depression, he should be referred to a psychiatrist for more intensive treatment. The physician's function with respect to such a patient will be to convince him and his family of the advisability of referral. The primary care physician may also be more successful than the psychiatrist in persuading them of the potential efficacy of electroconvulsive therapy, when it is indicated. In contrast to the growing acceptance of the use of drugs in the past decade, the widespread prejudice against the use of electroconvulsive therapy in general, and in the aged in particular, has increased. Yet, there is compelling evidence that, as opposed to psychopharmacological agents, fewer and less pernicious side-effects may occur in the aged patient suffering from an endogenous depression with electroconvulsive therapy. The prejudice against this modality ignores the demonstrated fact that it can be extremely effective and even life-saving in patients of any age group with intractable depression. Electroconvulsive therapy is indicated when there is a need for immediate relief of symptoms; when suicide appears to be imminent; when the patient's depressive symptoms include delusions and hallucinations,* when psychopharmacological treatment has failed; and/or when psychopharmacological treatment has produced serious adverse physiological side-effects.

MANAGEMENT OF THE SUICIDAL PATIENT. As a general rule, the suicidal patient should either be referred to a psychiatrist for further evaluation and treatment, or hospitalized. Both actions pose certain problems for the physician: Referral to a psychiatrist may be interpreted erroneously by the patient as a rejection and abandonment by the physician. Hospitalization, which is prescribed routinely for younger patients who are potentially suicidal, may present a dilemma with respect to the aged. On the one hand, uprooting the elderly patient imposes additional stress; on the other, keeping the patient at home, particularly if he lives alone, is a major risk. The need to protect the patient against his self-destructive impulses must take precedence over all other considerations. But the physician must also be aware that the risk of suicide in the aged remains high immediately following discharge from the psychiatric hospital, and for six months to a year thereafter. There is compelling evidence that most suicides subsequent to hospitalization occur in those aged patients who do not have an on-going relationship with a physician.[23] In a study of suicide rates among depressed patients subsequent to hospitalization, the correlation between suicide and a lack of continuity of care was higher than the correlation between suicide and the

* This applies particularly to male patients.

severity of the patient's original depression.[13] Therefore, the physician should be prepared to resume his relationship with the depressed aged patient after he is no longer under psychiatric care—even if he is not physically ill. But identification of the potentially suicidal patient remains the physician's most important task.

Most suicidal patients are ambivalent about their wish to die, regardless of their age. The suicidal individual contemplates such action because he feels he is faced with an insoluble dilemma; at the same time, however, he wants to discuss his predicament in the hope that he will be dissuaded from his intention—and persuaded that his dilemma is not insoluble. If the suicidal impulse is to be detected, the physician must encourage the patient to ventilate his feelings. Misconceptions on the part of the physician currently militate against such action: It is commonly believed that asking a patient whether he is preoccupied with thoughts of ending his life plants the seeds of suicidal behavior. To the contrary, such inquiries by the physician may forestall this action.

Hypochondriasis

The finding from recent gerontological studies that a large proportion of the aged suffer from hypochondriasis* is, we believe, open to challenge. It is our intention in this subsection to suggest an alternative interpretation of the data. Specifically, it is our impression that many elderly patients who manifest clinical features of hypochondriasis would nonetheless be diagnosed more appropriately as suffering from pseudo-hypochondriasis.

As pointed out in Chapter 5, the most prominent characteristic of the hypochondriac is a long-standing preoccupation with bodily concerns, accompanied by vague, shifting somatic complaints that are markedly exaggerated in relation to physical findings. A similar excessive concern with bodily function (of more recent history), which many gerontologists use as a cardinal criterion for diagnosis of hypochondriasis, might be regarded as normal in the aged. Given the biological changes inherent in the aging process, the frequent expression of vague somatic complaints by the elderly patient would not be considered extraordinary.

In both hypochondriasis and pseudo-hypochondriasis the preoccupation with bodily function replaces the individual's interest in external objects. Yet, paradoxically, both the hypochondriac and pseudo-hypo-

* For example, 33 percent of the population studied at the Duke Center were said to suffer from mild to severe hypochondriasis.[3]

chondriac attempt, on the basis of illness and suffering, to establish a regressive relationship with the physician, who, on another level, is perceived as a social contact. Patients in both groups have a paucity of social relationships. However, the elderly individual's social isolation is usually age-related; in the true hypochondriac the lack of viable social relationships is a consequence of life-long aberrant behavior.

The fact that the hypochondriac's somatic complaints are not significantly relieved by traditional medical treatment stems from his need to be sick in order to have prolonged and repeated medical contact. To this end, the hypochondriac incriminates "innocent" organs, and willingly submits to and even demands life-threatening procedures. When the clinical workup shows no organic pathology to account for the type or degree of symptomatology, the hypochondriacal patient responds to this reassurance with anger and an increase of complaints, insisting on further procedures. In contrast, the pseudo-hypochondriac's response to a favorable diagnosis is one of relief. He derives no comfort from the prospect of undergoing complex, costly, and often uncomfortable diagnostic and therapeutic procedures.

Finally, the true hypochondriac tends in the medical setting to manifest persecutory trends, that is, to level accusations of neglect, rejection, and incompetence against the physician. Such behavior is not characteristic of the aged pseudo-hypochondriac; nor does he have an inordinate need to verbalize guilt feelings, which is invariably found in true hypochondriasis.

It is not easy to distinguish between hypochondriasis and pseudo-hypochondriasis in practice, as is evident from the two cases described below. Nevertheless, if one proceeds on the premise that our formulation is accurate, it becomes apparent that a failure to make this distinction may worsen the patient's physiological as well as his psychological state.

> On his first visit to Dr. R.'s office, Mr. V., who was 75 years old, provided a nonstop recitation of his diffuse complaints, including his vision, his hearing, and his urinary system. After a complete physical examination failed to show any physical abnormality, Dr. R.'s suspicions were aroused. When he determined that Mr. V. had none of the other signs or symptoms of a depressive reaction and was able to rule out an organic mental syndrome, he began to give serious consideration to the possibility that Mr. V. might be a hypochondriac. He completed routine laboratory tests on Mr. V. and asked him to return in a week.
>
> When Mr. V. was informed that laboratory test findings were within normal limits, he reacted with great relief. He did not question the accuracy of Dr. R.'s diagnosis, nor did he press for further tests or

diagnostic procedures. He did express concern, however, about his behavior. Mr. V. felt that he had "blown up" his physical complaints, "made a mountain out of a mole hill," and he insisted that it wasn't like him to behave this way. He went on to confide in Dr. R. that he had always been a "happy-go-lucky" sort, with a fairly optimistic attitude. But his attitude seemed to have changed as he grew older. He had outlived everyone and everything that had been important to him. Now, instead of focusing on others, he focused on himself.

Miss Q.'s behavior was in marked contrast to Mr. V.'s.

Miss Q., a 67-year-old unmarried woman, was seen by Dr. G. only once. He formed a tentative diagnosis of hypochondriasis on the basis of subsequent phone calls and requests for medical information from a variety of sources.

On her first and only visit to Dr. G., Miss Q. presented multiple systemic complaints: She was dizzy, nauseous, had cramps, and she had been experiencing vaginal, rectal, and buccal mucosal burning sensations for six months. She also admitted that she had been feeling increasingly depressed, and that she lived alone and was estranged from her only living relatives. Dr. G.'s first task was to rule out any physiological basis for her complaints, and in fact all findings were within normal limits. After informing the patient that he could find nothing wrong with her, Dr. G. suggested that she return for another visit if she didn't feel better within a few weeks.

Dr. G.'s reassurance made little impression on Miss Q. The next day he received a phone call from the emergency room of a neighborhood hospital requesting information on his patient who had presented with a similar list of complaints, insisted that she felt sick and "limp" and was experiencing palpatations, shortness of breath, chest pain, and syncopal episodes. At this point Miss Q. was hospitalized for a suspected pulmonary embolism. In the hospital she was started on anticoagulants. When it became increasingly apparent after further physiological tests that her complaints were primarily psychogenic, Miss Q. was discharged.

In all probability, the fact that Miss Q. was told that she had no significant physiological dysfunction, that she was in good condition for her age, did not induce her to give up her "crusade." One can speculate that Miss Q. will continue to go from doctor to doctor in a never-ending search for the one physician who can find something seriously wrong with her.

Management. The most important aspect of management, then, is the need for the physician to differentiate between true hypochondriasis and pseudo-hypochondriasis, and to recognize concomitantly that certain aspects of the prescribed treatment for true hypochondriasis would be contraindicated in pseudo-hypochondriasis.

Once the presence of organic pathology has been ruled out, the physician's primary goal, in both hypochondriasis and pseudo-hypochondriasis, is to foster the patient's adaptation to the vicissitudes of aging. In both instances, a prerequisite for such adaptation is the physician's capacity to provide the patient with a supportive relationship. Beyond this universal, however, the physician adopts an "active" approach to foster adaptation in the pseudo-hypochondriac, and a "passive" approach to foster adaptation in the hypochondriac.

If reassurance does not halt the flow of somatic complaints in the pseudo-hypochondriac, it is useful to challenge the validity of his symptoms, to explore their possible emotional source, to confront him with the purpose they serve. The physician may then actively intervene to help the patient to identify and cope with the feelings that underlie his symptoms and/or, if feasible, encourage him to utilize his social network more fully.

In contrast, as we emphasized in Chapter 4, the symptoms of the hypochondriac, who depends on a conviction of illness to maintain his psychological equilibrium, should remain unchallenged; the physician assumes a passive stance with regard to psychological exploration, at least at the outset. Rather, the doctor's task vis-à-vis the true hypochondriac is to convince the patient that his interest in him extends beyond his symptoms. Once the patient is assured over time that his relationship with the doctor is not contingent upon illness and suffering, he may begin to talk about his emotional concerns. "Although complaints about symptoms remain, the steam goes out of them."[24]

The Organic Mental Syndromes

The point was made in Chapter 5 that organic mental syndromes frequently remain undetected. Yet, paradoxically, as is true of hypochondriasis, the frequency with which the organic mental syndromes have been *said* to occur in the elderly may be overstated.[3,25] Only one-third of the subjects in the Duke study manifested behavioral changes due to organic mental syndromes.[3]

The prerequisites for accurate diagnosis of an organic mental syndrome were discussed in detail in Chapter 5. But diagnosis of an organic mental syndrome in the aged also depends on the physician's recognition that a shift in normative values is necessary for this group, and, in fact, is essential for the accurate evaluation and interpretation of test findings.[25] Diagnostic accuracy depends, in short, on the physician's ability to construct an examination of the patient's mental status that will reflect sufficient knowledge of the neuropathophysiology of the normal aging process. For example, there is a growing literature in support of the contention that a vulnerable central nervous system is a normal feature of aging. In support of this view, Mason and others[26,27] have postulated an age-linked decline in adrenocortical function, as well as an age-linked increase in hypothalamic vulnerability. In other words, the aged patient may manifest an acute organic mental syndrome when "normal" psychological stress is imposed upon his already vulnerable central nervous system. The possible sources of such stress may vary widely: Physical disabilities of sudden onset, such as trauma, surgical intervention, infection, etc., may all evoke psychological stresses that cannot be dealt with easily by the aged individual. Even less threatening events may evoke psychological stress. For example, hospitalization for minor procedures, the need to change one's established routine, unfamiliar faces in strange places, even a brief separation from one's environment may compromise the vulnerable central nervous system. The elderly patient is frequently unable to deal with these events on a cognitive basis, to view them in perspective, to understand their meaning.

Management. Inasmuch as both dementia and delirium are precipitated by pathophysiological processes, identification and prompt treatment of these processes become the physician's first order of business. When the patient presents with delirium, the underlying process may be easily reversed, and in that event, mental functioning may be restored. For example, it is well known that delirium frequently occurs in the elderly as a consequence of the all-too-common practice of polypharmacy. In that event, it can best be treated by systematically eliminating as many drugs in the patient's regimen as possible or, at the least, reducing their dosage. When, however, the patient presents with dementia, in all probability the underlying pathophysiological processes cannot be reversed. Many attempts have been made to do so. For example, hyperbaric oxygenation has been used in an attempt to improve memory and other cognitive functions. A wide range of pharmacological agents have also been used for this purpose: stimulants and analeptics, vasodilators, anticoagulants, RNA-like compounds, vitamins, gonadal hormones, and beta-adrenergic blocking agents, i.e., propanolol.[28] It is the general consensus of gerontologists that the therapeutic efficacy of these procedures and agents has not been established.

In many instances, however, the psychological concomitants of this degenerative process can be minimized. But such efforts should not depend solely on the administration of psychopharmacological agents. It is now recognized that treatment of the chronic organic brain syndromes should consist in the combined use of psychopharmacological agents and other forms of psychological management, e.g., support and reassurance; behavioral modification; and environmental manipulation, including work with the patient's family.*

THE PHYSICIAN'S RESPONSE TO THE AGED PATIENT

Effective management of the elderly rests on two precepts: The first of these, which is referred to as the "vulnerability hypothesis," relates to the striking correlation between the physical status of the aged individual and his psychological, social, and economic status.† It follows, then, that the responsibility for the physical care of the aged patient cannot be separated from his psychosocial care, and vice versa. The responsibility for both, in the majority of these patients, falls by default to the primary care physician.

The second precept refers specifically to the physician's attitude toward this patient population. It is the consensus among gerontologists that one of the most important determinants of longevity for the aged is health maintenance. Current medical attitudes toward this patient group are antithetical to this goal. Although there is compelling evidence that the aged do not inevitably experience pathological declines in physical and mental capacities, or manifest intractable psychiatric symptoms (e.g., depression and "disengagement," hypochondriasis, and organicity), too many physicians cling to the stereotype of the elderly patient as being therapeutically hopeless. To automatically label the aged patient who is confused and disoriented as suffering from dementia, to automatically label the aged patient who is excessively preoccupied with his

* We believe that the specifics of the psychological management of this patient must depend on the issues presented by the individual patient. They have been discussed in general elsewhere in the literature.[29, 30]

† Thus the vulnerability hypothesis supports the bio-psycho-social theory of disease.

body as hypochondriacal, to automatically dismiss symptoms of depression in the elderly as indigenous to the aging process, is to do this patient population a gross injustice.

In large measure, the physician's attitudes mirror the attitudes toward the elderly that characterize our society. It is a society that rejects the elderly, that transforms an old person into a "nonperson." It is not surprising, then, that they may be rejected by their doctors as well. Unfortunately, the elderly patient who feels rejected, for whatever reason, frequently becomes more demanding as his feelings of rejection intensify, and his behavior then tends to legitimize the physician's stereotyped perception of the aged. Thus, the elderly patient often finds himself trapped in a vicious circle of rejection. When there is no hope of complete recovery, as is often the case, the patient finds that he has lost the right to have his physician try to make him feel better.

The physician's attitude toward the aged patient may have unconscious components as well: fantasies of omnipotence and of depletion, and the residual (unresolved) ambivalence that characterized his early relationships with his parents and grandparents. The aged patient will pose a threat to the physician's fantasies of omnipotence if the physician equates skillful treatment with cure. Because the goal of cure must often elude his grasp, he may tend to become less involved and less enthusiastic with regard to the management of the elderly patient.

The elderly patient may also undermine the physician's image of himself as indestructible. All too frequently, the physician unconsciously identifies, at least to some extent, with the deterioration that is inherent in the normal aging process. All of the stereotyped parameters of aging—the decline in intellectual power, in sexual capacity, in performance, the loneliness, the social ostracism—threaten the physician at every level of his concept of self. Even when the patient is able to make a relatively successful adaptation to his disabilities, when he accepts his growing infirmities as "part of life," the doctor may not be able to resist putting himself in the patient's position—and viewing that position in the worst possible light.

Although attempts have been made to lay to rest the universal image of the aged patient as chronically ill, as overwhelmed by psychological and social problems, the physician may continue to harbor the misconception that such patients will make excessive and inappropriate demands on his time, his resources, his physical and psychic energy. In short, he maintains the fantasy that they will take too much "out of him," that they will "suck him dry," that he will become psychologically and physically depleted if he allows himself to become too involved in their care.

Finally, it is a basic premise of developmental psychology that from time to time all children feel ambivalent toward their parents and grandparents. Contact with the aged patient may revive the conflicts, hostilities, and anxieties that characterized the physician's early child–parent relationships, and the aged patient may heighten these reactions if he assumes the role of parent vis-à-vis the physician or the physician casts him in that role. To ward off these feelings, the doctor may unwittingly treat the patient as a child rather than a competent adult, a person with his own identity. On the other hand, the physician may find it painful to care for the aged patient because in witnessing the dissolution of the body and/or mind of his patient (whether real or imagined), he is reminded of the inalterable changes which have occurred or will occur in his own parents and grandparents.

Given these powerful sociocultural and intrapsychic influences, it is not surprising that the physician may be tempted to distance himself, to "give up" on the aged patient. Unfortunately, all too frequently, this feeling is detected by the patient, who may then be tempted to give up on himself.

REFERENCES

1. Botwinick J: Aging and Behavior. New York, Springer, 1973, p 2
2. Miller DB, Lowenstein R, Winston R: Physician's attitudes toward the ill aged and nursing homes. J Am Geriat Soc 24:498, 1976
3. Palmore E (ed): Normal Aging. Durham, N.C., Duke University Press, 1970
4. Weiner H: Psychobiology and Human Disease. New York, Elsevier, 1977, p 584
5. Nowlin JB, Busse EW: Psychosomatic problems in the older person. In Wittkower ED, Warnes H (eds): Psychosomatic Medicine: Its Clinical Applications. New York, Harper, 1977, p 326
6. Butler RN: Geriatric medicine, editorial. Med World News, Feb 7, 1977, p 112
7. Garattine S, Marcucci F, Morselli PL, Mussini E: The significance of measuring blood levels of benzodiazepines. In Davies DS, Prichard BNC (eds): Biological Effects of Drugs in Relation to Their Plasma Concentrations. Baltimore, University Park Press, 1973, p 211
8. Bender AD: Pharmacodynamic principles of drug therapy in the aged. J Am Geriatr Soc 22:296, 1974
9. Gregerman RI, Bierman EL: Aging and hormones. In Williams RH (ed): Textbook of Endocrinology, Philadelphia, Saunders, 1974
10. Frolkis VV, Bezrukov VV, Duplenko YK, Genis ED: The hypothalamus in aging. Exp Gerontol 7:169, 1972
11. Hurwitz N: Predisposing factors in adverse reactions to drugs. Br Med J 1: 536, 1969
12. Botwinick J: Aging and Behavior. New York, Springer, 1973, p 51

13. Payne EC: Depression and suicide. In Howells JG (ed): Modern Perspectives in the Psychiatry of Old Age. New York, Bruner/Mazel, 1975, p 290
14. Dublin L: Suicide. New York, Ronald, 1963
15. Dublin L: Suicide: an overview of a health and social problem. Bull Suicidol, December 25, 1968
16. Shneidman ES, Barberow NL: Statistical comparisons between attempted and committed suicides. In Farberow NL, Shneidman ES (eds): The Cry for Help. New York, McGraw-Hill, 1965
17. Payne EC: Teaching medical psychotherapy in special clinical settings. In Zinberg NE (ed): Psychiatry and Medical Practice in a General Hospital. New York, International Universities Press, 1964
18. Bunch J: Recent bereavement and suicide. J Psychosom Res 163:361, 1972
19. McMahon B, Puch G: Suicide in the widowed. Am J Epidemiol 81:23, 1965
20. Dorpat TL, Ripley HS: The relationship between attempted suicide and committed suicide. Compr Psychiatry 8:74, 1967
21. Rachlis D: Suicide and loss adjustment in the aging. Bull Suicidol, Fall, 1970
22. Strain JJ: Psychopharmacological treatment of the medically ill. In Strain JJ, Grossman S (eds): Psychological Care of the Medically Ill: A Primer in Liaison Psychiatry. New York, Appleton, 1975, p 108
23. Motto J: Suicide attempts: a longitudinal view. Arch Gen Psychiatry 13:516, 1965
24. Altman N: Hypochondriasis. In Strain JJ, Grossman S: Psychological Care of the Medically Ill: A Primer in Liaison Psychiatry. New York, Appleton, 1975, p 76
25. Mattis S: Mental status examination for organic mental syndrome in the elderly patient. In Bellak L, Karasu TB (eds): Geriatric Psychiatry: A Handbook for Psychiatrists and Primary Care Physicians. New York, Grune, 1976, p 77
26. Mason JW: A re-evaluation of the concept of "non-specificity" in stress theory. J Psychiatr Res 8:323, 1971
27. Grad B, Kral VA, Payne RC, Berenson J: Plasma and urinary corticoids in young and old persons. J Gerontol 22:66, 1967
28. Eisdorfer C, Friedel RO: Psychotherapeutic drugs in aging. In Jarvik M (ed): Psychopharmacology in the Practice of Medicine. New York, Appleton, 1977, p 361
29. Howells JG: Family psychopathology. In Howells JG (ed): Modern Perspectives in the Psychiatry of Old Age. New York, Brunner/Mazel, 1975, p 253
30. Bellak L, Karasu TB: Geriatric Psychiatry: A Handbook for Psychiatrists and Primary Care Physicians. New York, Grune, 1976

Chapter 8

The Obese Patient

Gladys Witt Strain

The problems that face the primary care physician with regard to nutritionally dysfunctional patients—i.e., patients with eating disorders—are analogous to those that confront him with respect to the aged. Within the past decade, he has added an increased number of patients in both categories to his roster; all too frequently, his medical education and training have not equipped him to deal with the problems these patients present; consequently, the physician tends to perceive patients who must change their eating behavior as he perceives the aged, with some degree of hopelessness.

Gaps in the physician's medical knowledge, in combination with the therapeutic nihilism that characterizes his attitude toward both the elderly and patients with eating disorders, constitute major impediments to the management of these patient groups. The precise nature of the impediments to the appropriate treatment of the elderly were explored in the preceding chapter. Many of the variables identified there have relevance for our understanding of the clinical problems presented by the nutritionally dysfunctional and, in particular, the obese patient, who is our focus here.

To begin with, students at many medical schools do not receive adequate exposure to the etiology and management of eating disorders.* Until recently, nutrition was taught either by the basic scientist from the perspective of a metabolic schema, or by nutritionists or dietitians from the perspective of dietary intervention. Because little attempt has been

* There is some evidence of a recent reversal of this trend in medical school curricula.[1–4]

made, to date, to integrate these approaches, the medical student does not have a basic understanding of the biology of eating disorders. Furthermore, although the psychological components of nutritional dysfunction are universally acknowledged, they do not receive sufficient attention in medical school. Nor does the physician ever have an opportunity to acquire substantive knowledge of their etiology and management in the course of his clinical training. As a consequence of these gaps in his medical education and clinical training, the physician, once he has entered private practice, may not perceive these patients as a diagnostic or therapeutic challenge. And this is particularly true of the obese patient. In fact, because obesity does not necessarily require medication or surgical intervention, the physician may not even consider it a legitimate medical disease. Given this orientation, it is not surprising that the primary care physician may not be sufficiently familiar with the current status of nutritional knowledge, which, in the last five years, has undergone rapid expansion; nor is he equipped to evaluate the relative merits of new treatment modalities.

The decision to limit this discussion to the obese segment of the nutritionally dysfunctional population was based on three considerations. First, there has been a growing recognition over the past decade of the relationship between weight status and health status. Second, the overweight patient presents formidable difficulties in terms of the establishment and maintenance of a concordant doctor–patient relationship. Finally, physicians have been singularly unsuccessful in their attempts to manage this patient group effectively.

Our purpose in this chapter is to enhance the physician's knowledge of the pathogenesis of obesity, and to provide him with guidelines both for the psychological assessment of such patients and for the formulation of appropriate modes of intervention. It is our conviction that these precepts can be extrapolated to other forms of nutritional dysfunction—to medical conditions that necessitate a change in food choices, eating patterns, and life style.*

THE PATHOGENESIS OF OBESITY

Predisposing Biological Factors

It is generally recognized that there may be a genetic predisposition to body weight. Angel [5] and Gurney,[6] whose work is frequently

* At times, however, the management of certain forms of nutritional dysfunction—and anorexia nervosa immediately comes to mind—does not lie within the purview of the primary care physician. Such patients should be referred to a psychiatrist, at least for evaluation.

cited in support of this proposition, have demonstrated statistically that if both parents are stout, there is a 73 percent chance that their offspring will be stout; on the other hand, if both parents are lean, that chance is reduced to 9.1 percent. The nature of this predisposition has not been precisely defined.* Studies concerning possible inherited differences center on body type; adipose tissue cellularity; hyperphagia; taste sensitivity; hyperglycemia, hyperinsulinism; metabolic efficiency, i.e., hypometabolism; and enzymatic differences in lipogenesis and/or lipolysis.

In his classic studies, Sheldon [8] postulated that human beings could be characterized according to body type—i.e., as primary ecto-, meso-, or endomorph, and he hypothesized that inherited muscle mass distribution and bone structure could be correlated with specific personality traits. Sheldon also postulated that the primary ectomorph was destined to remain lean throughout his lifetime; that the mesomorph, with a well-developed muscle mass, was destined to accumulate fat tissue in later life, if there was a reduction in physical activity; that the endomorph would be fat, round, and sedentary throughout his life; and that the personality traits associated with each body type would also remain constant.

Research on the fat cell over the last ten years by such pioneers as Hirsch [9] and Björntorp [10] can be viewed as a refinement of Sheldon's theory. These workers have theorized that certain individuals have a tendency from birth to produce an increased number of fat cells.† Individuals who have an increased number of fat cells are overweight even when their fat cells are of normal size. An excessive number of fat cells can be an inherited trait, but infant feeding practices can contribute to cell number. In contrast, thin people have fewer fat cells. If their thinness is due to a pathological condition, they will still have a normal number of fat cells, but the cells will be smaller in size. The great majority of the population have a normal number of fat cells, which remains constant after maturity; however, the size of these cells can (and frequently does) increase in later years, as the proportion of body fat increases. This produces the more common adult onset obesity, in which the individual has a normal number of fat cells, but there is a marked increase in fat cell size.

* However, the recent studies of Garn and Baily [7] of twins raised in different households would implicate the environment rather than heredity.

† Five specific hypercellular conditions, all of which are rare, are known to be inherited: Laurence-Moon-Bardet-Biedlt (LMBB) Syndrome, Prader-Willi, Alstrom-Hallgren, Hyperstosis Frontalis Interna, and a triglyceride storage disease.[11]

Despite the apparent overall reliability of the fat cell hypothesis in classifying obesity, there is some doubt as to whether the fat cell itself is a dominant factor in determining body weight. When large fat cells from genetically obese mice were placed in lean mice, the cells became normal in size; when normal size fat cells from lean mice were placed in genetically obese mice, they became larger.[12] In other words, metabolic factors, other than those within the fat cell itself, may be important in determining body weight.

Studies of humans by Björntorp and his co-workers [13] have pointed up the need for a cautious interpretation of data derived from these animal studies, for their data indicate that a period of refractoriness to weight loss develops once the individual achieves a normal fat cell size. This finding may have important therapeutic implications: It is the consensus of many authors of numerous weight reduction studies that the prognosis is poor for individuals with childhood onset obesity who have both an increase in cell size and number. Yet the ability of the hypercellular individual not only to achieve weight loss, but to maintain weight loss over the long term, has also been reported in the literature.[14,15] Such data would seem to indicate that the postulated dominance of the fat cell can be overcome.

Other workers have approached the question of body weight regulation from another perspective. In *Biochemical Individuality,*[16] published in the 1950's, Roger Williams stressed the consistency with which the body maintains a stable weight. He used as an example the middle-aged man with little or no tendency to gain significant amounts of weight. All things being equal, his weight would remain stable over a 10-year period, or he might gain 5 pounds at most. This would mean that if he were moderately active over this 10-year period, he would have consumed 12,000 pounds of moist food. If his consumption differed from his requirements by 1 percent over the long term, he would gain (or lose) 120 pounds. Thus, the set-point machinery is remarkably accurate when it is operating normally. This applies to most individuals who, regardless of their weight status, maintain a stable weight without conscious awareness of their caloric intake.

Garrow [17] has approached the question of weight maintenance from still another perspective. Specifically, he emphasizes the vagaries of the body's response to known activity loads and energy expenditures. Those with experience in weight control programs are familiar with the patient who seems to defy the laws of thermodynamics. In some patients, energy intake can exceed energy expenditure without weight gain ("luxus consumption") for short periods of time. Others seem to obtain energy more efficiently from a given food source, or their energy expenditure for a given activity is more efficient than the expenditure of other individuals. Diet histories, 24-hour recall, and careful diet and activity records do not provide quantitative data that would explain these phenomena. Even in carefully controlled metabolic studies, intake does not always correlate well with energy expenditure. In some instances, as O. F. Pye pointed out in a personal communication, these findings may be a product of methodological error. It has also been suggested that these phenomena may occur as a consequence of enzymatic variations that contribute to the tendency to build up excess fat on a given energy load, and the decreased capacity to break down that fat when the body requires fat mobilization to meet energy needs. Nevertheless, as a general rule, when the energy intake exceeds the expenditure on a long-term basis, fat is deposited.

Other workers have interpreted data derived from studies of animal models as evidence of a possible genetic predisposition to hyperphagia. In both humans and animals, hyperphagia may be related to hyperinsulinism which has been related, in turn, to fat cell size. But in humans the compulsion to eat indiscriminately, and to eat quickly, may also be a product of maternal conditioning. Although numerous biological factors have been implicated in the genesis of aberrant weight status, they cannot, in themselves, explain this phenomenon. The psychological as well as the physiological factors that may predispose to a given disease must be investigated if the etiology of that disease is to be fully understood and an effective treatment plan formulated. In respect to obesity, studies of predisposing biological factors must be supplemented by studies of the psychological, as well as the social, economic, and cultural determinants of body weight abnormalities.

Predisposing Psychological Factors

Early Experience—Patterns of Mothering. The mother–infant relationship sets the stage for life-long patterns of eating behavior. If the mother responds appropriately, with food, to the infant's hunger signals, then hunger cues and the appropriate response to these hunger cues are reinforced and persist in the adult. If, on the other hand, the mother fails to discriminate between hunger cues, signals of nonspecific discomfort, and signs of the infant's need for bodily contact, she may provide food as a universal response to any signal of anxiety and distress. Then, in later life, the individual may use food indiscriminately as a means of coping not only with hunger but also with frustration, sadness, etc. Such an individual may develop a blunted internal awareness of his actual, i.e., physiological, need for food.*

> Miss B., 25 years old, was 5 feet 2 inches tall and weighed 290 lbs. The patient had been the long-hoped-for child of refugees who had suffered extreme starvation during World War II. As an infant, she had been exposed to what might be described as "forced feeding." A bottle was shoved into her mouth until she began to vomit. After the vomiting had subsided, the bottle was forced on her again. In later life, Miss B. never really "felt hungry"; yet she ate all the time. The correlation between the patient's early experiences and her subsequent eating patterns was confirmed by her behavior as a participant in a hospital-based program. An hour after she had finished an adequate lunch, Miss B. "had to have something to eat." Moreover, not surprisingly, she could not tolerate the liquid formula diet used to achieve weight loss in the research protocol.

When the preeminent quality of the mother–infant relationship is the mother's preoccupation with the provision and acceptance of food, her behavior may have crucial physiological and psychological sequelae. On the physiological side, regardless of the individual's constitutional endowment, during infancy and early childhood fat cells have the capacity to increase in number. If caloric intake is excessive during this stage of development, there may be a further increase in the number of fat cells, which would provide a possible physiological foundation for excessive body fat in the adult. On the psychological side, the mother's preoccupation with feeding may mean that the infant is deprived of other gratifications, e.g., affection, attention, etc., which may affect his personality development in general and further reinforce his interest and preoccupation with eating in particular. But, more importantly, the child is not provided with the psychological substrate of an essential ego function—an ability to control his impulses, to set limits, and to remain in control of his bodily demands. In this way, the psychologically deprived child may become the fat adult. Again, if the mother equates goodness and pleasure with eating, and, conversely, punishment and loss of status with not eating, she may inculcate these values in the child. These attitudes will also help to shape the child's self-image and body-image.†

* Evidence to support this hypothesis has been presented by Schacter,[18] Hashim and Van Itallie,[19] and others.

† There is, of course, another side of the coin. If the mother responds insufficiently to the child's hunger needs and there is a long-term minimal food

A number of conflicting findings have been generated by attempts to describe the psychological makeup of the obese individual. Bruch,[20] for example, has described two types of obese patients—those who suffer from "reactive obesity" (who ingest food as an emotional reaction to environmental stress) and those who suffer from what she terms "developmental obesity." In this latter group, emotional problems play a minimal role in the etiology of the disease. Certain authors conceive of obesity as a symptom of an underlying emotional illness.[15,21] Still other investigators have described obese individuals as reasonably well adjusted.[22,23]

This lack of consensus is evident as well in efforts to correlate specific personality characteristics with obesity. It has been speculated that, as compared to men of normal weight, obese men are more anxious, dominant, status-conscious, self-accepting, verbal, and "feminine." But Weinberg et al,[22] using psychological tests, found no support for these hypotheses.

The methodology used in research in this area can be criticized on two grounds. First, no distinction is made between psychological traits that play a predisposing role in obesity and those that occur secondary to the illness.* Nor have investigators always recognized the need to subclassify subjects within a single study according to time of onset of the disease and its severity. Individuals within these subgroups might be expected to present different psychological characteristics.

Given these methodological flaws, the conclusion that emerges from the literature to date is that obese individuals manifest diverse behavior patterns rather than a single discrete personality pattern.[11,25] The conclusion also emerges that the personality of the obese patient must be studied over time along with other physiological and psychosocial parameters. These variables, collectively and/or in relationship to one another, may then constitute predisposing factors in some individuals.

---

intake, this may provide a physiological basis for chronic underweight. Much more frequently in our affluent society, however, clinically significant underweight occurs as a result of distortions in the early mother–child relationship and the child's consequent rejection or rebellion against the mother's controlling behavior.

* This methodological problem, which is encountered in all of psychosomatic research,[24] could only be resolved, of course, if subjects at risk for obesity were identified before the onset of the disease. Until recently, such predictive studies were possible only for peptic ulcer, in which a specific physiological risk factor (i.e., the hypersecretion of pepsinogen) has been implicated. Obesity—in which hypercellularity of adipose tissue has been implicated as a physiological measure of risk—may now be studied in the same way.

Social, Economic, and Cultural Determinants

Under normal circumstances, as the child develops and matures, he becomes less vulnerable to maternal influences and more vulnerable to other people and his social, cultural, and economic environment. If economic factors limit the amount of food available to the young child, in later life he may attempt to compensate for this early deprivation. But perhaps the most important environmental determinants of eating behavior in the mother as well as the child are social and cultural. Social and cultural factors define an acceptable diet for the individual, i.e., his food preferences, the setting in which he elects to eat, and his pattern of food consumption. These factors, in combination with the nature of his early interaction with his mother, determine the meaning food has for the individual. For example, if the young child felt that his mother's love and approval were contingent upon his "good" eating behavior, and if this attitude is reinforced by cultural mores, he may, throughout his life, equate social acceptability with food consumption. If, in his culture, bigness in a man is equated with strength, power, and sexual potency, and bigness in a woman is equated with fertility and "giving," and is taken as a sign that her spouse can adequately provide for her, then social status for both will depend, to a large extent, on body weight. In such a culture the child will almost invariably be stimulated to eat in excess of his physiological needs. And these influences are so powerful that even if he is subsequently exposed to other cultural values, his early eating pattern may persist.*

ASSESSMENT OF THE OBESE PATIENT

The physician's assessment of the patient necessarily begins with an evaluation of his physical status. He needs, in particular, to establish the legitimacy of the patient's complaint with regard to his weight status. The physician with limited time and facilities will find the standardized height-weight tables, and the patient's weight history, together with his clinical observations, sufficient for this purpose in most cases. Once the patient's complaint has been confirmed, the doctor will, of course, want to identify any physiological determinants of obesity, which might include thyroid dysfunction, Cushing's syndrome, reactive hypoglycemia,† etc.

* These findings on the factors that are considered to predispose to obesity point up the need for further consideration of the classifications of adult versus childhood onset obesity.

† Reactive hypoglycemia is unique in that it can be modified by weight loss and/or the reduction of carbohydrates in the diet.[26]

Tests that the physician routinely administers to evaluate the general health of his patients are important for this group as well, for they enable the physician to determine the extent to which a patient's physical status has been adversely affected by his eating behavior. In addition, the doctor must attempt to determine during the initial phase of his evaluation of the patient whether his aberrant eating behavior is, in fact, a presenting symptom of frank psychiatric illness.*

At this stage in his medical and psychological assessment, the physician needs to decide whether he will act as a primary therapist or utilize the services of a trained nutritionist, dietitian, or self-help group. If he does not elect to use other professional and lay support systems, then he must go on to elicit other data on psychological and cultural factors that frequently are of overriding importance in the etiology and pathogenesis of obesity. This can be done by addressing straightforward questions to the patient in regard to his early weight status, whether he was breast-fed or bottle-fed, the weight status of his parents and siblings, and family attitudes toward body weight. He needs to learn about the patient's current food preferences, eating behavior, previous efforts at weight control, weight fluctuations, the duration of his problem, and possible precipitating events; his life style and occupation (including the amount of physical exercise he gets), and his economic status. During this informal history-taking, the doctor can draw crucial inferences regarding the nature of the patient's early experiences, his present psychological makeup, and the general quality of his relationships with others. He gains additional insight into the psychosocial factors that may have played a role in the genesis of the patient's obesity from his account of his current marital and family status, and from observations of the patient's behaviors in the clinical setting.

Finally, the physician needs to determine why the patient is seeking medical help at this particular time, and his expectations with regard to the duration and outcome of treatment. Such information provides important clues as to the degree to which the patient is motivated to participate in a weight-reduction plan.

The accumulation of these data need not be an onerous task. Taking a history of the patient's current eating behavior can be simplified by having him keep a record of his food intake over a seven-day period, with notations as to his mood and the extent of his hunger when he begins to eat, the kind and amount of food eaten, the rate at which it

* Excessive weight loss, anorexia, weight gain, binge eating, and food faddism can all be symptoms of the major psychiatric disorders described in Chapter 3, and, in fact, may be the only prodromal signs of the disorder.

Instructions to Patients for Completing Food Record

1. *Time:* Record the time you begin and the time you finish each meal or snack in the appropriate time block on the record form. Record the time as exactly as possible; e.g., 8:02 to 8:14, not 8:00 to 8:15. An entry should be considered a separate meal or snack if there has been a lapse of 15 minutes between bites.
2. *Place:* Record the place where you are eating. If at home–the specific room; if away from home–the place (restaurant, car, store, office, friends home, etc.) and whether at a counter, table, desk, etc.
3. *Physical position:* Use the following code: Standing (1), Sitting (2), Lying Down (3).
4. *With whom:* If alone write alone. If with one or more people, the number and relationship, i.e., husband, child, friend, strangers, etc.
5. *Associated activity:* Record anything that you're doing while eating such as reading, watching TV, talking, cooking, etc. If not engaged in any other activity, write in "eating only."
6. *Mood:* Record your mood before you begin eating. Use the first letter of whichever word most clearly coincides with your mood from the following list: Neutral, Content, Tense, Depressed, Angry, Happy, Bored, Fatigued, Rushed.
7. *Hunger:* Record your subjective feeling of hunger just *before eating.* Write down any number between 0 and 5 which describes your degree of hunger. 0 represents no hunger and 5 represents extreme hunger.
8. *Food and amount:* Record the name of the food and an estimate of either the weight of the food, the size of the portion or the number of pieces, so that caloric values may be determined.
9. *Meals:* Place an (M) next to those entries which you consider meals.
10. *Calories:* Look up the number of calories in the foods you eat.
11. At the bottom of each sheet, circle the number which corresponds most accurately with the percentage of entries made at the immediate time of ingestion (including just prior to or just after).

FIGURE 3

Food Intake Record. (Adapted from Jordan and Levitz: In Silverstone (ed): Obesity: Pathogenesis and Management, 1975. Courtesy of Publishing Sciences Group, with permission)

FOOD INTAKE RECORD

Date: ______________ Name: ______________

Time Start End	Place	Phys. pos.	Alone or with whom	Assoc. activity	M	H	Food and amount	Calories
6–11								
11–4								
4–9								

Percent of entries filled out right before or after eating 0 25 50 75 100 is consumed, where and when he eats, his physical position when eating, whether he eats alone or with others, and whether he engages in any associated activity while eating. An example of a form that is useful for obtaining these data is given in Figure 3.

Such records provide baseline information about energy intake and food preferences, and are a necessity in planning therapeutic intervention. Moreover, a food intake record augments the physician's psychological understanding of the patient. These advantages clearly outweigh the possible shortcomings of this form, which has been criticized on the grounds that the patient may record what he thinks the doctor wants to read. In fact, it is universally recognized that the overweight tend to under-report their food intake.* Nevertheless, completion of this form by the patient is the first step in a collaborative treatment effort.

INTERVENTION

Weight loss can be effected by a variety of measures—diet modification, drugs, surgical intervention, behavior modification, and psychological intervention.

Diet Modification

One can infer from the number of new diets that emerge each year, and are advertised as panaceas for the overweight, that no single diet has yet been developed that can provide a satisfactory solution to the problem of weight reduction. Most nutritionists agree that alterations in the proportion of fat, carbohydrate, and/or protein calories in a diet do not substantially affect the rate of loss of body fat.† [28] Any diet that prescribes an energy level below maintenance needs will result in weight loss. At the outset, however, the physician may have to correct certain preconceived notions the patient holds with regard to an appropriate reducing diet. For example, the physician may learn from the patient's food intake record that he is operating under the misconception that he can lose weight by eating only one meal a day, or that he can lose weight if he restricts his food intake to steak and salads. Apart from the

* It is currently estimated that even when diet histories are obtained by trained nutritionists, they have an inaccuracy for energy intake of ±30 percent.[11]

† Recent nitrogen balance and body composition data, obtained during protein supplemented fasting by Bistran and Blackburn, challenge this traditional concept,[29, 30] but further confirmation of these data is required.

fact that both of these eating behaviors may increase fat deposition, they do not necessarily ensure a lower caloric intake. Any patient who cannot consciously face the reality that his overweight is due to an ingestion of calories beyond his physiologic need should be referred for concurrent therapy to a nutrition specialist and a psychiatrist. The complexities of such denial and the inability to come to terms with blatant reality result in a poor prognosis. When weight loss is mandatory, the appropriate therapeutic intervention may be beyond the capacity of the primary care physician.

Generally, one plans a therapeutic dietary regimen by estimating the patient's caloric needs, which will depend, in turn, on his desirable weight, height, and customary level of activity.* The basic maintenance diet is then reduced by 1000 calories. At the same time, the primary care physician must be aware that there are inherent problems in this traditional approach to inducing weight loss. Accurate calorie counting and portion control are responsibilities delegated to the patient. But because of the obese patients' psychological set, there is a widespread tendency for them to underestimate the number of calories and the size of portions consumed. The physician may avoid these perils by prescribing a diet lower in calories than is actually required.† Apart from such considerations, in general, diets below 1200 calories are not nutritionally adequate. In those instances, vitamin and mineral supplements should be prescribed. In addition, clinical experience provides ample evidence that adherence to diets of less than 1200 calories is difficult for patients in the ambulatory setting.

Dietary compliance is fostered when the physician recommends a greater frequency of food intake, i.e., small meals, three or more times per day. Apart from the fact that this measure aids compliance, increased frequency of food intake will improve the patient's function in regard to glucose and cholesterol utilization.[32]

In contrast to long-term weight loss planning, at the outset the physician might prescribe a diet that constitutes a radical departure from the patient's customary eating behavior, and which departs sufficiently from his previous routine to mandate his focusing on what and how he eats.

The protein-modified fasting procedure,[30,33] which was recently in

* The American Dietetic Association, in conjunction with the American Diabetes Association,[31] has devised materials for use by the physician in explaining the diets he prescribes for individual patients.

† Even in the hospital setting, it is a fair assumption that the patient for whom a 600 calorie diet is prescribed, for example, may, in all probability, be served between 500 and 800 calories per day—unless, of course, he is placed in a research metabolic unit.

vogue, meets the criteria listed above. Moreover, it produces a significant weight loss, and thereby proves to the patient that he can indeed lose weight. The effectiveness of this procedure is further enhanced by the fact that it may produce a mild ketosis and, because it is low in fiber, provides less gut stimulus; both of these factors reduce physiological hunger. However, this procedure has certain major shortcomings. It mandates a continuing doctor–patient relationship, for, without medical supervision, it may be dangerous.* Furthermore, this diet will not enable the patient to learn new eating behaviors; consequently, weight loss is usually not maintained once the modified fasting procedure is terminated. With medical supervision, these shortcomings can be offset, to some extent. As the patient begins to approach his weight-loss goal, specific foods can gradually be incorporated into his diet to normalize his eating patterns and thereby ensure the long-term maintenance of weight loss.

Drug Intervention

The patient's inability to achieve weight loss may prompt the physician to prescribe an appetite suppressant. Of the available drugs, four have been identified as clinically useful by Silverstone:[28] diethylpropion, phentermine, fenfluramine, and mazindol.† The value of mazindol remains uncertain pending further clinical studies. Because it carries the risk of precipitating withdrawal depression, fenfluramine is contraindicated when there is evidence of depressive symptoms or a past history of a depressive episode.‡ For patients who are vulnerable to depression, diethylpropion in the long-acting form (75 mg daily) or phentermine (15–30 mg daily) are preferred drugs. On the other hand, fenfluramine (20–40 mg 3 times daily or 60–120 mg daily in the long-acting form) is particularly useful in the overactive, tense obese patient. However, intermittent administration of both diethylpropion and phentermine is recommended on the grounds that tolerance and dependence are less likely to occur with such a regimen.

* Long-term use of liquid protein hydrolysates has been associated with cardiac arrythmias and myofibril degeneration. On the other hand, the diet is so restrictive that patients rarely adhere to it long enough for its adverse physical sequelae to emerge. Nevertheless, a number of deaths have recently been attributed to the protein-modified fast, and these are currently under investigation.

† In a double-blind test, Atkinson and his co-workers[34] found no significant difference in effect between mazindol compound and a placebo.

‡ Fenfluramine has been found particularly useful in obese diabetics and is possibly the most effective anorectic in the management of phenothiazine-induced obesity.

Apart from the adverse reactions they may induce, these drugs will be ineffective for certain patients. Appetite suppressants have little or no value for those overweight patients who do not eat because they feel hungry, who, on the contrary, never actually feel hungry but overeat nonetheless. The appetite suppressant is also less effective for those individuals who are driven to eat primarily by external cues, as described by Schacter [18] earlier in this chapter. However, in double-blind, controlled studies, the drugs mentioned above have been shown to help with *early compliance* to a dietary regimen. They can also be appropriately incorporated into the therapeutic protocol, but only as part of a metabolically sound weight loss program. When their use is prolonged, these drugs frequently create new problems: The weight loss achieved thereby is not usually maintained on a drug-free regimen. The use of drugs raises the possibility of addiction. Such drugs place the patient at risk for a variety of physiological symptoms—hypertension, arrthymias, tachycardia, tachypnea. Finally, this approach, even though its use is time-limited, is not conducive to the patient's participation, beyond the ingestion of a pill, in his treatment.

Surgical Intervention

The great majority of clinically trained nutritionists believe that surgical intervention is still an experimental approach and should be reserved for the morbidly obese patient who has medical complications. Although a host of surgical methods are currently being evaluated, the most widely discussed and frequently used intervention developed for weight loss to date is the jejuno–ilieal bypass. The gastric bypass procedure, developed by Mason and his co-workers,[35] requires more extensive evaluation. The achievement of ideal weight is not the goal of these procedures; rather, surgery is performed to reduce the patient's disability to the point at which his excess weight is no longer incapacitating and potentially life-threatening. But even this limited goal is not generally achieved solely by these surgical procedures themselves; diet modification is often an essential adjunct to surgery.

> Miss S., a 400–pound, 31-year-old secretary with cellulitis, which required frequent intervals of bed rest, had failed consistently to adhere to a wide variety of diets. Because her disability was restricting her activities to an increasing degree, her physician finally succumbed to her pleas that he grant permission for a bypass. Following surgery, Miss S., who was under the misconception that her weight problem

had been solved, ate without restraint. In fact, she "ate through the bypass"—and maintained her preoperative weight.

The physician who is considering bypass surgery for his patient should be fully informed as to the potential dangers of the procedure, and he should carefully inform his patient of the possible complications and the practical problems the surgery may create. The patient must also recognize that he will not necessarily achieve a normal weight status as the result of the operation. When the bypass is performed in a general hospital setting, where the staff has limited experience with this specialized procedure, mortality can exceed 5 percent.[36] This rate is greatly reduced when the procedure is performed in a medical center by a staff with extensive experience in both the surgery and its postoperative management. Even under ideal circumstances, however, electrolyte imbalance, impaired liver function, gall bladder disease, arthritis, etc., may have their onset following the jejuno–ileal bypass. (Many of these metabolic problems have not been observed in the gastric bypass procedure. However, as noted above, this procedure is still under investigation.) In any event, given their potential hazards, the physician and his morbidly obese patient must decide whether the benefits of the bypass outweigh the risks involved.

Behavior Modification

Dietary compliance, drug therapy, surgical intervention can all be enhanced by a behavior modification plan designed to meet the needs of the individual patient. The physician can formulate such a plan by drawing on the patient's food intake record, and on the information he has gleaned and the inferences he has drawn from the patient's account of his life style. These data point up the patient's aberrant eating patterns and their origins, and provide clues for their possible alteration. For example, it is axiomatic that eating at an appropriate time, in an appropriate place, with others, and only when one is hungry can foster weight control. If the patient consistently violates these "golden rules," the physician must first make him aware of what he is doing, and then, to the extent that it is possible and necessary, explore the reasons for his behavior. The obese patient may eat alone most of the time, while he is watching TV or reading, and these behaviors may blunt his awareness of his actual food consumption. Even when the psychogenesis of the patient's aberrant eating behavior is extremely complex, at times a mundane recommendation by the physician may produce therapeutic benefits.

> Mrs. I., a 38-year-old nurse, who had been unsuccessful in her efforts to lose weight via self-help groups, consulted her physician for nutritional guidance—as a last resort. The patient's food intake record revealed that she usually ate standing up. The physician's recommendation that she sit down whenever she ate made her aware, for the first time, of how often and how much she ate. This awareness proved to be the first step in a successful weight loss program.

The patient's sedentary life style may also have to be modified, for exercise is an integral part of any weight loss program. Two factors may impede the physician's efforts in this regard. For the patient whose body mass makes any movement laborious, compliance with the physician's instructions to stand rather than sit, walk rather than ride, climb steps rather than take an elevator, may present major difficulties. Even the moderately overweight patient who is physically capable of intensive exercise, e.g., swimming, dancing, jogging, etc., will often resist such recommendations because he is ashamed to be seen in a bathing suit or a tennis outfit; in fact, he is ashamed to be seen in public without a coat. The physician may deal with these patients in several ways. When resistance is particularly strong, he may concentrate on diet until increased exercise becomes more feasible. At that point, he can confront the patient with the fact that one approach will not work without the other, that diet modification will be ineffective in the long run unless it is supplemented by exercise, and vice versa. Once there is some indication that the patient is more receptive to an exercise program, the physician can then strengthen his motivation by assuring him that it is physically safe for him to engage in the prescribed activity. The fear that exercise may precipitate a heart attack is common among obese patients and must be refuted by firm data accumulated in the course of the physician's careful physical assessment of the patient. The physician can also strengthen the patient's motivation by providing precise instructions as to the kind of exercise he is to engage in and the duration of such exercise. An exercise program that provides an additional element of control in the patient's life may have the further advantage that it fosters self-discipline—and adherence to a dietary routine.

The physician's efforts to foster his prescribed regimen may be furthered by the patient's participation in a self-help group such as Weight Watchers, Overeaters Anonymous, or Take Off Pounds Sensibly (TOPS). Theoretically, such groups are intended to and do serve a primary therapeutic function. Some patients, for a variety of reasons, will not be able to benefit from their services; others may find participation in such a group possible if it is a prescribed adjunct to the physician's therapeutic efforts.

Psychological Intervention

We propose that none of these measures—diet intervention, drugs, surgery, or behavior modification—can be truly effective unless the physician supplements them with psychological interventions. Our focus here will be on the nature of the doctor's psychological interventions, and the use of the doctor–patient relationship as a vehicle for such treatment.

By and large, the success of the physician's attempt to induce diet modification is contingent upon two interrelated factors: the extent to which the patient is motivated to lose weight, and the extent to which he is capable of adapting to the prescribed treatment regimen. The doctor's efforts in both of these areas, i.e., to foster motivation and adaptation to the therapeutic regimen, will be complicated by a variety of factors. Among the more significant, we would include the psychological status of the overweight individual and the sociocultural issues that may impede treatment progress, and the doctor's response to his overweight patient—that is, his ability to adapt to the patient and his illness.

With regard to the psychosocial status of obese patients it has been our experience that those individuals who seek medical help do have certain common psychological characteristics that have not been sufficiently identified. Generalizations carry with them the risk that the importance of treating each patient as an individual may be minimized, but elucidation of the psychological characteristics observed in obese patients may ultimately be helpful in formulating plans for therapeutic intervention. The first of these is the strong need of the obese patient for an external control, which can, of course, be viewed as an indication of immaturity and/or a derivative of deep dependency needs. Second, this group of patients typically uses food as a means of dealing with psychological stress. Third, contrary to common belief, these patients are motivated to seek medical help not predominantly by narcissistic concerns but by their fear of premature death as a consequence of their obesity. While some patients do experience self-loathing and a poor self-image, this is not universal. For those patients who express feelings of worthlessness and self-deprecation, and for those who manifest a strong correlation between stress and binge eating, psychotherapy may be helpful.[37] For the great majority of patients, however, we have found that the most effective therapeutic tool in the management of the obese patient is the doctor–patient relationship within the primary care setting.

To develop the therapeutic alliance, the physician must stress at the outset that the patient has a chronic disease requiring medical supervision. The patient's need for an external control may or may not be visible. The point is that when strong dependency needs exist, the patient may not perceive his essential role in the therapeutic process. Typically, he accepts minimum responsibility for the success of his program and prefers to believe that the onus for the treatment rests primarily on his physician. The physician must define the therapeutic roles in such cases. The weight loss process is the responsibility of the patient; the doctor is there to assist and encourage this process. In contrast to those patients whose dependency is visible, others attempt to ward off their passivity through displays of excessive independence, aggressive behavior, and efforts to control the doctor by dictating their own therapeutic protocol. For example, they may insist on a particular diet regimen or demand that, rather than a diet, the physician give them a pill that will "kill" their appetite; or they may be convinced that bypass surgery is the only solution to their problem.

Another major obstacle to an effective treatment regimen may be the "fear of success." It is an interesting paradox that, while the fear of dying may have motivated the patient to seek medical help initially, the prospect of weight loss may give rise to one or several of the psychological stresses which are universally evoked by other acute and chronic medical illnesses. Specifically, weight loss may pose a threat to the patient's sense of integrity and/or evoke fear of the loss of or injury to a body part, fear of the loss of love and approval, of control of developmentally achieved functions, fear of pain, or reactivate feelings of guilt and shame.

Fear of the Loss of Integrity and/or Fear of Loss of or Injury to Body Parts. Mention was made earlier of the fact that the overweight patient, whose eating habits are culturally determined, may equate bigness with strength and power, with fertility or virility. Loss of weight would then be regarded, unconsciously, as synonymous with the loss of his integrity. The imposition of dietary restrictions which are antithetical to the patient's social and cultural values may further intensify this fear. The patient whose sense of integrity is contingent, at least in part, on his weight status may also perceive weight loss as a mutilation of his body or as the loss of a body part. On a psychological level, he may perceive his fat mass as a body part.

Fear of Loss of Love and Approval. If the love and approval of a parent or spouse are contingent upon excessive food intake, dieting may evoke fear of the loss of love and approval of these important persons.

Fear of the Loss of Developmentally Achieved Functions. Many patients give histories of weight change in late adolescence, when they were achieving sexual maturity. At this stage of development, the weight change may serve as a defense against feelings (and the expression) of sexuality; at the same time, the excessive weight may be perceived as a protection against sexual advances. If this conflict has not been resolved, then weight loss may be equated with increased feelings of sexuality, with sexual availability, and the feared expression of sexual impulses.

> Miss X., a 35-year-old librarian, had been overweight for the last ten years. During this time she had seen countless doctors and tried innumerable diets and even psychotherapy for weight loss, without success. When she was quite resigned to being fat for the rest of her life, two factors made her decide to try one more time: She felt that unless her personal appearance improved, she would not get a promotion at her job, and she developed a "crush" on her boss. Motivation and a skillful, interested physician proved an effective combination. Miss X. lost a substantial amount of weight in the first six months she saw Dr. Y. and was able to exercise remarkable self-discipline in regard to her eating behavior.
>
> Her weight loss continued slowly but steadily for seven months, at which point she became increasingly anxious. The reasons for this anxiety were conscious, in part. Miss X. felt that despite her success in the past, she would not be able to continue to adhere to her prescribed diet, and that everything would just "fall apart." The second cause for her anxiety presented a much greater therapeutic hazard. Before she had gained so much weight, Miss X. had led a very promiscuous sex life. And all of her affairs ended with her being rejected. Thus, she associated sex with being hurt and abandoned. Her weight loss revived this association. Being thin was equated with sexual availability, which meant that she might once more become emotionally vulnerable. What Miss X. was not totally aware of, of course, was that this was a wish, as well as a fear. Nor was she fully aware of her fear that she would express her sexual impulses. Thus, she feared she would lose control on two fronts: that she would begin to eat again, and begin to express her sexuality again. Unfortunately, but predictably, Miss X. reached a point where the need to cope with her anxiety forced her to abandon her weight reduction plan.

The male patient may be beset not only by fears of loss of sexual control, but also by fears of impotence. The achievement of normal body weight, which would make him aesthetically more desirable, might also expose his sexual inexperience or incompetence, or, in his fantasies, transform him into a "sex maniac" unable to control his sexual impulses.

The fear of loss of control may take another form as well: The patient who feels that to attempt to alter his eating patterns would be to put to the test his developmentally achieved capacity to tolerate frustration may be afraid of failure.

Fear of Pain. The patient may be convinced that the deprivation or reduced intake of food may cause somatic pain, particularly gastrointestinal pain or discomfort. These fears may or may not be based on fact; and even when there is pain, it may not have a physiological origin.

The Activation of Feelings of Guilt and Shame. If the patient feels, consciously or unconsciously, that his aberrant weight status is justified punishment for his "sins," weight loss may constitute a threat to his psychological homeostasis. Alternatively, he may anticipate feelings of guilt and shame if the prescribed changes in food selection and eating patterns violate his cultural and social mores. Or failure to follow the medical regimen or anticipation of such failure may evoke feelings of guilt and shame that will preclude any further attempts to achieve the therapeutic goal.

The physician's awareness of these possible psychological stresses may help him to focus his support: He may have to deal with the modification of stress to achieve effective weight loss. It must be pointed out that if the psychological stresses assume such proportions that the patient's psychological homeostasis may be threatened by weight loss, diet modification may require concurrent psychotherapeutic intervention. Actually for the majority of patients, however, a focus on eating behavior and food selection—external factors, per se—is sufficient to assist the weight loss process. Insight therapy is seldom indicated solely on the basis of moderate obesity. However, over the long term, the patient's internal cuing and his accustomed responses to these signals must be modified for weight maintenance.

Family attitudes that may play an etiological role in the patient's aberrant eating behavior may also perpetuate that behavior. For example, if the husband feels insecure in his own sense of identity, he may encourage his wife to persist in her pathological eating patterns lest she demand increased social contact with others. The efforts of the woman to lose weight may be impeded by her children as well—by the adolescent daughter who is in competition with her mother, or by the son who fears he will not be able to maintain control if his mother becomes sexually desirable. Actually, most female patients recognize, at some level, that their weight change may alter family relationships significantly, either in fact or in fantasy. This is no less true of the obese man. The prospect of his attainment of normal weight may be perceived by his wife as a threat if she feels physically and sexually inadequate, and equates leanness with virility in the male or sexuality with youth. She may then attempt unconsciously to sabotage his weight loss program. The response of the extended family to his efforts to lose weight may also be a determinant of therapeutic success.

When it is evident that family attitudes present a real obstacle to treatment progress, the physician may have to meet with the spouse or arrange to see the entire family to discuss the problem. Such family interviews are also indicated when the patient, no matter how well motivated, is not able to tolerate the stress that accompanies adherence to the therapeutic regimen.

THE PHYSICIAN'S RESPONSE TO THE OBESE PATIENT

The physician's first task is to correct the misconceptions he may hold with regard to the obese patient population. The first of these—which is all too prevalent among the medical profession—is the tendency to view obesity as a result of a lack of discipline, rather than a legitimate medical disease. A corollary to this misconception is the erroneous belief, particularly when these patients are refractory to treatment, that obesity is a purely psychological problem. Admittedly, psychological factors do play a role in its etiology and pathogenesis. However, the effective management of the obese patient requires medical skills as well as psychological intervention. It is important to note in this connection that the great majority of obese individuals do not manifest major psychiatric morbidity. Nor does major psychiatric morbidity necessarily occur as a concomitant of weight reduction procedures. Contrary to general belief, studies of formerly obese patients who had undergone bypass surgery showed only limited adverse psychological reactions.[38,39]

A second misconception is the belief held by many physicians that the patient, having achieved the desired weight loss, will be able to remain at that weight level without further support. Obese patients suffer from a chronic disease, and, as is true of any other chronically ill patient, they require ongoing medical contact and supervision.

Careful consideration of the psychological and physiological factors that may predispose to obesity, and of the factors that may impede the effectiveness of therapeutic intervention, permit the formulation of guidelines for treatment: The long-standing habits and life-long patterns of eating behavior which have given rise to the patient's illness will not be modified without an investment on the part of the physician of considerable time and energy. He must be prepared to deal with the difficult behaviors that are characteristic of obese patients. For example, such patients unwittingly or deliberately present inaccurate reports of their food intake. They are notoriously remiss in keeping appointments, arriving on time, or in following the doctor's directions (e.g., to keep a food intake record, to collect urine specimens, etc). If the physician permits such behaviors to irritate him to the degree that he loses his respect for the patient as a person, treatment will be compromised. He can best convey his respect for the patient as an individual by letting him know implicitly or explicitly that he expects him to assume a degree of responsibility for his treatment. In so doing, the physician also minimizes the irritation such behaviors might evoke in him.

Perhaps the greatest impediment to the effectiveness of treatment stems from the challenge these patients present to the doctor's fantasies of omnipotence. The fact that this disease does not respond readily to his clinical skill—and may not respond at all—the difficult behavior of these patients, the fact that progress frequently alternates with regression, and that even when he does achieve a therapeutic success, it may be short-lived, all undermine the physician's self-image as the "powerful healer."[40] Perhaps because obesity presents such a threat to the physician's fantasies of omnipotence, he is reluctant to recognize it as a chronic medical disease, tends to view this patient population as emotionally disturbed and maintains that their treatment does not fall within his province. It may also explain the hostility many physicians feel toward these patients and the alacrity with which doctors condemn them for not exerting enough "control." Not only must the physician be able to accept with equanimity the problems these patients present in terms of their management, he must have also resolved his fantasies of omnipotence sufficiently to be able to accept the fact that some patients will simply not be able to lose weight or maintain a weight loss. Once he has come to terms with his clinical vulnerability he will be able to demonstrate his therapeutic effectiveness by offering these patients a continuing relationship and support.

REFERENCES

1. Frankel RT: Nutrition education for medical students. J Am Dietet Assn 68:513, 1976
2. White PL, Mahan LK, Moore ME (eds): Conference on Guidelines for

Nutritional Education in Medical Schools and Post Doctoral Training Programs (Williamsburg, Va). Chicago, AMA, 1972
3. Vitale JJ, Hodges RE: Teaching nutrition in medical schools. Am J Clin Nutr 30:795, 1977
4. Blackburn GL, Bistran BR: Careers in nutrition from the clinical viewpoint. Nutr Rev 34:97, 1976
5. Angel JL: Constitution in female obesity. Am J Phys Anthropol 7:433, 1949
6. Gurney R: Hereditary factor in obesity. Arch Intern Med 57:557, 1936
7. Garn SM, Baily SM: Fatness similarities in adopted pairs. Am J Clin Nutr 29:1067, 1976
8. Sheldon WH: Atlas of Men. New York, Harper, 1954
9. Hirsch J: Adipose cellularity in relation to human obesity. Adv Intern Med 17:289, 1971
10. Björntorp P: Effects of age, sex and clinical conditions on adipose tissue cellularity in man. Metabolism 23:1091, 1974
11. Bray G: The Obese Patient. Major Prob Intern Med, Vol. 9. Philadelphia, Saunders, 1976
12. Ashwell M, Meade CJ, Medawar P, Sowter C: Adipose tissue: contributions of nature and nurture to the obesity of the mutant mouse (ob/ob). Proc R Soc Lond [Biol], 195:343, 1977
13. Björntorp P, Carlgren G, Isaksson B, Krotkiewski M, Larsson B, Sjostran L: Effect of an energy-reduced dietary regimen in relation to adipose cellularity in obese women. Am J Clin Nutr 28:445, 1975
14. Kempner W, Newborg BC, Peschel RL, et al: Treatment of massive obesity with rice/reduction diet program. An analysis of 106 patients with at least a 45 Kg weight loss. Arch Intern Med 135:1575, 1975.
15. Bruch H: The psychological handicap of obesity. In Bray GA (ed): Obesity in Perspective, vol. 2 part 2. DHEW (NIH) 75–708, 1976, p 111
16. Williams RJ: Biochemical Individuality. New York, Wiley, 1956
17. Garrow JF: Energy Balance and Obesity in Man. London, North Holland Publishing, 1974
18. Schacter S: Obesity and eating: Internal and external cues differently effect eating behavior of obese and normal subjects. Science 161: 751, 1968
19. Hashim SA, Van Itallie TB: Studies in normal and obese subjects with a monitored food dispensing service. Ann NY Acad Sci 131:654, 1965
20. Bruch H: Eating Disorders: Obesity, Anorexia Nervosa and the Person Within. New York, Basic Books, 1973
21. Swanson DW, Dinello FA: Follow-up of patients starved for obesity. Psychosom Med 32:209, 1970.
22. Weinberg N, Mendelson M, Stunkard A: A failure to find distinctive personality features in a group of obese men. Am J Psychiatry 117:1035, 1961
23. Sucsek RF: The group approach to weight reduction: 2. Psychologic aspects of obesity and group weight reduction. J Am Dietet Assoc 30:442, 1954
24. Weiner H: Psychobiology and Human Disease. New York, Elsevier, 1977

25. Johnson SF, Swenson WM, Gastineau CF: Personality characteristics in obesity: Relation to MMPI profile and age of onset of obesity to success in weight reduction. Am J Clin Nutr 29:626, 1976
26. Bacchus H: Essentials of Metabolic Diseases and Endocrinology. Baltimore, University Park, 1976, p 66
27. Jordon HA, Levitz LS: A behavioral approach to the problem of obesity. In Silverstone TS (ed): Obesity: Pathogenesis and Management. Acton, Mass, Publishing Sciences Group, 1975, p 155
28. Silverstone TS: Obesity: Pathogenesis and Management. Acton, Mass, Publishing Sciences Group, 1975
29. Bistran BR, Blackburn GL, Stanbury JB: Metabolic aspects of a protein-sparing modified fast in the dietary management of Prader-Willi obesity. New Eng J Med 296:774, 1977.
30. Bistran BR, Blackburn GL, Flatt JP, Sizer J, Schrimshaw NS, Sherman M: Nitrogen metabolism and insulin requirements in obese diabetic adults on a protein-sparing modified fast. Diabetes 25:494, 1976
31. American Diabetes Assoc and American Dietetic Assoc: Exchange Lists for Meal Planning, 6000 Fifth Ave, New York, N.Y. 10020, 1976
32. Young CM, Hutter LF, Scanlan SS, Rand CE, Lutwak L, Simko V: Metabolic effects of meal frequency on normal young men. J Am Dietet Assoc 61:391, 1972
33. Genuthe SM, Castro, JH, Vertes V: Weight reduction in obesity by outpatient semi-starvation. JAMA, 230:987, 1974
34. Atkinson RL, Greenway FL, Bray GA: Treatment of obesity: comparison of physician and nonphysician therapists using placebo and anoretic drugs in a double-blind trial. Int J Obesity 1:113, 1977
35. Mason EE, Printen KJ, Hartford CE, Boyd WC: Optimizing the results of gastic bypass. Ann Surg 182:405, 1975
36. Faloon WW (chair): Symposium on jejuno-ileostomy for obesity. Am J Clin Nutr 30:1, 1977
37. Stunkard AJ: Obesity. In Reiser MF (ed): American Handbook of Psychiatry. New York, Basic Books, 1975
38. Castelnuovo-Tedesco P, Schiebel D: Studies of superobesity: II. Psychiatric appraisal of jejuno-ileal bypass surgery. Am J Psychiatry 133:26, 1976
39. Solow C, Silberfarb PM, Swift K: Psychosocial effects of intestinal bypass surgery for severe obesity. New Eng J Med 290:300, 1974
40. Spikes J, Holland J: The physician's response to the dying patient. In Strain JJ, Grossman S (eds): Psychological Care of the Medically Ill: A Primer in Liaison Psychiatry. New York, Appleton, 1975, p 138

Chapter 9

The Intrafamilial Environment of the Chronically Ill Patient

Obviously, the physician's understanding of the patient's response to chronic illness cannot rest solely on the insights he has acquired into the patient's intrapsychic functioning. The primary care physician knows from first-hand experience that such a "linear" approach, which focuses on the patient, his emotions, and their effect on his physiological status, must be expanded to accommodate an "open systems" model that enables his understanding of the system of the patient, the family, and their interactional patterns. He knows that perception of the patient as part of a larger sociocultural network is an essential ingredient of his awareness of the individual patient's psychological status.

As is true of the linear approach, the open systems model, as employed by Minuchin,[1] seeks to identify the symptom, the precipitating event, and the factors that maintain the symptom. In contrast to the linear approach, however, Minuchin emphasizes that family interactional patterns, as well as intrapsychic phenomena, may trigger the onset and/or hamper the subsidence of psychophysiological processes; that illness may disrupt family organization, or serve as a homeostatic mechanism that regulates family interactions.

The open systems approach becomes operational when its components are viewed as discrete entities. To the extent that it shapes the individual's response to the "normal" vicissitudes of life, the intrafamilial environment may initiate illness in a variety of ways. Schmale and the Rochester group [2] concluded from their pioneer study that real or imagined separation and loss, when they give rise to "helplessness-hopelessness," "giving in-giving up," are common occurrences prior to the overt manifestation of illness, and that such sense of loss is usually experienced in regard to a family member.

Other investigators have attempted to codify specific family-related life events that may contribute to the onset of physical illness. For example, Holmes and Rahe,[3] who correlated actual or anticipated life events (positive and negative) that require social readjustment with the onset of illness (Fig. 4), found that among the events listed, the three most potent were family-related—death of a spouse, divorce, and mari-

LIFE EVENT	MEAN VALUE*
1. Death of spouse	100
2. Divorce	73
3. Marital separation from mate	65
4. Detention in jail or other institution	63
5. Death of a close family member	63
6. Major personal injury or illness	53
7. Marriage	50
8. Being fired at work	47
9. Marital reconciliation with mate	45
10. Retirement from work	45
11. Major change in the health or behavoir of a family member	44
12. Pregnancy	40
13. Sexual difficulties	39
14. Gaining a new family member (e.g., through birth, adoption, oldster moving in, etc.)	39
15. Major business readjustment (e.g., merger, reorganization, bankruptcy, etc.)	39
16. Major change in financial state (e.g., a lot worse off or a lot better off than usual)	38
17. Death of a close friend	37
18. Changing to a different line of work	36
19. Major change in the number of arguments with spouse (e.g., either a lot more or a lot less than usual regarding child-rearing, personal habits, etc.)	35
20. Taking on a mortgage greater than $10,000 (e.g., purchasing a home, business, etc.)	31

FIGURE 4

*The Social Readjustment Rating Scale. (From Holmes and Rahe: J Psychosom Res 11:213, 1967, with permission) *Mean value refers to the value assigned to the life event, based on the frequency with which that particular event preceded illness in the population studied.*

LIFE EVENT	MEAN VALUE*
21. Foreclosure on a mortgage or loan	30
22. Major change in responsibilities at work (e.g., promotion, demotion, lateral transfer)	29
23. Son or daughter leaving home (e.g., marriage, attending college, etc.)	29
24. In-law troubles	29
25. Outstanding personal achievement	28
26. Wife beginning or ceasing work outside the home	26
27. Beginning or ceasing formal schooling	26
28. Major change in living conditions (e.g., building a new home, remodeling, deterioration of home or neighborhood	25
29. Revision of personal habits (dress, manners, associations, etc.)	24
30. Troubles with the boss	23
31. Major change in working hours or conditions	20
32. Change in residence	20
33. Changing to a new school	20
34. Major change in usual type and/or amount of recreation	19
35. Major change in church activities (e.g., a lot more or a lot less than usual)	19
36. Major change in social activities (e.g., clubs, dancing, movies, visiting, etc.)	18
37. Taking on a mortgage or loan less than $10,000 (e.g., purchasing a car, TV, freezer, etc.)	17
38. Major change in sleeping habits (a lot more or a lot less sleep, or change in part of day when asleep)	16
39. Major change in number of family get-togethers (e.g., a lot more or a lot less than usual)	15
40. Major change in eating habits (a lot more or a lot less food intake, or very different meal hours or surroundings)	15
41. Vacation	13
42. Christmas	12
43. Minor violations of the law (e.g., traffic tickets, jaywalking, disturbing the peace, etc.)	11

tal separation. In fact, of the 33 life events listed, 16 are directly related and all the others may be indirectly related to family interaction. This thesis has been supported by Meissner,[4] who contends that "disruption or disequilibrium within the family system" may be a major source of psychological stress, which acts as an intervening variable between environmental events and illness in the individual.*

* Thus, as Jackson [5] has pointed out, the onset of illness, in itself, can be used by the physician as a barometer of the family's psychosocial status.

Holmes [6] also found that life changes, when these occur in sufficient quantity, can even precede the signs and symptoms of common maladies, e.g., colds, low-grade fever, headache, and so forth. Furthermore, Holmes's finding that individuals experience "streaks," i.e., "cluster days," of illness, would seem to militate against the possibility that disease strikes at random. The number of life changes an individual experiences may also heighten his vulnerability to accidents. A significant proportion of the group studied by Holmes who suffered accidents had accumulated an excessive number of life changes.

Proponents of the open systems approach further emphasize that once the individual becomes ill, the cause-effect relationship is reversed: The patient, rather than his family, then becomes the potentially pernicious influence. As Livsey [7] has pointed out, the patient then has the "power" to contribute to the onset of physical or psychological dysfunction in one or several family members—and to the disintegration of the family as a unit. And, by the same token, the family has the "power" to adversely influence the patient's capacity to adapt to his illness.

These data underscore the potential importance of the systems model. It is not our aim in the chapter, however, to provide a detailed discussion of the clinical application of this model; indeed, such a discussion lies beyond our competence. Our approach to psychological dysfunction in the medically ill remains primarily a psychodynamic one. But this orientation does not preclude consideration of the clinical significance of the complex interactions of the system of the patient and the system of his family. The physician's ability to evaluate the patient's intrapsychic functioning in the context of the system of his family, will enhance his psychological capacities with regard to the individual patient.

> John was the oldest son of immigrants, to whom he was very attached. Parents and son lived close by and saw each other often socially. But, in addition, John dropped in on his parents almost daily to report on his family and his job, and to check up on them. And his parents, who were proud of their son, looked forward to these visits. Their pride was understandable. John's parents had worked hard all their lives and valued hard work, perseverance, and achievement. And, at the age of 46, John seemed to be fulfilling his parents' goals—which had become his own. Although he was one of several vice-presidents of a large corporation, he stood out because he tried harder than his peers, worked longer hours, was more competitive. Work was John's life. And his life style was condoned not only by his parents, but by his wife as well. John had married a woman who admired ambition and achievement, and who took his preoccupation with his job for granted. And, like his parents, she accepted signs of strain or

excessive fatigue in her husband as part of life. Even his children had learned not to make demands on their father, that he had more important things to do.

John's acute life crisis occurred after he had been associated with his company for 7 years. There was an opportunity for advancement to a position that was highly coveted by John and his peers, although it meant relocation. John dreaded leaving his parents; but he also felt it was terribly important to get this promotion, and his wife agreed.

While John awaited the verdict of his superiors, he was plagued by a number of somatic complaints. He began to be aware of how tired he felt; he experienced diffuse discomfort in his chest from time to time; he noticed he was short of breath even on customary exertion. As his appetite diminished and his discomfort persisted, he began to feel that something was wrong. His wife dismissed these complaints as manifestations of anxiety; she felt he was worried about whether he would get the job, and if he did, whether he would succeed.

When John was awakened at 3 in the morning by acute radiating chest pains which persisted, and were accompanied by nausea, sweating, and palpitations, his symptoms could no longer be dismissed as trivial. Yet, even then John was reluctant to call the doctor, and his wife did not urge him to do so until the pain became so severe that he had to ask her to telephone Dr. Y., who told them he would order an ambulance and meet them at the hospital. John's illness was diagnosed promptly in the emergency room as an acute myocardial infarction, and he was transferred to the coronary care unit.

There was no doubt that John was seriously ill, and he seemed to be aware of this. Yet, his anxiety focused not on whether he would live or die, but on whether he would lose his chance for promotion.

There is no conclusive evidence that John's addiction to work, his competitiveness, and his anxiety to get ahead precipitated his heart attack. Nor is there conclusive evidence that the possible separation from his familial environment, and, in particular, the loss of regular contact with his parents, played an important etiological role in the onset of his disease. Both factors may have been involved. John manifested the characteristics of the "Type A" personality described as vulnerable to coronary heart disease. But he was also preoccupied with anticipated important life changes—the uncertainty as to whether he would get his promotion and, the fear if he did, of separation from and loss of his parents.

Having a heart attack had many complex implications for John. It was, of course, perceived as a threat to his survival; yet in a sense it offered an easy solution to his dilemma: If he died, the decision regarding his promotion, which meant relocation and separation from his parents, would be taken out of his hands. On the other hand, he needed to deny his symptoms because of his fear of passivity; if he were an invalid, all of his past achievements would count for naught. Finally, to admit to being ill would be to admit to losing control over his career, his family—and his destiny. No feature of John's intrafamilial environment could counteract these fantasies, with the result that for any one or several of these reasons John delayed seeking medical help after he developed significant symptoms.

Actually, John's behavior is not uncommon. Hackett [8] found that 50 percent of the patients in the sample he studied failed to respond promptly to symptoms of a myocardial infarction; and many of these patients died subsequently because of an inability, due to psychological factors, to obtain the medical care that may have saved their lives if it had been provided early enough. Hackett ascribes this behavior to denial. We suggested several other possible explanations in Chapter 1. And when this behavior is viewed within the specific context of family interactions, one can speculate that the patient's failure to obtain medical help may be an attempt to punish or control significant members in his family.[9] On an unconscious level, John may have resented his wife's apparent indifference to his dilemma, and even his parents for their excessive emphasis on work. Such patients ordinarily try not to delay indefinitely since it is not their ultimate purpose to "hurt," i.e., kill themselves. Unfortunately, however, their judgment as to how long they can safely delay is not always accurate. Greene and his co-workers,[10] who studied the characteristics of early and late responders to chest pain found that early responders were more likely to initiate medical care on their own; a family member or friend usually initiated medical contact for late responders. John's case was atypical in this regard. Although his wife did eventually initiate medical contact for him, she did so at his request.

As Shindell et al [11] has pointed out, a layman—and, in particular, a key family member, affects not only the initial utilization of medical services, but also has an impact on the acceptance of medical diagnosis and on patient compliance with a prescribed treatment plan. The family may be the only source of information for the patient who needs to deny illness, to the extent that he seems to be out of touch with his body sensations; who needs to be completely self-reliant, and who tends to ward off passivity and dependence by limiting his contact with the doctor. Quite possibly, given his drive to achieve, John might have gone back to work prematurely, worked too hard, etc. Ideally, his wife would have intervened to enhance compliance with an appropriate regimen. But, in this case, there is a possibility that John's wife may have encouraged his noncompliance—one way or another. Moreover, one can anticipate that John's maladaptive convalescent behavior would meet with his parents' tacit approval. This speculation gains currency when one considers the failure of his wife and parents to pay proper attention to his prodromal symptomatology which illustrates the quality of their interactions.

The preceding clinical example is exceptional because it demonstrates the relationship between individual and family psychodynamics at every phase of illness, with the exception of diagnosis which was readily established in John's case. In contrast, the accurate diagnosis of depression, and, in particular, identification of the potentially suicidal patient, may rest on information supplied by family members. Information from the patient can be verified and augmented by his family, who can be asked whether the patient has suffered a recent loss; whether he has always been a depressed individual, and pessimistic about life; whether the onset of his depression coincided with the onset of his illness or followed shortly thereafter; whether he has manifested certain vegetative signs of depression, e.g., weight loss, loss of appetite, etc. They may also have some awareness of the degree of frustration and unhappiness the patient is experiencing.

The family may play a particularly crucial role in the diagnosis of the elderly patient who presents numerous vague somatic complaints without remarkable physical findings. If, according to family members, the patient has a life-long history of repeated contacts with clinics and physicians, has submitted willingly to a wide variety of diagnostic and therapeutic procedures, and findings have always been within normal limits, the possibility that the patient may be a "true" hypochondriac must be considered (in the absence of positive physical findings). If, on the other hand, his family reports that the patient's preoccupation with bodily function is of relatively recent onset, and can be related to certain physiological and/or psychosocial stresses, one would be less likely to make a pre-emptory diagnosis of hypochondriasis.

Biographical data from the family can be equally helpful in the accurate diagnosis of a chronic organic mental syndrome and its differentiation from delirium. They may know whether the patient's confusion, disorientation, memory loss, and impaired judgment had a sudden onset, suggestive of delirium, or whether these cognitive deficits are of long duration, suggestive of dementia.

On the other hand, information transmitted by a family member may cloud diagnosis.

> Mrs. G., a 66-year-old widow, lived with her daughter, son-in-law, and two teen-age granddaughters in a four-room apartment. The patient was brought to the doctor's office by her daughter, who was also present during the initial interview. Mrs. G. complained that everything hurt her; she had no appetite, couldn't sleep at night, and woke up exhausted in the morning; she just had no interest in life

any more. The daughter augmented this list of complaints with a certain alacrity: Her mother was forgetful; she kept losing things; she made inappropriate comments in front of company; she was always intruding; she had no judgment about when she should join the family and when they should be alone; and she couldn't follow instructions.

Dr. M. did a complete physical on Mrs. G. and, when physical findings were negative, suspected she might be suffering from a depressive reaction or a chronic organic mental syndrome. The results of a mental status examination ruled out that possibility. All of Mrs. G.'s mental functions—memory, judgment, orientation, etc.—were essentially intact. Furthermore, the patient revealed none of the vegetative signs of depression. But there was no question that she presented a depressed mood. And Mrs. G. had some insight into the dynamics of her problem. She wasn't really part of her daughter's family, she felt like an outsider, taking up too much space, interfering with her granddaughters' social life. Yet, there was no alternative. She couldn't afford to live by herself, her son-in-law certainly couldn't afford to supplement her income, and she couldn't reconcile herself to the prospect of spending the rest of her life in a home for the indigent aged.

Mrs. G. was unable to communicate her despair to her daughter in words, and used symptoms instead. Because her daughter misinterpreted these symptoms, Dr. M. was confronted with contradictory diagnostic data.

PSYCHOLOGICAL ASSESSMENT OF THE FAMILY

By and large the physician proceeds on the basis of two premises, both of which are open to challenge. The first premise states that certain types of families are better suited to sustain an ill family member. The second postulates that families that function "badly" prior to the onset of a chronic illness may be unable to adapt successfully to that illness once it has been established. With regard to the first of these premises, it is a fair assumption that the nuclear family might be more effective in a therapeutic capacity than a single-parent family, and that the extended family might offer more than the nuclear family. In fact, each of these types of family can pose specific problems for medical care. In theory, the internal structure of the nuclear family is one of the first lines of defense against stress. But today the nuclear family has very few members; often it has a weak internal structure, and it may be isolated from members of the extended family. In that event, it may not be equipped to cope with illness and dysfunction in a family member. In fact, there is some question as to whether the American nuclear family, as it is currently structured, can even sustain its healthy members.[12] The problems the one-adult family and the single-parent family may present in this regard are self-evident. But the extended family and the two-adult family are not immune from these problems. The point is that no type of family, regardless of its structure, can escape the difficulties presented by medical illness in a family member, particularly when that illness is disabling and chronic.

With regard to the second premise, as might be expected, in general, families that function badly are less able to cope with the chronic illness of a member than are families who would be considered to function well; there are exceptions, however. The crucial determinant seems to be whether the family has evolved satisfactory ways of coping. For example, the wife in a "doll house marriage" may cope with life by depending entirely upon her husband, to the degree that she is unable to alter this posture even when he develops a physical dysfunction that requires him to become the dependent one. Her inability to alter her customary role, while it may appear on the surface to be maladaptive, actually serves an important supportive function with regard to her husband. For her continued reliance on his judgment, her perception of him as the strong man of the family, may enable him to maintain his self–esteem.

In other instances, however, "pathogenic" modes of interacting may impede rather than foster adaptation. Such a situation might obtain, for instance, when illness serves as a homeostatic mechanism that regulates family interactions. In that event, in their need to maintain homeostasis, the family may, consciously or unconsciously, foster the patient's noncompliance with the medical regimen (and his maladaptation to chronic illness).

Just as the physician must resist the temptation to generalize with regard to the chronically ill patient's response to his illness, he must guard against generalization with respect to the efficacy of modes of family functioning. His concern is with the psychological orientation of the *individual* family as a unit, the meaning the illness of the *individual* patient holds for his family, with the nature of family relationships, and, in particular, with the quality of his patient's interactions with specific family members.

The Life Cycle of the Family

A number of parameters—among them, the stage in the family's life cycle at which the illness occurs—can be used to evaluate the family's response to the patient's illness and the psychological sequelae of this response for the patient. In a sense, the concept of a family life cyçle, which has been postulated by Shindell and Oberembt,[11] is analogous to Erickson's concept of the individual life cycle.[13] Specifically, these authors identify eight major events that can serve to delimit stages in the family's development:

1. Selection of a mate and the legitimization of the relationship, e.g., through marriage;
2. Realization of the process of establishing a new family as distinct from the background families of the couple;
3. Arrival of the first child, and establishment of husband-father and wife-mother roles;
4. Individuation of first child—not just as an extension of the parents—including developing sexual identity;
5. First child's entry into school;
6. First child's adolescence;
7. Surrendering first child, decreasing family structure, facing retirement;
8. Coping with death of one's spouse and survivor's task of continuing the family.

Considered in the context of this broader conceptual framework, we come to understand that the psychosocial stresses evoked by chronic illness and the responses of the patient and his family to these stresses will depend, in large measure, on the stage at which the illness occurs in the evolution of the family. For example, had John's heart attack occurred at a later stage in his family's life cycle—at his retirement, after he had made his mark—neither he nor his wife might have perceived it as such a threat; in which event, he might have initiated medical contact more promptly, and been more apt to comply with the constraints imposed during the convalescence stage of his illness.

The Quality of Family Relationships

Confirmation of the findings derived from the numerous studies of bereavement, i.e., that loss of the object plays a major role in the onset of physical disease, has come from an unexpected quarter: Hinkle and his co-workers,[14] who have focused on the correlation between the quantity and quality of "interpersonal life events" and vulnerability to illness, have concluded from their studies that a more isolated person, one who is less involved with other people, may be less prone to illness than an individual who has close ties to others. In short, the individual's vulnerability to disease as a consequence of bereavement or any other life change will depend on the meaning that event has for him. In a classic frequently cited study, Hinkle [15] observed that while some displaced Hungarians undergoing relocation were prone to illness, others remained surprisingly healthy despite the stress and personal turmoil of revolution and immigration.*

Singer's concept [17] of engagement–involvement as a central issue in psychophysiological phenomena is in accord with Hinkle's theory. At any given moment, each individual appears to manifest an estimable level of engagement or nonengagement with his fellow man, his surroundings, and his inner self. The degree of this involvement with his human and non-human environment may affect his physiological functioning, favorably or unfavorably; that is, it may reduce or increase his vulnerability to disease.

Once chronic illness is established, the psychological stress it produces in both the patient and his family, can be viewed from the same vantage point of engagement–involvement. In Chapter 2 we hypothesized that the onset of chronic illness evokes eight basic stresses in every patient. But the intensity of these stresses will depend on the degree to which the patient is emotionally involved with his family —and with himself. By the same token, the intensity of the stresses evoked in a given family by the illness of a member depends on the degree to which the family is involved with its sick member—and with each other. The degree of "engagement–involvement" then becomes an important criterion of the quality of family relationships.

These background data permit the formulation of guidelines that allow for a more comprehensive assessment of the psychodynamics of the patient's intrafamilial environment. For example, there may be a correlation between the engagement–involvement of family members and the stage in the family's life cycle at which the chronic illness occurs.

> Mr. and Mrs. F., who had been married for 46 years, had become increasingly disinterested in one another. Actually, they had never been very involved with one another, but their discordance had not

* Hinkle [16] concludes, on the basis of his many long-term studies of this phenomenon, that 30 percent of any given population will have 70 percent of the illness that occurs in that population, and that the vulnerability to illness is well established by adulthood.

been as apparent earlier in their marriage. Mr. F.'s work and his wife's preoccupation with raising their children and acting as homemaker had kept them sufficiently busy and distant, so that they were able to maintain a fairly concordant relationship. Mr. F.'s retirement and the exodus of their children resulted in drastic changes in the structure of their family. For the first time in their lives, Mr. and Mrs. F. found themselves alone and together. They were forced to talk to each other, and their lack of warmth and caring for each other was apparent despite their long association and the experiences they had shared.

When Mr. F. developed crippling arthritis, he wasn't unduly upset. He didn't particularly care, for example, whether he appeared less attractive to his wife. Nor was he distressed by the prospect of being placed in a nursing home. Mrs. F. performed routine nursing functions for her husband, but she made no real attempt to support him psychologically. In fact, most of the time, she was able to view him with what might be regarded as clinical detachment.

Intrafamilial modes of interaction can also be conceptualized in terms of the developmental tracts referred to earlier. By and large, an individual's premorbid character traits will mesh on a manifest, as well as a latent level, with the character traits of other family members. For example, when a man has an excessive need to demonstrate his independence and authority (on a manifest level), his wife and children may assume a dependent, passive posture. But once that individual has developed a chronic illness, there may be a dynamic alteration in this customary mode of interaction. As a general rule, a shift of roles within the family unit results in interpersonal as well as intrapsychic stress in its members. The stress may arise from unexpected sources, however.

Mr. E. was a construction foreman who boasted that he had forty people working under him. His wife and children worked under him as well. When he came home after a hard day's work, regardless of how busy his wife had been during the day, he expected to have his beer poured, and the whole family to assemble at a prescribed time for dinner.

Mr. E.'s incapacitating emphysema forced a major change in the family's life style. Financial pressures made it necessary for Mrs. E. to go to work and for his older children to get part-time jobs. Initially, Mr. E. attempted to maintain his role as captain of the regiment and expected his family to carry on as before. Very early on, however, there was rebellion in the ranks. Mr. E.'s illness had given his wife an opportunity to break out of the bind he had placed her in, and she took great pleasure in asserting her rights. Once they saw that it worked for their mother, the children were quick to emulate her.

The psychological consequences for Mr. E. were catastrophic. Predictably, the behavior of his family exacerbated all the stresses he experienced as a consequence of his illness. On the other hand, his illness diminished the stresses his family experienced as a consequence of living with him. Thus, Mr. E.'s chronic illness resulted in a healthy reorganization of the family unit, which may ultimately exert a salutory effect on Mr. E. as well. More specifically, Mr. E.'s illness necessitated a shift in roles that permitted other family members to express their needs more fully without a conflict of the intensity they had previously experienced. Mr. E. may, in turn, come to realize that his attitude toward other family members was unrealistic. Whereas any attempt to alter his behavior in a healthy state would have given rise to conflict within himself, his illness would give him license to become kinder, more considerate, less dominating, without losing face.

With the onset of chronic illness, latent character traits which have pernicious psychological and physiological sequelae may come to the surface.

> Mr. and Mrs. G. both gave the impression of being independent, active adults—until Mr. G. had an acute myocardial infarction. During his convalescence, all of Mr. G.'s passive, dependent wishes came to the surface and provided Mrs. G. with an opportunity to give full expression to her own longings to be in control and to dominate her environment. As a result, long after Mr. G. was physiologically ready to resume his normal activities, he was still being fed and "mothered" by his wife.

Alterations in premorbid modes of intrafamilial interactions, can, of course, take many other forms as well. The permutations and commutations are incalculable. The task of the physician is to identify the specific form the alteration takes in the individual family and to observe the psychological sequelae of this alteration in his chronically ill patient.

Provided all of the elements of the patients' intrafamilial environment are available to him for evaluation, the physician can determine, on the basis of his assessment of the quality and quantity of his patient's relationships with individual family members, and his impression of the family's response to the patient and his illness, who is best qualified to assume responsibility for the patient's management. He may conclude that responsibility for the patient's care can best be assumed by the extended units within the social network or by a health care facility, as opposed to involvement of the patient's nuclear family.* He may conclude that no individual member of the nuclear family or the extended family should assume sole responsibility for the patient's management, or that a particular family member might best bear the onus at one phase of the patient's illness, and another member at a subsequent phase.

> Mrs. X. had a very different kind of relationship with her two daughters. Mary, the eldest, had for several years tended to infantilize her: She telephoned her mother every day to check up on her, tried to supervise her activities, and, in general, assumed the role of parent. Alice, on the other hand, was very much involved in her own life and assumed that her mother was of a similar mind. Their relationship had the quality of friendship. Therefore, it seemed logical to Dr. K. that Mary would be good psychologically for her mother during the posthospital convalescent phase following an operation for the replacement of her aorta. Alice, on the other hand, might be expected to encourage Mrs. X. to "get going again," during the active rehabilitation phase of her convalescence.

Finally, an assessment of the family would necessarily include the identification of those members who are at risk for psychological and/or physiological dysfunction as a consequence of the patient's chronic illness. Certain groups are particularly vulnerable in this respect. Data presented earlier point up the high vulnerability to disease among the bereaved aged. As might also be expected, young children are particularly vulnerable to psychological dysfunction following the serious illness or death of a family member—even a member of the extended family.

Given the complexity of the data that the physician accumulates in the course of his assessment of the family system, he might profit from the use of a genogram,[20] which can facilitate their codification. Briefly described, the genogram is a visual presentation of the structure of three generations within a single family: the nuclear family, children, and grandparents. Via symbols, numbers, and words, it incorporates general information, e.g., names and addresses of individual family members, birthdates, and deathdates, and these data enable the physician to de-

* For example, studies have shown that some asthmatic children and some children who fail to thrive do better when they are separated from their families.[18, 19] The intrafamilial environments are so pathogenic in these cases that remaining in the family unit imposes a greater stress on the patient than does separation from it.

termine the location and availability of specific family members when necessary. Other types of general information are included as well, e.g., socioeconomic data, religious preferences, and ethnic background. But the genogram also includes more complex data regarding, for example, the frequency of contact and the nature and quality of the relationships between individual family members. Thus relevant themes and patterns inherent in the relationships of the various constituents of the extended family unit, and in particular those patterns which may lead to pathology, emerge. For example, these data may help the physician to determine whether his patient will maintain an active stance because it is syntonic with the present family system. In that event, the alteration of that stance, although it is medically indicated, would, presumably, exacerbate a latent conflict which may, itself, prove pathogenic.

In addition, the use of this device facilitates the codification of medical data. It provides the doctor with a visual record of the family's current illnesses, as well as those they sustained in the past. More important, perhaps, it can accommodate information regarding the sick family's reaction to and mode of coping with physical illness. To illustrate, if heart disease has been a frequent cause of death, the doctor needs to learn something about the family's attitudes toward heart disease. If the physician is concerned about the family's response to the anticipated death of a patient, he may find historical data reassuring. If the family was able to cope with severe illness and/or death in the past, they may react similarly to current misfortune. If, on the other hand, the death of a family member precipitated a major disruption in the family system in the past, the physician should be alert to the possibility that it may evoke the same response again.

In summary, a carefully constructed genogram provides the physican with a "birdseye" view of the three-generation family, its constituents, their characteristics, and their potential capacity to function as allies in his efforts to minimize the patient's disability. Its usefulness lies in the fact that it encourages the physician to make observations and ask questions that a less structured, narrative family assessment might obscure. At the same time it provides the physician with a succinct and permanent record, which can be altered and refined over time, of the patient's sociocultural environment.

MANAGEMENT

Just as understanding of the patient's psychological status must extend beyond consideration of his intrapsychic functioning, interventions to enhance adaptation to chronic illness must extend beyond modification of the patient's intrapsychic environment to include modification of the patient's extrapsychic environment. Although Minuchin's formulations [1] derive from his work with children with psychosomatic illnesses, his concepts and applications of the open systems model reflect this orientation, and have particular relevance for the management of adverse responses to adult chronic disease that arise from the intrafamilial environment.

Viewed within the framework of the open systems model, psychological management can be aimed at the patient, the family, the feedback processes inherent in the family's transactional patterns—or all three. Minuchin sees as the goal of psychological intervention the minimization of the pathogenic forces within the family system, and four major pathogenic characteristics in particular: enmeshment, overprotection, rigidity, and the lack of conflict resolution. Modification of the patient's intrafamilial environment can be enhanced by the doctor's awareness of the parameters of the family's optimal adaptation to a sick member, delineated by Beallor [21] as follows:

1. The ability of the family to accept the fact that the patient may regress physically and mentally as a consequence of his illness.
2. Their ability to help him ward off the stresses evoked by his illness.
3. Their ability to tolerate the patient's expression of his fears and feelings, e.g., that he is going to die, that he will never be the man he once was, that he will never recover, etc.
4. Their ability to enlist the patient's basic trust, i.e., his confidence that they will not abandon him, and at the same time to support his efforts to function as autonomously as possible.
5. Their ability to mobilize outside support on behalf of the patient when necessary.

Perhaps the physician's most important task in educating the family with respect to their role in the management of the chronically ill patient is to correct any misconceptions they may have with regard to the patient's physical and mental capacities. A chronically ill, bedridden woman does not necessarily have to relinquish her premorbid family role. She can still supervise her children's activities and run her household, albeit in a supervisory capacity, but the family must support her in these pursuits. By the same token, the family—acting on information received from the doctor—would abstain from criticism, explicit or implicit, of the patient who in fact is incapable of resuming her former roles.

The extent to which the family is able to adapt to role change and reallocation may be a potent factor in the prevention of the patient's social and psychological withdrawal—and ultimately of the feelings of "helplessness-hopelessness," "giving in-giving up," which frequently initiate chronic illness, and may at times exacerbate it once it has been established. More specifically, based on his knowledge of the patient's physical status, the physician can inform the family when the patient's dependent-passive stance is physiologically essential. The family can then reduce the conflict inherent in this stance, and thereby reduce the patient's potential for assuming a pseudo-independent hyperactive stance which may be life-threatening. When regression in the service of adaptation is either excessive or insufficient, the family may have the capacity to facilitate the necessary modifications in the patient's behavior.

At other times, the physician's task may be to convince a family in conflict that the patient should not be maintained at home, that therapy might be effected more easily in a professional milieu. And this may pose an even more difficult problem, particularly when family members are so involved with each other that they cannot step back to judge a situation objectively, or take appropriate action because the mere contemplation of such action gives rise to overwhelming feelings of guilt.

> Mr. A., a 47-year-old man, lived with his wife and three young children, to whom he was devoted. He prided himself on the fact that he was a good son, a good husband, and a good father; therefore, when his own father suffered a stroke, he automatically offered to assume the responsibility for his posthospitalization care.
>
> Mr. A.'s father presented difficult nursing problems: He was incontinent, his speech was badly impaired, and he could not feed himself easily. The major burden for his case fell to Mrs. A., who, on the one hand, liked and admired her father-in-law, and, on the other, was infuriated with her husband for putting her in this predicament. Mr. A.'s conflict was even more intense. He had strong positive feelings for his father but empathized with his wife. As time went on, and the patient did not improve, the A.'s marriage became increasingly strained, and even the children began to resent the presence of their grandfather.

Both Mr. and Mrs. A. realized, of course, that the sensible thing to do was to place Mr. A.'s father in an institution. They weren't able to take this step, however, until it was specifically recommended by the primary care physician. In a sense, his recommendation legitimized their wish.

At times, particularly during the initial stage of a chronic illness, the fantasies that surround it—in both the patient and his family—may be more devastating than the effects of the illness itself. Under these circumstances impulsive decisions can be made and actions initiated that may have dire and irrevocable consequences.

> When Mr. C.'s illness was diagnosed as multiple sclerosis, the first thing he did was read all the professional literature available to him on that disease. He then informed his wife, who was expecting their first baby in three months, that he wanted a divorce.
>
> Mr. C. was also convinced that his illness would ultimately interfere with his life-long ambition—to practice medicine. And he had another concern: He was sure that because of his illness, and his consequent inability to practice medicine, he would incur the disapproval of his parents, who "expected great things" of him. These concerns weighed so heavily on Mr. C. that he thought of committing suicide, which he felt was preferable to waiting for the disease to cripple and blind him.

The primary care physician was aware of Mr. C.'s anxieties, and was able to share these with his family. In the course of his discussions with them, he discovered that the patient's wife and his parents shared many of Mr. C.'s misconceptions about his disease. Mrs. C. was certain that her husband would be blind, incontinent—a helpless cripple—before the year was out. If she stayed married to him, she would be taking care of two babies. His extremely religious parents felt that he must have done something wrong to get such a terrible disease. And, on another level, they too felt that his life was over; he would not be able to study medicine, he would not, in fact, be able to pursue any vocation. Once the physician had corrected these misconceptions, he was able to help the family to make a concerted effort to alleviate the patient's stress. Mr. C.'s wife assured him that she wanted their marriage to continue, and added that she felt he was overreacting to his diagnosis. His mother and father made him feel that their love and approval was not contingent on his choice of profession or the state of his health. And they too, somehow, made him feel that his reaction was extreme and inappropriate.

The family can perform a particularly vital function in regard to the management of the aged patient. All too frequently, however, strained relationships between the elderly patient and members of his family make them unavailable to the physician. When a relationship with an adult child is all that remains to the elderly patient, it is difficult for him to tolerate the ambivalence that is frequently a component of such relationships. And this, in turn, imposes a burden upon the child. The patient's preoccupation with self—his constant complaints of fatigue, vague aches and pains, or physical limitations—may alienate even the most devoted members of his family, who take such complaints at face value and interpret his behavior as an expression of the patient's desire to be left alone. So, in effect, the aged individual extrudes his family from his life.

THE PHYSICIAN'S RESPONSE TO THE FAMILY

The family's ambivalence toward the patient may be intensified by the physician's attitude. The physician may, for example, resent sharing information with regard to the patient with family members. He may be reluctant to encourage them to participate in the patient's care to the family. Or he may resort to coercion as a means of informing the family of its "duty" to a sick member. If the family is made to feel guilty, if the physician's recommendations do not take their own needs and capacities, as well as those of his patient into account, he will heighten their ambivalence. If he is a strong proponent of family involvement, he may be so hostile toward the family who does not actively participate in the care of his patient, that he makes no attempt to understand the roots of their indifference or attempt to alter their attitude. And, of course, his anger with the family who unintentionally sabotages his treatment plan may be so extreme as to discourage them from any further attempt at participation in the patient's care. Each of these responses—the physician's explicit or implicit disapproval of the family, his reluctance to elicit their cooperation, or his use of coercion to that end—may militate against the implementation of an effective treatment plan.

The physician's maladaptive response to the patient's family may be circumvented, to some extent, by a review of the genogram of his own family.[22] Just as a genogram of the patient's family can highlight potentially pathological attitudes, patterns, and processes, a genogram of the doctor's family can enable him to gain the necessary emotional distance from his expectations of how family members ought to respond to medical crises. To a large extent, these expectations are based, of course, on his own family's medical history, their typical reactions to medical illness, and, in general, their modes of relating.

> Dr. V. had been a great favorite of his widowed grandfather, and he had felt especially close to the old man who spent long hours telling him stories about his own youth, his rise to success, and even about the inexorable changes, losses, and disappointments that had con-

> fronted him in his later years. This fondness for older people extended to his medical practice as well, so that when Mrs. T. told him she was unwilling to have her father live with her, he was visibly annoyed. In fact, Dr. V. was annoyed to the degree that he didn't hear Mrs. T.'s explanation for her inability to accommodate her father: Her apartment had only one bedroom, and the fact that she had two small children who kept her busy would not allow her to provide him with the nursing care he required.

Perhaps if Dr. V. had not been biased toward old people, and suspicious of their "neglectful" children, he might have felt that a nursing home was the most favorable solution to his patient's problem. Instead, he made Mrs. T. feel guilty, and this increased her negative feelings toward her father.

REFERENCES

1. Minuchin S: Families and Family Therapy. Cambridge, Harvard University Press, 1974
2. Schmale AH: Relation of separation and depression to disease. I. A report on a hospitalized medical population. Psychosom Med 20:259, 1958
3. Holmes TH, Rahe RH: The social readjustment rating scale. J Psychosom Res II: 213, 1967
4. Meissner WW: Family dynamics and psychosomatic processes. Fam Proc 5:142, 1966
5. Jackson DD: Family practice. A comprehensive medical approach. Compr Psychiatry 7:338, 1966
6. Holmes TH: Presentation at the University of West Virginia, Charleston Division, April 2, 1977
7. Livsey CG: Physical illness and family dynamics. In Lipowski ZJ (ed): Psychological Aspects of Physical Illness. Basel, Karger, 1972, p 237
8. Hackett TP, Cassen NH: Factors contributing to delay in responding to the signs and symptoms of acute myocardial infarction. Am J Cardiol 24:651, 1969
9. McCord W, McCord J, Verdin, P: Familial correlates of psychosomatic symptoms in male children. J Hlth Hum Behav 1:192, 1960
10. Greene WA, Moss AJ, Goldstein S: Delay, denial and death in coronary heart disease. In Eliot RS (ed): Stress and the Heart. New York, Futura, 1974
11. Shindell S, Salloway JC, Oberembt CH: A Coursebook in Health Care Delivery. New York, Appleton, 1976, p 33
12. Moulton R: Some effects of the new feminism. Am J Psychiatry 134:1, 1977
13. Erickson E: Childhood and Society. New York, Norton, 1950
14. Hinkle LE, Jr.: Presentation at Montefiore Hospital and Medical Center, 1972

15. Hinkle LE, Jr.: Motivations of the individuals who took part in the uprising. Second seminar on the Hungarian Revolution of October 1956. New York, Society for the Investigation of Human Ecology, 1958
16. Hinkle LE, Jr., Christenson WN, Kane FD, et al: An investigation of the relationships between life experience, personality characteristics, and general susceptibility to illness. Psychosom Med 20:278, 1958
17. Singer MT: Presidential Address. Engagement–Involvement: A central phenomenon in psychophysiological research. Psychosom Med 36:1, 1974
18. Knapp PH: Acute bronchial asthma in the asthmatic child. In Schneer HI (ed): The Asthmatic Child. New York, Hoeber, 1963
19. Powell GF, Brasel JA, Raiti S, Blizzard RM: Emotional deprivation and growth retardation simulating idiopathic hypopituitarism. N Engl J Med 276:1279, 1967
20. Ferber A, Mendelsohn M, Napier A (eds): The Book of Family Therapy. New York, Science House, 1972
21. Strain JJ, Beallor G: The liaison model as a viable alternative to consultation and referral methods. (In preparation)
22. Guieri P, Fogarty T: Study your own family. In Ferber A, Mendelsohn M, Napier A (eds): The Book of Family Therapy. New York, Science House, 1972, p 445

Part III

Extensions of the Model of Psychological Medicine

Chapter 10

The Future of Psychological Medicine

There is a growing awareness among physicians that a critical ingredient of medical treatment is psychological care. The question remains, however, as to who should administer such care, how it should be administered, and which patients are "eligible" for psychological intervention. The material presented thus far may give rise to serious misunderstanding on this score: We may have created the impression that the future of psychological medicine rests with the primary care physician, the internist, the physician in family practice, etc. It would be a major error if our book conveyed this message. For, in fact, the provision of psychological care cannot be limited to physicians who engage in a particular type of medical practice, or to a particular patient population; nor can it be limited to a particular medical setting.

Many medical patients are cared for by specialists; many patients will require treatment in an inpatient acute illness setting and/or a tertiary care setting at some point in their lives. Furthermore, in these settings psychological care should, in our opinion, be administered by every member of the health care team, all of whom can make an important contribution to, or undermine the patient's psychological well-being. Thus unless medical practice is restructured *throughout* medicine to accommodate psychological as well as physiological principles, patient care will still fall far short of the ideal. Because the implementation of a model of psychological medicine in an inpatient and/or tertiary care unit requires some basic knowledge of the organization and structure of these settings, we now proceed within a different frame of reference. If only by implication, we are saying that the adoption of a psychological approach to medical care depends not only on the predilection of the individual physician, but also, to a large extent, on the philosophy and organization of every sector of the teaching hospital, for that is where the future of psychological medicine ultimately rests.

The fact is that patients in the acute inhospital setting and the tertiary care unit often have the greatest need for psychological understanding. Yet such understanding may not be available to them from the staff of either the hospital ward or the tertiary care unit. For despite the consensus that exists as to the validity of the bio-psychosocial theory of disease, this approach has not yet been sufficiently incorporated into the fabric of patient care in the contemporary teaching hospital in either its inpatient or its technologically-oriented ambulatory facilities.

Several pioneer programs have been developed to foster such an approach to medical care in the institution-based setting. Ham and his colleagues were instrumental in the development of a medical training program designed to foster holistic ideals at Case Western Reserve University. Engel,[1] Romano,[2] and Bibring and Kahana,[3] have all made notable efforts to provide medical students, residents, fellows, and attendings with a core knowledge of human behavior that would enhance their awareness of the psychological needs of their patients. Ross and Levine [4] attempted to train internists to view and understand the patient as an integral unit. The development of other programs which seek to bring the bio-psycho-social model into focus as a standard of medical practice is currently in progress under the aegis of workers in social medicine, family practice, community medicine, and behavioral medicine at almost every major medical teaching center in this country.

In the two chapters that follow we shall report on specific attempts to integrate psychosocial and physical care in an inpatient teaching hospital setting and in technologically-oriented tertiary care settings. Chapter 11 is an account of an effort to incorporate psychological concepts into medical care on the in-patient service at a particular hospital, Montefiore Hospital and Medical Center. In Chapter 12 we report on experiments in two technologically-oriented ambulatory tertiary care centers which have a similar goal. In the first instance we have drawn, once again, on our experience at Montefiore. The second experiment reported in Chapter 12 was conducted in Switzerland, and is of special interest in the context of this book because its central aim was to integrate the primary care physician into the protocols of the tertiary care setting, so that he could continue to offer his patient psychological as well as physical care. Once the primary care physician was provided with the knowledge essential to the monitoring of the tertiary care center therapeutic protocols, he was able to incorporate tertiary care knowledge into his decentralized primary care practice.

As mentioned above, we are well aware of the potential effectiveness of other members of the health care team in respect to the psychological well-being of the patient. Many programs, including those described in the ensuing chapters, currently provide for the psychological training of medical and nursing personnel. Provided he is able to establish a liaison with the house staff on the inpatient service, the primary care physician can provide the staff with information regarding his patient's psychosocial status that they would not otherwise be privy to. In the tertiary care unit, in some instances, the primary care physician can participate actively in the care of his patient; in others, he can enhance the knowledge of the specialist and health care workers who attend his patient's psychosocial needs. Thus, insofar as he is able to foster a psychosocial orientation, the intervention of the primary care physician in these settings can indirectly benefit those patients who do not have their own primary care physician. He cannot solve their dilemma completely, however. The issues the psychosocial management of this patient group raises sustain our interest in the psychological training of medical and nursing personnel, and heighten our conviction that optimal medical care requires the application of psychological principles at every level of medical practice. Yet, in keeping with our orientation throughout this book, the physician remains our protagonist.

REFERENCES

1. Engel G: Psychological Development in Health and Disease. Philadelphia, Saunders, 1962
2. Romano J: Teaching of psychiatry to medical students. Lancet 2:93, 1961
3. Bibring G, Kahana R: Lectures in Medical Psychology. New York, International Universities Press, 1968
4. Ross WD, Levine M: Training in psychosomatic medicine. In Deutsch F (ed): Advances in Psychosomatic Medicine, Vol. 4. New York, Hafner, 1964, pp 14–22

Chapter 11

The Application of Psychological Concepts in the Hospital–Inpatient Setting

James J. Strain and David Hamerman

Inpatient hospital facilities are utilized, to a growing extent, for the acutely ill who must be monitored constantly, for those patients who require complex surgical procedures, and/or for those patients who require extensive diagnostic workups. Thus, in recent years, the general hospital has taken on the characteristics of an intensive care unit, where, typically, the focus is primarily—and often exclusively—on physiological aspects of patient care.

The primary care physician will continue to maintain contact with his hospitalized patient, of course; but for the most part that patient will be cared for by the hospital staff, and, in particular, by the resident. In the contemporary teaching hospital, bureaucratized systems of patient care and house staff rotations on the inpatient service, understandably limit the resident's opportunities to relate to the patient as an individual. Patients rotate as well. It is not uncommon for a patient who is admitted to the hospital for chest pain to be transferred three, four, or even five times in the course of his hospital stay.

> Mr. T. was admitted from the emergency room to a medical ward for chest pain and questionable EKG abnormalities. Twenty-four hours later, he was transferred to the coronary care unit with an evolving myocardial infarction. After three days in the coronary care unit, he

This chapter is an amended version of a paper entitled: "Medical-Psychiatric Teaching Rounds (Ombudsman Rounds)," tentatively scheduled for publication in the *Annals of Internal Medicine,* April 1978.

was moved to the intermediate coronary care unit, for close but less intensive observation. Four days later, he was transferred back to a medical ward, but not the one to which he had been admitted. One week later, the patient had stabilized. Accordingly, he was transferred, for the fifth time, to the self-care rehabilitation unit in preparation for discharge.

The fact that Mr. T. was transferred to five different settings in the course of his hospital stay meant he was cared for by as many residents and interns—none of whom might have had an opportunity to provide him with psychological support, which is a product of ongoing and insightful medical care.*

The effects of staff and patient rotation may be just as pernicious for the resident. During his brief contact with a given patient, the resident has only limited opportunities to gain an awareness of that patient's psychological responses to his medical illness (and of the possible psychological precipitants of his illness); as a result, his interest in the psychological components of medical care will inevitably wane.[1] This tendency will be reinforced by the perception of the "teaching" medical patient as one who has been hospitalized for an acute identifiable, reversible, medical dysfunction. The resident's attitude is strengthened by the attending physician, who attaches major importance to his ability to diagnose and treat such patients successfully, for he himself is most skilled in the diagnosis and treatment of interesting, "difficult" cases. Such cases are a source of satisfaction because they give him an opportunity to discourse on the biological aspects of medical illness, and because many of the problems presented are reversible. Ordinarily, the most prestigious faculty conduct medical attending rounds on the inpatient services. Paradoxically, however, this prestigious role model may not be primarily involved in direct and continuing patient care and may not have the time, background, or experience for encouraging exploration of the psychosocial factors that also preoccupy the medically ill patient.

This description of the acute inpatient service in the contemporary teaching hospital points up the formidable impediments to the incorporation of psychological medicine in such a setting. However, despite these impediments, the need exists to alter current patterns and to develop a more comprehensive approach to patient care. The medical psychiatric teaching rounds described below evolved as a consequence of these considerations.

* Cases such as this one strengthen the misconception that technological care and psychological medicine are antithetical concepts. Inasmuch as the technological care Mr. T. received prolonged and may have even saved his life, he was provided with the most humane care available.

THE INFUSION OF PSYCHOLOGICAL PRINCIPLES ON THE ACUTE INPATIENT SERVICE: OMBUDSMAN (MEDICAL-PSYCHIATRIC) ROUNDS

The distinction drawn between physiological and psychological concepts in the approach to patient care begins early in medical school,[2] * and is continued in postgraduate clinical training programs.[8] Thus, for example, mind-body dualism is perpetuated in the contemporary teaching hospital, where psychological and social problems are typically assigned to the psychiatrist and social worker, respectively (in the standard consultation and referral models), while the medical staff remains preoccupied with pathophysiological issues.

The Chairman of the Department of Medicine and the Director of Liaison Psychiatry † at a particular teaching hospital (Montefiore Hospital and Medical Center), decided to undertake a joint effort to make psychological and social issues an integral part of clinical training by instituting psychiatric–medical teaching rounds, which we have termed "ombudsman rounds."

The ombudsman program was initially established at Montefiore separate and distinct from liaison psychiatry teaching rounds in response to the request by the house staff for additional help and support in resolving intrastaff disputes and clinical problems. In addition, an attempt was made to insure continuing communication among the house staff, nursing staff, social workers, and psychiatrists on the medical wards.

The liaison psychiatry teaching program offered weekly conferences for house staff and nurses on each of the medical wards to enhance their psychosocial orientation. However, because attendance at these conferences was not mandatory, they had relatively little impact. An obvious solution was to combine the ombudsman and liaison psychiatry rounds. The objectives of the ombudsman rounds were then expanded to include the exploration of psychosocial problems in individual patients, as well as medical issues and staff interactions. Patient interviews and staff interchange provided the ward staff with a dynamic understanding of the mechanisms underlying the fears, anxieties, and hostility expressed by the patient to the staff, and by the staff to the patient. Ombudsman rounds also enabled ward staff members to go beyond the

* Many medical schools are presently addressing this problem by placing greater emphasis on the teaching of psychological and social issues.[3–7]

† Liaison psychiatry is a subspecialty of psychiatry that has as its primary goal the dissemination of knowledge, skills, and attitudes regarding the psychology of the medically ill to the medical staff and other health care workers.

routine aspects of patient care, and to deal with their feelings and values regarding their patients. The rounds on each medical ward were conducted under the aegis of a medical attending (ombudsman) and liaison psychiatrist.

Characteristics of the Ombudsman and Liaison Psychiatrist

The six medical attendings who serve as ombudsmen represent a broad spectrum: senior and junior staff members, those with inpatient and outpatient responsibilities, specialists and primary care physicians, and full time and voluntary attendings. The ombudsmen are asked to assume a responsibility for which there are no specific guidelines or formal training, and one radically different from their accustomed role as ward attending. They are required to co-chair a discussion of the interrelationship between psychosocial and physical factors in the patient, on the one hand, and of the existence of conflicts that may be inherent in certain staff attitudes on the other. They must deal with the apparent indifference toward their efforts of some staff members, who may be reluctant to participate and will have to be "rounded up." The ombudsmen also need to develop a close interpersonal working relationship with the liaison psychiatrists with whom they continually interact before, during, and after the conferences. Ideally, in time, they will provide much of the psychosocial explanations themselves, with the liaison psychiatrist acting as a resource person.

Ultimately, each ombudsman develops a unique style in the conduct of his or her rounds. Although it is difficult to generalize about the personality characteristics that promote proficiency in fulfilling the role of ombudsman, some of the qualities that enhance their capacities include an ability to be empathetic with patients and staff, an appreciation of the importance of psychosocial issues in medical care, a willingness to identify and understand house staff problems, an interest in ward routine, leadership skills to mobilize staff members to form a cohesive team, and competence in the practice of medicine.

To be effective, the liaison psychiatrist must see himself as a colleague on the medical ward, rather than as an occasional consultant. Paul Kaufman[9] has observed that

> . . . frequently, the psychiatrist must pass through a kind of test, to see if he still is really a doctor and thus a colleague; and this involves more than simply demonstrating factual knowledge—

> the willingness to pitch in and assume responsibility is more important. However, demonstrating the possession of an adequate medical background and the ability to recognize gaps in one's current usable information is often a vital first hurdle to be passed in developing a useful relationship with the house staff.

The liaison psychiatrist also needs to demonstrate clearly that his psychological formulations follow from the actual clinical material. Discursive, ambiguous, inconclusive patient evaluations, for which psychiatrists have a well-known penchant, generate hostility on a busy acute medical ward, where internists have a penchant for precise, concrete, conclusive diagnosis and treatment protocols. The liaison psychiatrist's capacity to fulfill these functions will be enhanced if he possesses the following characteristics:

Self-esteem. The ability of the liaison psychiatrist to confront and resolve complex problems that challenge his capacities must be a major source of satisfaction, rather than the instant approval of his colleagues. If his sense of self-esteem is not regulated internally, the psychiatrist is vulnerable to two types of dysfunctional reactions: anger and/or depression. He may then be tempted to withdraw or to be too aggressive and critical.

Activity. The ability of the liaison psychiatrist to maintain an active stance is a second determinant of his proficiency. The liaison psychiatrist is constantly under pressure to give opinions, make decisions, and solve problems, all of which may be crucial to his ability to maintain an alliance with the medical staff. But he must, at the same time, be sufficiently passive to be able to listen. The liaison psychiatrist should not react with fear or avoidance in highly charged situations in which he is challenged by the staff, nor should he be afraid to elicit affects in patients or staff when necessary.

Independence. The liaison psychiatrist must be able to think and synthesize creatively "on his feet." If he is to convince the medical staff that he has something meaningful to offer, he must be able to make independent judgments, take independent action—and to accept the consequences of his interventions. On the other hand, he must also be able to tolerate dependence in the medical staff members as he attempts to help them become more autonomous in their efforts aimed at psychological support of their patients.

The Organization and Structure of the Ombudsman Rounds

Ombudsman rounds consist of two distinct phases—the pre-ombudsman meeting and the ombudsman rounds, per se.

The Pre-Ombudsman Meeting

The ombudsman, head nurse, liaison psychiatrist, the medical residents, and the social worker meet a day or two prior to the weekly ombudsman rounds for several purposes.

1. To review the ward routine and functioning during the previous week; to discuss certain administrative issues, e.g., the institution of a new nursing procedure, a new social service form, use of the psychiatric outpatient department, etc.
2. To evaluate interstaff relationships, e.g., house staff–nursing, social service-house staff, etc.
3. To discuss the optimal use of the forthcoming rounds.

In accordance with the basic thrust of the ombudsman program, the participants in the pre-ombudsman meeting identify and select for presentation a series of medically ill patients who highlight universal psychosocial–medical issues and/or currently present urgent management problems, such as noncompliance, character trait disturbances (excessive passivity or activity), organic mental syndromes, depression, hypochondriasis, family reactions to medical illness, the appropriate use of psychotropic medication. An informed consent is then obtained from the patient selected to join the ward staff at ombudsman rounds to discuss his reactions to illness and hospitalization. In the case of the private patient, it is not enough to obtain the patient's consent to be interviewed; the private attending's permission must also be secured, and he is invited to attend and participate in the rounds.

The Ombudsman Rounds

Once a week, one hour of regularly scheduled medical attending rounds is devoted to ombudsman rounds. The personnel at this meeting include the ombudsman, house staff and medical students, the liaison psychiatrist, social worker, ward charge nurse and staff, ward monthly attending, ward secretary and unit manager, patient representatives,* and representatives of the hospital administration.

Pre-Interview Discussion. Once the group has assembled, the ombudsman and/or psychiatrist announces the name of the patient (who is not yet present) states the focus of the presentation, and invites comments from the staff regarding their perception of the patient, difficulties his care presents, and their impression of his reaction to his illness and hospitalization. The interviewer is selected from among the members of the ward staff, e.g., house staff, social worker, nurse, or psychiatrist. The group makes suggestions to the interviewer with regard to areas they would like explored.

The Interview. The patient is brought in, introduced to the group, and seated next to the interviewer. A typical greeting might be: "Good morning, Mr. M. How are you today? You remember we spoke to you about coming to this meeting, and the staff is very grateful to you for coming. We would like to ask you a few questions." At the end of the interview, the patient is asked if he would mind if other staff members asked him some questions, or if he has questions of his own for the staff. The ombudsman and the liaison psychiatrist attempt to correct the patient's misconceptions as well as answer his questions, if they can. When the interview is concluded, the patient is thanked and escorted back to his room.

Post-Interview Discussion. The ombudsman or psychiatrist begins the discussion by asking the group what their responses were to the patient. Once these have been elicited, the psychiatrist and ombudsman attempt to formulate a psychosocial–medical understanding of the patient's behavior and to synthesize a treatment plan that encompasses all aspects of his care–psychological, social, and medical. Through such understanding, they attempt to help the patient adapt to his illness and, at the same time, to help the staff adapt to the paient.

Post-Meeting Followup. We try to have one of the members of the group, i.e., a nurse, social worker, or resident, visit the patient shortly after the conclusion of the interview to learn of the patient's reactions and to deal with any problems or questions that may have emerged. Ideally, at the post-meeting followup, the staff member attempts to

* Patient representatives transmit the needs of the patient to their families, medical personnel, and hospital administrators.

assess ongoing patient behavior, further correct misconceptions, and provide psychosocial support in areas where the need for such support has become obvious from the rounds or followup. The accumulation of psychosocial data throughout the patient's hospital stay permits confirmation of the accuracy of the original psycho–social–medical formulations, and, when indicated, further refinement of the therapeutic intervention.

CLINICAL EXAMPLES

It is difficult to convey the actual tone and conduct of the ombudsman rounds by a single, abbreviated clinical example. The following three cases are representative of the spectrum of problems that might arise during these rounds. In the first two, who were staff patients, the relationship between the patient's behavior and his medical illness emerged with particular clarity, and the treatment protocol was influenced by the staff's enhanced understanding of the patient's psychosocial problems.

> Mrs. L., a 23-year-old asthmatic Puerto Rican woman, had been hospitalized for medical supervision while she was being withdrawn from steroids. Mrs. L.'s husband had abandoned her and their 4-year-old daughter; and her parents, with whom she had virtually no contact, lived in Puerto Rico.
>
> The resident, Dr. F., had requested that Mrs. L. be interviewed because she continued to demand prednisone although "she could get along without it," and because she refused all attempts to persuade her to participate in a withdrawal program. According to Dr. F., this patient equated pills with attention, and used her illness and medication to control both her environment and him. Dr. S., another resident on the ward, questioned the effectiveness of Dr. F.'s approach to the patient. He agreed that Mrs. L.'s behavior was inappropriate and difficult, but he also felt that getting angry or arguing with her was not the answer. Dr. S. felt this patient needed to be referred to a psychiatrist.
>
> When Mrs. L. was introduced at the rounds, she was asked directly by the interviewer why she couldn't "get off" her medication. To the surprise of both Dr. F. and Dr. S., the patient replied that she wanted to because the pills were making her "old and ugly," but that she was afraid she would die if she stopped taking steroids. The questioning then took on a more personal quality. Following Dr. S.'s earlier suggestion that Mrs. L. needed psychotherapy, the patient was asked about her social and emotional life, whether there was anyone she could depend on or turn to, and how she felt about herself. In her answers to these questions, Mrs. L. emerged as a lonely, frightened,

> isolated individual, who felt rejected but unconsciously invited rejection—by her parents, whose letters she would not answer; by her neighbors, whose invitations she would not return; and by her doctor, whose suggestions she would not listen to. Mrs. L. seemed determined not to allow herself to be "manipulated," even in the service of parental support, friendship, or recovery.

After the interview was concluded, there was a greater expression of empathy for Mrs. L. (at least in contrast to the irritation voiced in the pre-interview discussion). Dr. S., who had indicated his sensitivity to Mrs. L.'s distress, continued to maintain that he did not have the "skills to deal with a patient like this." Two crucial guidelines for Mrs. L.'s management emerged, however. First, the patient obviously needed to be helped to correct her misconception that she would die unless she was given prednisone on a long-term basis. Second, it seemed equally apparent that Mrs. L. might benefit from a constant relationship with a physician, who could provide the reassurance—over a period of time—that she required to be able to comply with a withdrawal program. Such a relationship would alleviate her feelings that she was alone and helpless and would reduce her dependence on prednisone—the only thing she could depend on to keep her going.

The conference also allowed a more precise explanation of Mrs. L.'s needs. Dr. F. and Dr. S. both expressed surprise at how they had misread Mrs. L.'s behavior. Dr. F. said, "I pegged her wrong; I thought she was just being difficult. She's really frightened, confused, and very alone—another side of her came through I hadn't seen." More importantly, the view of Mrs. L. that emerged at the ombudsman rounds led Dr. F. to take a different approach to his "uncooperative, manipulative" patient. Furthermore, the house staff realized that this patient's psychosocial problems, which appeared to be "deep" and insoluble initially, might actually require only minimal psychotherapeutic intervention as part of the ward treatment plan, an intervention that could be provided within the context of a continuing doctor–patient relationship.

At times, a patient presents very complex problems that can only be approached and aired in a preliminary way during the hour allocated for the rounds; such patients require extensive followup.

> Miss T., a 40-year-old diabetic woman for whom dialysis was mandatory, refused to permit insertion of a shunt because she felt she had nothing to live for. The patient's behavior—and her expressed wish to die—had generated anger and despair in the staff.

Miss T. had been diagnosed as diabetic three years earlier, and since then her condition had worsened rapidly; she had developed severe complications, including blindness, a nephrotic syndrome, and renal failure. In the course of the interview, it became clear that the major cause of Miss T.'s depression was not only her growing incapacity but her extremely close relationship with her family. Miss T. was afraid that the gravity of her illness would soon make her incapable of taking care of her parents and, indeed, would require this elderly couple to be totally responsible for her care. Actually, her parents, with whom she had lived all her life, had been responsible for her care even before she became ill. Miss T.'s response to her parents when they came to visit her confirmed her dependence on them. Parents and daughter squabbled constantly because, Miss T. complained, her parents didn't seem to be aware of the extent of her increasing incapacity. "I certainly can't do the things they think I should be able to do."

After the interview, the ombudsman observed that the patient needed someone, other than her parents, to whom she could respond and who would support her. Similar comments were made by others, but it was difficult to understand what approach to take with her negativistic and uncooperative behavior. The liaison psychiatrist further clarified the psychodynamics of Miss T.'s response. He suggested that the major cause of Miss T.'s distress could be her overwhelming fear of what would happen to her if she outlived her parents. Her irritation with her parents might then be understood as an expression of her need to be close and affectionate, and at the same time to assert her independence. The ward staff had to begin to get Miss T. to shift her involvement from her parents, who were really in no position to care for her, to someone better qualified to assume the role of caretaker, and her parents needed to allow her to do this. Perhaps if she were provided with a surrogate parent, e.g., through placement in a foster home or health-related facility, Miss T. could derive enough security from that relationship to agree to the insertion of a shunt and dialysis which could then prolong her life even beyond that of her parents.

In the final example, the staff's reactions to a patient's severe illness and prolonged hospitalization, and the conflicts that may be inherent in the staff's relationship with the patient's private attending were examined.

Mr. N., an elderly man, had undergone radical surgery the previous year for the removal of a nasopharyngeal carcinoma, which required an indwelling tracheostomy. Following surgery, he had developed a series of complications, including a myocardial infarction, a urinary tract infection, candida meningitis, and bone marrow suppression secondary to therapy. The patient was now totally withdrawn, depressed, and had developed contractures and bedsores. He was not brought in for the interview.

The intern who presented the patient, by her own admission, had "reached the end of her rope." Dr. D. expressed the enormous sense of futility the staff felt in its efforts to keep this patient alive. She pointed out that the patient was a "mass of sores," had no veins, and had recently been given a transfusion through an apparent vein in the finger. "Every time I go into the room, I hate it, and I feel that his face is like a Jesus looking at me and hating me for what I am doing to him." She felt guilty, depressed, and exhausted, looked for support, and did not know whom to turn to. Dr. D. perceived her interaction with the patient's private primary care physician as unfavorable. She considered him authoritarian and arbitrary, and resented his insistence that she continue drug therapy without giving her an opportunity to share with him her grave misgivings about what she was doing to the patient.

To further complicate the problem, the social worker pointed out that as a result of the delay in obtaining a Medicaid number for the patient, his transfer to a chronic care facility was being held up. His transfer was also being delayed by his primary care physician, Dr. Y., who did not feel Mr. N. should be transferred from an acute treatment setting while he will still salvageable. Dr. Y. pressed his point with vigor: This patient had remarkable physical resilience; he had pulled out of one crisis after another when the house staff had written him off, and there was a good chance that he would pull out of this crisis too. At this point, the ombudsman reassured the primary care physician that no precipitous action would be taken with regard to his patient. He then turned to the intern, who had somehow faded into the background, and commented (with obvious feeling): "We really need to give you interns more help in dealing with the enormous problems treating the dying, the elderly, and the chronically ill present."

This vignette illustrates another aspect of ombudsman rounds. It provides staff members with an opportunity to express, in a personal way, conscious feelings that arise in the course of patient care and which markedly influence their capacity to deal with their patients and with their colleagues. (In addition, a staff member's unconscious response to a patient may emerge in the course of the ombudsman rounds, and, in that event, the psychiatrist is provided with an opportunity to help him cope with this response and thereby achieve optimal adaptation to his patient.)

DISCUSSION

Given the limitations inherent in the acute medical ward setting for such teaching, it is our conviction that ombudsman rounds serve a function even if they only heighten the staff's awareness of those psychosocial factors that predispose, initiate, and perpetuate disease, as well as the psychosocial reactions that are typically evoked by illness and hospitalization. The staff's interaction during and after the patient interview creates a climate of interest in these factors. The liaison psychiatrist provides a synthesis of the psychosocial data that facilitates an interpretation of the patient's behavior.

The ombudsman rounds also provides a forum for discussion of the feelings that arise within the house staff regarding such personal and professional issues as deciding whether a patient should be resuscitated in the event of a cardiac arrest, how the disoriented elderly can best be cared for, whether the use of heroic measures is indicated in terminal disease, how to deal with the noncompliant patient, and how to cope with one's inability to arrive at a diagnosis. These issues have the greatest clinical relevance, but are seldom confronted in the course of traditional medical training. Such issues do not lend themselves to formal didactic presentation; they are too far-reaching, and, as opposed to didactic material, do not fit into a theoretical framework, and cannot be taught by routine methods. In short, ombudsman rounds create a setting in which anxieties, conflicts, and stresses in patients, as well as in their doctors, can be examined—where the approach to medical care is enhanced by moving beyond physiological content to an awareness of the psychological needs of the patient and his doctor.

It is difficult to judge how successful ombudsman rounds have been. One such attempt, a preliminary study to assess the impact of the ombudsman program on staff attitudes, was conducted recently.* Specifically, we sought to determine the group's responses to the program, and to identify their expectations. In addition, we wanted to determine how learning in a group situation, such as ombudsman rounds, is af-

* This study was done under the direction of Marilyn Margon, Coordinator of Educational Development for the Residency Program in Social Medicine at Montefiore Hospital and Medical Center.

fected by the group's composition and the "student's" position in that group.

To this end, a questionnaire was developed and presented to most of the house staff by the Chairman of Medicine at a meeting, thereby insuring its prompt return. The questionnaire was also distributed to nurses, social workers, unit secretaries and managers, and patient representatives. All members of the health care team were told that the purpose of the questionnaire was to assess their perception of the effectiveness of the ombudsman-psychiatry teaching rounds.

Many of the respondents felt that the program offered a unique opportunity with regard to medical and nursing education and hospital teamwork. Specifically, the responses of house staff and nurses were assessed in regard to four main issues: sensitivity to psychosocial aspects of patient care, staff cooperation, inter-staff communication, and individual impressions of the value of these meetings (Table 1). Nurses, as a group, were most positive about the influence of the rounds. But on the whole, the house staff also expressed positive attitudes to the four issues evaluated. Indeed, the house staff and nursing staff were far more receptive than anticipated to psychosocial concepts, especially given the many impediments, mentioned earlier, to their routine inclusion in the acute inhospital teaching and medical care processes. And, as a matter of fact, over 60 percent of the interns, first-year residents, and nurses reported that the ombudsman meetings had favorably affected their level of job satisfaction and/or their job performance. The four social workers and three patient representatives canvassed were unanimous in their approval of the program. Only the second-year residents (who were least involved in the rounds) were relatively unenthusiastic about the program's achievements.

In response to open-ended questions included in the questionnaire eliciting recommendations for future program development, it was suggested that the organization and structure of the ward be altered to facilitate routine followup and reinforcement on cases and topics discussed at rounds, and that the purpose of each meeting be stated with greater clarity before rounds. Admittedly, there were several limitations to the design of this study. First, since the questionnaires were anonymous, it was impossible to follow up on those staff members who did not respond. Second, the use of a structured interview rather than a questionnaire would have increased, refined, and enhanced the data collected. But, at the very least, the survival of this program over the past three years has established it as a "traditional" conference which the staff attend with the same regularity as they do more conventional medical grand rounds or chief of service rounds. Furthermore, the

TABLE 1
Assessment of Staff Attitudes Toward Medical - Psychiatric Teaching Rounds (Ombudsman Rounds)

	PGY–1 (N = 19)	PGY–2 (N = 28)	PGY–3 (N = 13)	Nurses (N = 38)
I. Sensitized Me to Psychosocial Aspects of Medical Care				
Yes	57% (11)	43% (12)	23% (3)	81% (30)
No effect	43% (8)	57% (16)	77% (10)	19% (7)
II. Cooperation among Staff				
Encourages	57% (11)	50% (14)	46% (6)	76% (29)
Discourages	0	0	0	0
No effect	43% (8)	50% (14)	54% (7)	24% (9)
III. Communication between House staff and Other Ward Staff				
Improved	63% (12)	50% (14)	38% (5)	73% (27)
Not affected	37% (7)	50% (14)	62% (8)	27% (10)
Weakened	0	0	0	0
IV. Value of Ombudsman Meetings				
Very valuable	6% (1)	4% (1)	7% (1)	13% (5)
Valuable/some value	68% (13)	60% (17)	46% (5)	76% (29)
Not valuable	26% (5)	36% (10)	46% (6)	10% (4)

majority of interns and residents have demonstrated enhanced skill in interviewing and in analyzing patient responses. Some persist, however, in their view of these rounds as potentially "damaging" to patients, or intrusive, "solely for teaching purposes." The elicitation of sexual material by the psychiatrist, when the need for such data is indicated, is most often the spark that ignites house staff indignation. When the interview elicits profound emotion—e.g., when the patient cries or expresses despair over a serious or fatal illness, aging, or an intolerable life situation—the house staff may protest that the patient is being unnecessarily "exposed." We attempt to deal with the staff's resistance to probing the patient's intense feeling states on another level. We discuss with them their unrealistic fears that they will "hurt" the patient, or that the patient (or they themselves) will be hopelessly overwhelmed by such feelings. At the same time, the ombudsman and liaison psychiatrist need to impress upon the house staff the necessity for such action if their patient is to be understood—and helped. By and large, post-round interviews conducted by the house staff confirm the value of these "painful" psychological interviews. The staff cannot fail to be impressed by the frequency with which patients express their gratitude for giving them an opportunity to talk about what is really bothering them.

Ombudsman rounds provide a designated time and place where compassion can be expressed and experienced on the part of the staff toward the patient, and toward each other. Indeed, we have observed that those conferences which appear to have moved the staff to its most positive expression are those where the staff has been deeply affected by its interaction with the patient. Thus, we view these rounds as a vehicle for reducing the intellectualization of psychosocial issues, and for the elimination of still another "dichotomy," identified by Engel between the "technician-physician" and the "compassionate physician."[10] If medical schools plant the seeds of mind-body dualism and post-graduate clinical training perpetuates this orientation, then the ombudsman rounds are an essential mechanism to offset these influences, which can "nurture humaneness" and simultaneously provide "systematic attention to the scientific disciplines of human behavior in health and disease."[10] We have concluded on the basis of these considerations that . . . exposure to the ombudsman rounds provides an invaluable teaching experience for the future physician.

Ombudsman rounds promote psychosocial–medical interviewing, evaluation, diagnosis, and the management of the medically ill under the tutelage of a medical attending, on medicine's time, with the liaison psychiatrist serving as a resource behavioral scientist. Thus, in a very real sense, this program provides a forum on an acute medical ward within an academic department of medicine for a "new medical model—the bio-psycho-social model" which more adequately addresses the needs of the medically ill.[11]

REFERENCES

1. Strain JJ, Grossman S: The precepts of liaison psychiatry; Building the alliance. In Strain JJ, Grossman S (eds): Psychological Care of the Medically Ill: A Primer in Liaison Psychiatry. New York, Appleton, 1975, pp 3, 184
2. Engel GL: Enduring attributes of medicine relevant for the education of the physician. Ann Intern Med 78:587, 1973
3. Bruhn, JG, Naughton J: Effect of a course in internal medicine on the attitudes of first-year medical students. J Med Educ 44:504, 1969
4. Gorell AH, Stoeckle JD, Lazare A: Teaching the clinical interview: An experiment with first-year students. J Med Educ 49:957, 1974
5. Rezler AG: Attitude changes during medical school. A review of the literature. J Med Educ 49:1023, 1974

6. Cluff LE: New settings for medical education. Pharos 38:2, 1975
7. Engel GL: The education of the physician for clinical observation. J Nerv Ment Dis 154:159, 1972
8. Honig PJ, Liebman R, Malone C, Koch DR, Kaplan S: Pediatric-psychiatric liaison as a model for teaching pediatric residents. J Med Educ 51:929, 1976
9. Kaufman P: Consultation services. International Psych Clin 3:123, 1966
10. Engel GL: Care and feeding of the medical student: The foundation for professional competence. JAMA 215:1135, 1971
11. Engel GL: The need for a new medical model: A challenge for biomedicine. Science 196:129, 1977

Chapter 12

The Implementation of Primary Care Concepts in the Technologically-Oriented Ambulatory Setting

Most physicians will concede that the incorporation of the bio-psycho-social model into patient care as provided on the acute medical ward of a teaching hospital represents no small achievement. As we have seen, the obstacles to the practice of holistic medicine in this setting are formidable. The integration of psychological medicine into patient services provided in a technologically-oriented setting may be even more difficult. The participation of the primary care physician will, of course, benefit the patient in this regard; unfortunately this is not always feasible. Another group of patients—who are in the majority—are deprived of psychological care simply because they do not have a primary care physician. With respect to the latter group, efforts need to be made to foster the specialist's awareness of the psychosocial stresses evoked not only by the patient's chronic illness, but by his treatment. Efforts need to be made, in short, to increase the psychological competence of the nephrologist, oncologist, cardiologist—the specialists who administer such settings and are responsible for staff attitudes toward these patients.

Two pilot projects representative of each of these approaches are described in this chapter. Following a brief account of background material, we begin with a discussion of the means by which the psycho-social knowledge of the administrators of the technologically-oriented clinic can be heightened and channeled. We proceed then to a discussion of the ways in which the primary care physician's participation in his patient's treatment at this phase of his illness can be enhanced.

OVERVIEW

The Patient Population

We have selected for discussion two groups of patients who must be seen in technologically-oriented clinics: renal dialysis patients who may be machine-dependent for the rest of their lives, and cancer patients who require time-limited cobalt bomb treatments. Patients in both these groups are under tremendous stress and are among those populations who are most in need of a supportive relationship with their doctor, based on his understanding of their psychological status. The technologically-oriented clinic offers major "advantages" in terms of patient care; but the provision of adequate psychological services is not among them.

The Treatment Setting

In contrast to the inpatient hospital setting, the ambulatory clinic setting appears, at first glance, to present certain features that are conducive to the practice of psychological medicine: The attending physician assigned to a technologically-oriented ambulatory clinic is not usually rotated to other clinic settings; he is permanently assigned to the unit. Nor do patients rotate from service to service, from clinic to clinic, from doctor to doctor. However, despite the physician's extended tour of duty and the long-term "availability" of his patient (ranging from several weeks to a lifetime), the attending physician has only a minimal involvement in the patient's routine treatment—on both a psychological and physiological level. Rather, provision of the patient's physiological treatment and the day-to-day emotional support these patients frequently require falls—by default—to the technician, who, himself, is a product of the technological revolution.

The factors that underlie the ascendency of the technician to a position that approximates that of primary caretaker merit brief elaboration. The attending physician tends to assume a supervisory–executive role in this setting. Typically, the nurse serves as "unit manager" of the technologically-oriented clinic, and this move upward to administration compromises her availability for her traditional patient care function. In short, the formal duties of the medical and nursing staff may preclude their involvement in the psychological care of these patients. Finally, although the social worker might logically be expected to provide continuity of psychological care, the provision of concrete services which she performs in accordance with her prescribed role may leave her little time to dispense the ongoing emotional support that would promote these patients' psychological adaptation to their catastrophic medical illness. As a consequence of these alterations in the traditional roles of the nurse and physician, and the limitations imposed upon the activities of the social worker, the technician has more contact—physical and psychological—with the patient than any other member of the health care team.

Physiological and Psychological Characteristics of the Machine-Dependent Patient

Renal patients on dialysis and cancer patients receiving cobalt bomb treatments have certain physiological and psychological characteristics in common. First, they suffer from a life-threatening illness with an uncertain course. Second, many are enraged by the knowledge that their survival depends on the use of a machine "ordered" by a doctor, particularly since the physician who holds their lives in his hand may not be directly involved in their treatment, per se, and invariably delegates the "hook-up" to others. Third, their machine dependence exacerbates the eight universal psychological stresses to which these patients are vulnerable as a consequence of their chronic illness. Their self-esteem is inevitably diminished by the realization that they can no longer rely on their own (physical) resources, that, in effect, a faceless machine has become the "master of their destiny." Fear of separation from the machine becomes a major issue. In addition, fear of further loss of body parts, of loss of the love and approval of others who no longer perceive them as autonomous individuals, and a preoccupation with past "sins" of omission or commission, to which they can attribute their misfortune, frequently come to the surface.

On the other hand, renal dialysis patients and cancer patients differ significantly in respect to the nature of their machine-dependency experience. As noted above, the renal dialysis patient is machine-dependent for the rest of his life; the cancer patient is machine-dependent only for a period of several weeks, although he may require follow-up treatment on occasion. Treatment for both patient groups is, as noted earlier, administered by a technician. But the renal dialysis patient is under the long-term care of a nephrologist, who, because of the intensity, duration, and vicissitudes of treatment, might be expected to function as his primary care physician. The cancer patient, although his treatment is supervised by a radiotherapist, during the relatively brief period of cobalt treatment, may be deprived of direct contact with the physician.

The problem of providing psychological care for the renal patient might be solved if the nephrologist who has contact with these patients over the long term were trained to assume responsibility for the total care of the patient, especially if that patient has no other physician. With respect to the cancer patient, adequate psychological care during this stressful phase of treatment might best be achieved if the primary care physician participated actively in the physiological care of his patient.

THE INTEGRATION OF PSYCHOSOCIAL CONCEPTS AND MEDICAL TREATMENT IN A RENAL DIALYSIS SATELLITE*

Psychological Status of the Chronic Renal Patient

While technological advances in treatment have prolonged the lives of many patients with chronic renal disease, the quality of life is known to be impaired as a concomitant of such treatment. The psychological reactions to renal dialysis have been discussed at length in the literature. Abram,[1] for example, has described the patient's initial reaction to dialysis—as toxic apathy clears—as euphoric. As the problems inherent in the treatment procedure become more evident, however, anxiety appears. Subsequently, conflicts centering on dependency emerge, and at this point the patient begins to wonder whether life is worth living. Viederman,[2] who has enhanced our insight into the inner life of the renal dialysis patient, has elucidated his problems in particularly vivid terms:

> The patient has surrendered his autonomy, his clothes are removed, privacy is denied, intake and elimination become subject to the orders of others. There is no dietary freedom. The dialysis bath comes to symbolize the womb and birth, and a love-hate relationship develops with the machine.

According to Levy,[3] approximately two-thirds of all male patients report some form of sexual dysfunction as a concomitant of chronic renal failure and/or dialysis treatment which further compromises their self-esteem. In addition, the patient must cope with adverse mental reactions. Cognitive deficits occur that are symptomatic of renal dis-

* This pilot program is described in greater detail in Strain JJ, Langer S: "Blueprint for Psychological Care of Patients with Chronic Renal Disease" (in preparation).

ease; his sensorium alters from day to day depending on his physiological status, e.g., disequilibrium syndrome, azotemia, etc., and/or as a consequence of drugs commonly administered to such patients, e.g., imuran, prednisone, and psychotropic medication.

Several authors have discussed the psychological characteristics of these patients from another perspective, i.e., in terms of adaptive and maladaptive coping patterns, and elucidated the relationship between adaptive capacity and sociocultural background.[1-9] For instance, Landsman[10] maintains that the greatest psychological challenge for the chronic renal patient is the need for him to erect a realistic set of expectations and goals. His dilemma stems from the peculiar characteristics of this illness. After its initial impact, the renal patient finds himself "adrift somewhere between the worlds of the sick and the well." Unless he appears to be severely disabled, society may expect the renal patient to resume his former activities where he left off at the time of the hospitalization. Too often, society fails to recognize that even when the patient looks well, and is fairly comfortable, the mere fact that every aspect of his life has been altered by his dependence on dialysis automatically eliminates him from the ranks of the healthy. Because he may not look sick, but certainly cannot be described as healthy, the renal dialysis patient remains a "marginal man," engaged in a continuing inner struggle to arrive at an appropriate self-image. The problems posed by renal patients who are in psychological crisis, i.e., who are considered suicide risks, have also been discussed.[11-13]

It is recognized that the psychological care generally offered this patient population is inadequate to the task of reducing the stresses that renal disease and its treatment typically evoke. Indeed, several workers have recommended that a psychiatrist be permanently assigned to, or work in conjunction with renal dialysis units.[14-18]

There is also a general consensus, based on these studies, that the nephrologist and his staff need to be trained in psychological medicine. The two major obstacles to the implementation of such a training program for nephrologists are their strong physiological orientation, and the renal patient's attitude toward psychosocial intervention. The nephrologist's concern centers, appropriately, on maintaining physiological homeostasis and on the preservation of life. He tends, therefore, to discount the patient's adverse psychosocial response to his illness and treatment, and this tendency is legitimatized by the patient's assessment of his maladaptive behavior: Typically, the patient does not view his behavior as indicative of the presence of psychiatric dysfunction. Rather, he thinks of himself as being understandably upset, anxious, disturbed, etc., and balks at a psychiatric label. There is some justification for this feeling. The concerns that beset the renal patient are very real: Will he be able to work again? Will his kidney shut down? What would happen to him in an emergency if his nephrologist were not available? Regardless of the patient's premorbid emotional status, stresses of this nature and magnitude would be expected to evoke some maladaptive response. In any case, the patient with chronic renal disease, who is understandably preoccupied with the physical aspects of his illness, is not usually motivated to seek psychiatric help through normal channels.

Moreover, his reluctance to enlist the services of a psychiatrist is strengthened by practical considerations. Often, the patient with chronic renal disease must spend part of at least three days a week on the dialysis machine, and may be unable to report for work (if he can work) on those days. It would be unrealistic to expect him to visit still another medical setting within a single week for psychiatric treatment.

The Teaching Program

The model described below was constructed to promote the expanded function of the nephrologist and his team in the medical setting. Briefly, this teaching program incorporated measures that made it feasible to assign a liaison psychiatrist to the renal dialysis unit at a specific teaching hospital.* Essentially, we anticipated that the psychiatrist would disseminate psychological knowledge and skills to the nephrologist (and his staff) with sufficient effectiveness, so that in time they would be able to function fairly autonomously in the psychological sector. Specifically, the goals of this program were to transmit information that would enable the medical staff to adopt a psychophysiological approach to the renal dialysis patient—to anticipate and prevent the development of psychological symptoms (primary prevention); to treat psychological symptoms which stem from adverse reactions to the stresses that are universally evoked by chronic renal disease and its treatment by dialysis (secondary prevention); and to forestall the recurrence or worsening of these psychological symptoms (tertiary prevention).[19]

The teaching program was established in conjunction with the medical director of the renal dialysis satellite center, who was assisted thereby in the incorporation of psychological medicine into the operation of the technologically-oriented treatment facility. To this end, he

* This program was established at Montefiore Hospital and Medical Center by the author, in his capacity as Director of the Psychiatric Liaison Service of that institution.

was encouraged to utilize those characteristics of the center that parallel the features that are the hallmark of the primary care concept: (a) continuity of care, (b) coordination of medical care and, (c) the provision of psychological as well as physiological care. We deviated from the primary care concept in that the program took into account the fact that just as the administration of technologically sophisticated medical care, such as renal dialysis, requires a team approach, several members of the team will need to administer psychological care under the aegis of the medical director. The team approach is particularly efficacious when all its members are psychologically-oriented, and one individual is expected to establish a meaningful relationship with the patient. Although realistic considerations may prevent the nephrologist from functioning as the primary psychological caretaker, the team is most effective when he functions as its leader.

To help the medical director and his staff achieve their goals, it was necessary for the psychiatrist to alter his customary role in the hospital setting, i.e., that of consultant. Thus, patients at the Satellite Center were seen in conjunction with members of the team, at times, even while renal dialysis was in progress. First, the psychiatrist needed to become an observer and "student" of a new patient group, who presented a new set of bio-psycho-social medical problems. Second, he agreed to act as teacher to the team within this milieu to enhance their capacity to manage the psychosocial aspects of their patients' dysfunction. Third, the psychiatrist encouraged his colleagues to devise a system of medical-nursing-social service patient records that would include psycho-social-biological data. The ready availability of such data would facilitate the identification of critical situations: suicidal ideation, noncompliance, sexual dysfunction, reactions to psychopharmacological agents, organicity, psychobiological reactions to stress and life events, and manifest psychological symptoms, e.g., depression and anxiety, and their physiological correlates, psychogenic pain, work inhibitions, and intrafamilial issues. And, once such situations had been identified, the psychiatrist also attempted to demonstrate how patients who were resistant to psychological intervention could best be managed.

> After an unsuccessful transplant which had produced multiple postoperative complications, Mr. R. became markedly depressed. The patient was 37 years old, single, and had worked as a carpenter until this occupation was counterindicated because of his illness. His symptoms, which were typical of depression, included subjective feelings of hopelessness, lowered self-esteem, a diminished interest in outside activities, and a tendency to withdraw from his family and friends.
>
> These symptoms, which had become evident while Mr. R. was

hospitalized, had become more intense following his discharge, and had persisted for the two years he had been on dialysis. Yet, he continued to resist all attempts to persuade him to seek psychiatric treatment. The nephrologist had more or less "given up" on Mr. R. He was firmly convinced that this patient would continue to refuse psychiatric help and would never overcome his depression without such help.

After the installation of the teaching program, the liaison psychiatrist sought to alter what appeared to be a "hopeless" situation by taking every available opportunity to establish rapport with Mr. R. (These informal meetings, which soon took on the character of psychotherapeutic sessions, were often conducted while the patient was on the dialysis machine.) After several such sessions, in which Mr. R. verbalized the devastating effects of his failed transplant and its stormy postoperative course—and discussed his impotence—he appeared to be less distressed. Over the next several months, his depressive symptoms continued to abate; he began to see his family and friends more often, and he began to feel less helpless and hopeless. Moreover, his work inhibition diminished to the extent that he was able to accept a referral for vocational rehabilitation.

In addition, the medical team needed to be made aware of the fact that because funding agencies have come to recognize that reimbursements should be made for psychological, as well as physiological care, the psychiatrist's services were supported (in part) by fees generated from patient interviews done conjointly with the medical, nursing, and technical staff.* In other words, this program could serve as a paradigm, at present for other renal dialysis satellite centers, and quite possibly for a variety of tertiary care units in the future.

Organization and Structure of the Renal Dialysis Unit. The Renal Dialysis Satellite Center, which was the setting for the teaching unit, is a 60-chair ambulatory clinic located three blocks from Montefiore Hospital and Medical Center. A total of 150 patients come to the Center three times a week for dialysis.

The Center does not differ in organization and structure from the technologically-oriented clinics described earlier. Medical treatment is administered under the joint supervision of a nurse who is not directly involved in patient care, but acts as the unit manager, and two nephrologists who are in charge of the facility. The social worker attached to the unit is available for consultation and provides concrete services.

* Under Public Law 92–603, Medicare payments of up to $250 per year are available for psychiatric services to all chronic renal dialysis patients, regardless of age, for one year post surgery.

The teaching programs provide for weekly psychosocial teaching conferences which are attended by the Center's medical director, nursing supervisor, social worker, the unit manager, and the liaison psychiatrist. Training at these conferences focuses on those issues that have particular relevance for this population, e.g., the detection of anxiety, depression, and organicity, and modes of dealing effectively with these disorders, such as the use of psychotropic drugs,* receive extensive (and intensive) coverage. In addition, the psychological reactions of individual renal patients are explored in depth: These patients are interviewed before the group, management plans are formulated, and, subsequently, followup observations are compared with initial impressions and responses to the psychosocial treatment protocol. An important aspect of these teaching rounds is the examination of staff attitudes, conscious and unconscious, toward these complex patients and toward the teaching program which gave rise to new conflicts. Initially, the social worker felt strongly that all the patients and families she referred for psychological evaluation should be seen and cared for by the psychiatrist; that is, she wanted him to officiate as a consultant. In marked contrast to the acute inhospital medical ward, the nurse at the Satellite Center did not offer patients bedside care. Rather, it was the technicians, whom she supervised, who had close contact with and the confidence of these patients. Therefore, it was decided, with the approval of the medical director and the nurse, that the psychiatrist would conduct ongoing conferences with the technicians.

The technicians were given a brief orientation as to the nature of psychological reactions that occur secondary to the stress of chronic illness and medical treatment. They were then asked to describe the responses and behavior of their patients. What kinds of questions did their patients ask? What did the technician usually do and say when a patient cried, said she couldn't go on, or became openly hostile and aggressive? At the outset it was apparent that most of the technicians handled the feelings of their patients, and their own feelings, by the simple expedient

* It should be noted that the use of psychotropic drugs may give rise to major physical and psychological problems in chronic renal disease. For example, with regard to the minor tranquilizers that are frequently administered to this patient group, nephrologists are not always aware of the important fact that Valium is fully metabolized nonrenally, whereas Librium is not, raising the possibility of toxicity.[20] Furthermore, the nephrologist may not be aware of the fact that the therapeutic effects of these drugs may be attenuated by a variety of factors, e.g., drug-drug interaction, the dosage prescribed, excretion rates, and alterations in the patient's mental state. In addition, the psychotropic drugs can, themselves, cause alterations in mental status which can exacerbate an existing delirium or dementia.

of ignoring them—by sticking to the business at hand, i.e., manning the dialysis machines as efficiently and quickly as they could, in order to keep talk to a minimum. But after several weeks of case presentations, the direct interview of selected patients, and, at times, individual precepting sessions, there was an obvious change in the attitude of this group: The technicians showed a great capacity to empathize and talk with patients. Moreover, with training, they became knowledgeable enough to be able, when necessary, to refer their patients to other members of the team more skilled in the management of the psychological problems the technicians had identified.

The psychological issues that confounded the technicians were analogous to those raised by other members of the team. The technicians wanted to know how to manage the crying patient, the angry patient, the noncompliant patient; they wondered whether they should accept presents from their patients, and whether the patient was attempting through such gestures to "buy" better care; whether it would be appropriate for them to function as mediators between patient and doctor, e.g., act as an "agent" for the patient who wanted more time with his doctor, or was afraid to tell his doctor about sexual problems or mental clouding.

Although the liaison psychiatrist had made his position clear from the outset, the nephrologists at the satellite unit continued to hope for some time that he would assume total responsibility for the psychological care of all patients served by the unit. In addition, they harbored an initial expectation (which was also doomed to disappointment) that the liaison psychiatrist would be able, within a relatively brief period of time, to effect improvement in the psychological functioning of these patients, i.e., that he would function as an omnipotent healer. A third paradoxical feature of the nephrologists' initial response to the teaching program consisted in their resistance to their status as students, although they had previously agreed to enter into a pedagogic relationship vis-à-vis the liaison psychiatrist. These resistances were lessened after the teaching program had been in existence for approximately one year. The nephrologists then began to spend more time with patients and to demonstrate a greater willingness to work on psychological issues. They accepted the fact that the psychological care, of Mr. R., for example, was a continuing process that fell into their province.

The social worker underwent a similar transformation in regard to her orientation. Initially, it will be recalled, the social worker, like the nephrologist, expected the psychiatrist to assume responsibility for the treatment of these patients. Instead she was encouraged to regard the psychiatrist as a teaching colleague, rather than solely as a source of referral. In other words, the social worker was encouraged to move well beyond her traditional function on behalf of the medically ill in the institution-based setting.

As a result of this teaching program a health care team emerged that thought in terms of holistic patient care: Staff and patient requests for psychological evaluation and planning increased. In addition, the work performance of the social worker, the technician, and even the nurse, was altered to reflect what could realistically be done to enhance their patients' emotional well-being. Following the tenets of the primary care approach, an attempt was made to coordinate satellite and inhospital care, when hospitalization was required. But perhaps the greatest achievement of the program consisted in the change of attitude effected in staff members with regard to this patient population. Behavior was viewed as adaptive or maladaptive, rather than "good" or "bad."

THE INTEGRATION OF THE PRIMARY CARE PHYSICIAN INTO A TECHNOLOGICALLY-ORIENTED TREATMENT SETTING FOR CANCER PATIENTS

Psychological Status of the Cancer Patient

As noted earlier, the psychosocial stresses to which all chronically ill patients are vulnerable as a consequence of their illness are compounded in the machine-dependent patient by the stresses evoked by treatment. Thus, when the cancer patient must undergo cobalt therapy, his uncertainty regarding the outcome of his illness is heightened—and his anxiety is exacerbated—by his fear of pain, disfigurement, abandonment, and death. Through his alliance with the doctor the patient can gain a realistic appraisal of his situation, which may diminish the frightening thoughts and fantasies that emerge during the machine-dependent phase of treatment, and can, at times, be more painful than his cancer. Primary care physicians recognize the need for continuity of care at this phase of the patient's illness. And many do continue to be actively involved in the patient's management. However, by and large, medical practice in the tertiary care facility has not yet been organized to accommodate the ongoing participation of primary care physicians.

On the physical side, radiotherapy may cause fatigue, anorexia, skin changes, nausea, vomiting, and alopecia. On the psychological side, the need for radiotherapy is interpreted as prognostically significant, so that the patient's ability to tolerate the physical side-effects of treatment is weakened at the outset. The environment of the outpatient radiotherapy clinic does little to alleviate the stress that the candidate for such treatment is experiencing. In fact, the environment in which treatment is administered may exacerbate his anxiety and his feelings of abandonment and hopelessness. Regardless of his financial status, the seriously ill cancer patient is expected to enter a strange environment, administered by strangers, and to sit with strangers while he waits alone to be led to machines operated by technicians he has never seen before and who know nothing about him other than the number of rads he requires and where they should be placed. Nor will their knowledge of him or their interest in his psychological reactions to treatment increase on subsequent visits. The technician in the radiotherapy clinic, like the surgeon, maintains an "affective neutrality" toward his patients, which is essential if he is to do his job efficiently.

No clinical example could adequately convey the response of the cancer patient who, without the support of his primary care physician, must submit to a technological treatment modality he doesn't understand, which he knows may produce frightening side-effects, and which, in any event, may not halt the progress of his disease. The fears universally experienced by such patients emerge most vividly when they are described in the patient's own words. The transcripts presented below of interviews conducted by a psychiatrist at the radiotherapy clinic of a major teaching hospital provide a compelling argument for psychological medicine.* Both of the patients whose interviews are summarized below had recently undergone mastectomies.

MRS. B.—SECOND COBALT TREATMENT SESSION

> It's been very nerve-racking for me. When they mark you up, you look like an Indian on the warpath. It really bothers me that I'm not able to wash that area, or use a deodorant or anything. I hate that. The after-effects were bad too. Maybe they won't be as bad today, because this is my second session. But I'm determined to see this through. I have a lot at stake. I want to get this over with and get back to living. I've just got to lick this.
>
> Well, here I am for my second treatment, but I'm going to need thirteen more. That seems like such a long time. My family has been great to me. That's why I say I have to think positively, that I have to lick this. I'm so glad the weather's been nice since I've been coming for these treatments. That helps a little.

* We are indebted to Jimmie Holland, M.D., for making these transcripts available.

I don't like the after-effects, but I guess that's part of it. Take that, or don't come at all. That's the way I figure. When you've been having those treatments, the technician says, "this will take three minutes," but to me, it seems like an eternity. The first session I had three treatments, on three different machines—three different positions, in two different rooms. Doesn't that seem long for the first time? I suppose I'll just have to get used to it.

I was very nervous about coming here the first time, and I'm nervous now too about coming, and especially about having to wait. And I don't really like the position I'm in on the table; it's that slanting position. This arm hurts when I have to keep it in that position when they have the machine on. My new surgery doesn't hurt me except if I keep my arm in that strange position.

There's another thing that bothers me too. When they told me I needed the treatments, I really wanted to know the reason why. Well, my surgeon explained it sort of, and I thought, "If he thinks I should have it, I'll just have it. If it's the best thing for me, how can I object?" I'll just have to get myself together and reconcile myself to the fact. But it is so awful when you are all alone, and there is nobody to talk to about the treatments, and the way they make you feel. Deep down, I know my doctor is interested in me, but sometimes I have the feeling that outside of my family—and they don't know much more than I do—nobody really cares about me. If I were still seeing Dr. D., I would be able to talk to him, and I know he would try to answer my questions. But once they found out that I needed this operation, he sent me to a specialist, and I guess I'm not his patient anymore.

MRS. M.—FIRST COBALT TREATMENT SESSION

I'd be happy to tell you how I feel about being here, but I have to go back to my operation. First of all, I think that after you've had a biopsy, you should be visited by a person who's had the same operation and knows what the after-effects will be. I also think that if you're going to be given cobalt treatment, this should be explained to you. It's terribly hard to be thrown into a course of treatment with absolutely no understanding why such treatment is necessary. I know all about X-rays; I know about Roentgen, I know about Rutherford, I know what they've done with X-rays, what they have done with the alpha, beta, gamma particles, so naturally I feel very upset about being deprived of any information of why I have to have this treatment, and what benefits they think it will have for me.

Today, when I got here, I talked to two doctors and found out that neither of them had seen the pathologist's report on me. I really feel that they're a disgrace to the medical profession. Even my family doctor hadn't seen the pathologist's report! I think he should have been interested enough to insist that they send it to him. People say my surgeon is a wonderful surgeon; well, he may be a great technician, but when he treats a patient, he forgets that that patient is a whole person, that she has a mind as well as a body. He doesn't realize that I need to understand what happened to me; I need to understand why this treatment is considered necessary. I finally persuaded the surgeon to talk to me, and he told me that the treatment is necessary because they didn't remove as much of the cancerous tissue as they might have, and they think that there is a special affinity of cancer cells with this type of radiation. The remaining cancer will be wiped out, and the radiation will also prevent any further cancer.

I think this place is terrible, too. You have an appointment for ten o'clock and you come early for it, and give your name to a clerk. She tells you to put your name on a list and sit down. You wait, and wait some more. I was reading a book and didn't hear her call my name. If I hadn't just happened to look up at that moment, I might still be sitting here.

I could suggest a procedure that would be much better. First of all, there should be an initial meeting between the patient who just had a mastectomy and a person who has experienced it. The American Cancer Society says this exists. In my case, it didn't. I didn't know anything about where to get a prosthesis, how to use one, whether one kind was better than another. Even if they can't arrange those visits, they could hand out printed sheets to mastectomy patients giving them the information they need to know. And they need to tell you what type of further treatment you will require, and give you concise reasons why you will need that particular treatment. That's what I would like to know. If your surgeon is too busy to talk to you, that could be accomplished with mimeograph sheets too. After all, they have diet sheets, you know, for people who have to be on salt-free diets and whatever. Alright, I'm a person who has had a mastectomy, who needs information. It doesn't have to be a scientific explanation—just enough explanation to help me understand what's happening to me. Maybe then I wouldn't be so terribly frightened. I never really appreciated my family doctor before. He may not have been a great specialist, but he was always willing to fill me in on what was happening to me. Because of the way medicine is organized in this country, the family doctor has been pushed out of the picture. But the "experts" who have taken over haven't been able to fill his shoes.

Obviously, Mrs. B. and Mrs. M. coped with their anxieties in very different ways. Perhaps, Mrs. B.'s most conspicuous characteristic was the attempt she made to present a facade of optimism. Mrs. M. appears from this transcript to have erected intellectual defenses against her anxiety. She used anger as well—anger with the radiotherapists at the unit, with the receptionist, with her primary care physician, and with her surgeon. In all probability, some of her allegations were unfounded. For example, one might question her statement that neither of the radiotherapists she had talked to at the clinic were familiar with the pathologist's report of her condition, that her primary care physician was not aware of the contents of the pathologist's report; or that he wasn't interested in what happened to her. However, the question of whether Mrs. M.'s allegations were valid or not is not the issue here. Rather, the issue is that both Mrs. M. and Mrs. B. had an urgent need for psychological support in this machine-dependent phase of their illness, and that such support was not available to them from any quarter.

Impediments to the Practice of Psychological Medicine in the Radiotherapy Unit

In theory, psychological support for the cancer patient undergoing radiotherapy might be forthcoming from one of three sources: the technician, the oncologist, or the primary care physician. A program designed to provide psychological training for technicians, so that they might be able to meet some of the needs of this patient population would be feasible. This is true of the oncologist as well, although his role is traditionally that of consultant and protocol provider. However, because of the brief duration of the machine-dependency of this patient group, we feel that the primary care physician is best qualified to bear the major responsibility for their psychological care.

By definition, the primary care physician is involved at every phase of the patient's illness. This means that he would be involved in preparing the patient for this particular technological phase of treatment; he would be aware of the patient's response to radiotherapy, and be informed of any side-effects the patient may suffer. The problem, of course, is that the primary care physician, who by virtue of his prolonged association with the patient is in an ideal position to fulfill the patient's psychological needs at this point, is not usually institution-based.

Moreover, if the primary care physician is to be involved in the patient's care during the machine-dependent phase and to function as his primary physician once his surgery and his institution-based phase of treatment is completed, he must have the physiological as well as the psychological knowledge that will enable him to maintain a "therapeutic relationship" with the patient.

The Basel Experiment

Modern diagnostic and treatment modalities for cancer require special knowledge, which is constantly evolving and expanding as new basic research findings become available. It would not be feasible, as medical practice is presently organized, to expect the primary care physician to possess this specialized knowledge or to administer to all the physiological needs of the cancer patient. It has been suggested, however, that the primary care physician become involved in a step-by-step "decision tree" approach that would enable him to provide the latest chemotherapeutic methodologies under the tutelage of cancer experts. A team from the University of Alabama in Birmingham has initiated such a program.[21] An equally impressive experiment, designed to enable the primary care physician to maintain a therapeutic (psychological as well as physiological) relationship with his cancer patients, was developed at the Kantonsspital at Basel, Switzerland.* The outpatient clinic of the Oncology Center of the Basel University Clinics can serve as a paradigm for the implementation of continuity of comprehensive health care.†

Organization and Structure of the Oncology Center. The Basel Oncology Center works with cancer institutes in Switzerland and elsewhere to accumulate information, which is then disseminated to the primary care physician, who is incorporated into the clinic treatment program. It also integrates information provided by the primary care physician regarding patient (records, family history, etc.) into its own data bank.

The staff of the center includes representatives from a variety of groups who meet regularly to implement its objectives, the most prominent of which is the establishment of practical guidelines for the diagnosis and treatment of various forms of cancer. These guidelines are

* The author acquired firsthand knowledge of this experiment through his work with G. Nagel and J. Sartorious in Switzerland. In addition, he participated in the preparation of a report of this model demonstration.[22]

† This approach was modeled after a program developed at Roswell Park, New York.

then made available to the primary care physician, in the form of protocols which are revised and updated at regular intervals.

The institution-based outpatient department puts theoretical knowledge received from the Center to practical use. However, in so doing, it strives to avoid further fragmentation of health care services that would ensue if its staff were to monopolize management of the cancer patient. Therefore, the primary care physician is encouraged to participate in such management. More specifically, he is advised to relinquish responsibility for the technical care of the patient during the limited period when he is undergoing a course of radiotherapy, and when the optimal dose of a chemotherapeutic agent for a particular patient is under study for the titration of its therapeutic effectiveness, versus its toxic, potentially fatal side-effects. These procedures must be supervised by an institution-based facility. However, the primary care physician is encouraged to continue to provide his patient with psychological support during these technologically-oriented phases of treatment, because ultimately the primary care physician—via his constant presence, his long-term relationship with the patient, and his knowledge of the patient's psychological makeup—is best qualified to help his patient (and the patient's family) to weather the psychological stresses that inevitably arise during these phases of treatment.

This model has certain psychological advantages for the physician, as well as the patient. The physician who participates in the treatment of a dying patient whom he has known and cared for over the years may be under considerable stress. These stresses are alleviated, to a large extent, by his alliance with the Oncology Center. The fact that the physician followed the protocols of a "renowned" oncologist will serve to mitigate his feelings of impotence, inadequacy, and guilt, in the event of the patient's deterioration and/or death; the use of the treatment and consultation services of the prestigious Center mitigates his feeling that he alone has "failed" the patient. Moreover, he is less likely to be the sole target of the anger of the patient who is seriously ill or dying of cancer. Instead, the patient (and his family) may direct their anger over treatment failure, toxic side-effects, and disability toward the institution-based facility, with the result that the positive doctor–patient relationship, built on hope and trust, is preserved.

Although the nature of the treatment provided, and its duration, will vary, there is compelling evidence that the population of machine-dependent patients will increase in the next decade. Some patients will require treatment for relatively brief periods; others will be machine-dependent for the rest of their lives. The setting in which treatment is provided will vary as well. In all probability, severe burn patients will always have to receive institution-based treatment. But one can speculate that in the future some forms of radiotherapy will be provided in the primary care physician's office; and there is a growing trend toward the use of renal dialysis machines in the home. One variable remains constant, however. Regardless of the nature of treatment, its implications for prognosis, or the setting in which it is provided, such treatment will evoke intense psychological stress in the patient and these stresses can best be dealt with by the physician who has maintained a relationship with the patient over time.

While the stresses, fears, and anxieties the machine-dependent patient is heir to may be more intense, they do not differ in essence from those evoked by other forms of chronic illness. Further, the ways in which the machine-dependent patient attempts to cope with these stresses —through noncompliance, pseudo-independence, excessive activity, etc.—do not differ essentially from the coping mechanisms used by other chronically ill patients. The resolution of these behavioral problems—the patient's ability to adapt to his illness, and the physician's ability to adapt to the patient—will hinge on the physician's capacity to incorporate the principles of psychological medicine, as elucidated throughout this book, into his medical practice.

REFERENCES

1. Abram HS: Psychiatric reflections on adaptation to repetitive dialysis. Kidney Int 5:67, 1974
2. Viederman M: The search for meaning in renal transplantation. Psych 37:283, 1974
3. Levy NB: Sexual adjustment to maintenance hemodialysis and renal transplantation. National survey by questionnaire: preliminary report. In Levy NB (ed): Living or Dying, Adaption to Hemodialysis. Springfield, Ill., Thomas, 1974, p 127
4. Foster FG, Cohn GL, McKegney FP: Psychobiologic factors and individual survival on chronic renal hemodialysis—A two year follow-up: Part I. Psychosom Med 35:64, 1973
5. Viederman M: Adaptive and maladaptive regression in hemodialysis. Psych 37: 68, 1974
6. Viederman M: Psychogenic factors in kidney transplant rejection: A case study. Amer J Psychiat 132:957, 1972
7. Abram HS: The "uncooperative" hemodialysis patient: A psychiatrist's viewpoint and patient's commentary. In Levy NB (ed): Living or Dying, Adaption to Hemodialysis. Springfield, Ill, Thomas, 1974, p 50

8. DeNour AK: Role and reactions of psychiatrists in chronic hemodialysis programs. International J Psych in Med 4:6375, 1973
9. Freyberger H: Six years' experience as a psychosomaticist in a hemodialysis unit. Psychother Psychosom 22:226, 1973
10. Landsman MK: The patient with chronic renal failure: A marginal man. Ann Int Med 82:268, 1975
11. McKegney FP, Lange P: The decision to no longer live on chronic hemodialysis. Am J Psychiatry 128:267, 1971
12. Kemph JP: Psychotherapy with patients receiving kidney transplant. Am J Psychiat 124:623, 1969
13. Kemph JP, Bermann EA, Coppolillo HP: Kidney transplant and shifts in family dynamics. Am J Psychiatry 11:1485, 1969
14. Kaye R, Leigh H, Strauch B: The role of the liaison psychiatrist in a hemodialysis program: A case study. Psychiat in Med 4:313, 1973
15. Cazzullo CL, Invernizzi R, Ventura R, et al: Psychosomatic implications in chronic hemodialysis. Psychother Psychosom 22:341, 1973
16. Fielding JM, Grounds AD, Mellsop M: Psychiatrists' role and staff stresses in a renal homotransplantation unit. Med J Aust 1:66, 1974
17. Cramond, WA, Knight PR, Lawrence JR: The psychiatric contribution to a renal unit undertaking chronic hemodialysis and renal homotransplantation. Br J Psychiatry 113:1201, 1967
18. Abram HS: The psychiatrist, the treatment of chronic renal failure, and the prolongation of life: I. Am J Psychiatry 124:1351, 1968
19. Caplan G: Principles of Preventive Psychiatry. New York, Basic Books, 1961
20. Strain JJ: Psychopharmacological treatment of the medically ill. In Strain JJ, Grossman S (eds): Psychological Care of the Medically Ill: A Primer in Liaison Psychiatry. New York, Appleton, 1975, p 108
21. Medical World News, December 27, 1976
22. Nagel G, Santorious J: An innovative approach to the management of the cancer patient: The outpatient clinic model. Presentation at The Basel University Oncology Center, Basel, Switzerland, June 1975

Author Index

Subject Index